A DREAM OF DEATH

HOW SOPHIE TOSCAN DU PLANTIER'S
DREAM BECAME A NIGHTMARE AND
A WEST CORK VILLAGE BECAME
THE CENTRE OF IRELAND'S MOST
NOTORIOUS UNSOLVED MURDER

RALPH RIEGEL

GILL BOOKS

Gill Books

Hume Avenue

Park West

Dublin 12

www.gillbooks.ie

Gill Books is an imprint of M.H. Gill & Co.

978 07171 8671 6

Proofread by Jane Rogers

Printed by ScandBook AB, Sweden

This book is typeset in Adobe Garamond with chapter headings in Oswald.

The paper used in this book comes from the wood pulp of managed forests. For every tree felled, at least one tree is planted, thereby renewing natural resources.

'In the Eye' from *A John Wayne State of Mind* by Ian Bailey © Ian Bailey 2020

A CIP catalogue record for this book is available from the British Library.

5 4 3 2 1

Ralph Riegel is the southern correspondent for Independent Newspapers, Ireland's biggest newspaper group, covering the region for the *Irish Independent*, *Sunday Independent*, *Evening Herald* and Independent.ie. His work has also featured in the *Independent* (UK), the *Daily Telegraph*, the *Belfast Telegraph* and the *Cork Examiner*. He is a regular contributor to RTÉ, Virgin Media One, the BBC, Channel 4 and Newstalk. He is a graduate of DIT.

A Dream of Death is his ninth book. Four were bestsellers, including the Number 1 bestseller *My Brother Jason*, published by Gill Books. His book *Commando* was the focus of a Sky TV documentary. *Hidden Soldier* inspired the RTÉ series *Hostile Environment*, starring Liam Cunningham.

A native of Kilworth, he lives in Fermoy, Co. Cork, with his wife, Mary, and three children.

ACKNOWLEDGEMENTS

This book would have been impossible without the support, cooperation and generosity of a large number of people over many years.

I am particularly grateful to the Bouniol and du Plantier families for their kindness and openness over almost twenty-three years of covering developments of the investigation into Sophie Toscan du Plantier's death. Despite the horrific loss they suffered, they have been astonishingly generous with their time since I first began reporting on this tragedy in 1997. I will never forget how, in the midst of their grief, Georges and Marguerite Bouniol, as well as Marie-Madeleine Opalka, Pierre-Louis Baudey-Vignaud, Bertrand Bouniol and Jean-Pierre Gazeau, displayed unfailing kindness and patience.

Similarly, I'd like to thank Ian Bailey and his solicitor, Frank Buttimer, for taking phone calls and queries at the most inopportune times over the years. When on many occasions they were not able to formally comment on matters, they were both unstintingly helpful and understanding.

Author and playwright Michael Sheridan wrote *Death in December* in 2002 and was the first to bring much of the Sophie Toscan du Plantier story into the public domain. My work on the 2003 libel hearing for the updated edition of *Death in December* was my first publishing project and I remain forever grateful to Michael for that.

Special thanks to both Barry Roche, Southern Correspondent for the *Irish Times*, and Paul Byrne, Southern Editor for Virgin Media (formerly TV3). Barry has worked on this story since the very beginning in 1996/1997, and I am deeply grateful for all his help and expert advice. Paul is also a fount of knowledge on the case and has been incredibly generous with his expertise.

Similar thanks for all their help and advice to *Irish Sun* Southern Correspondent Ann Mooney; 96FM Chief News Reporter Fiona Donnelly; Cork freelance extraordinaire Olivia Kelleher; the *Irish Examiner* journalists Eoin English, Noel Baker, Eddie Cassidy and Michael Clifford; my predecessor at the *Irish Independent*, Dick Cross; Tom MacSweeney, former Southern Editor of RTÉ; both Mike and Daragh McSweeney of Provision; and Castletownbere photographer Niall Duffy.

Much of the material in this book I have covered over the years as part of my work for the *Irish Independent*. For those parts I was not directly involved in covering, I am indebted to the following: Shane Phelan, Dearbhail McDonald, Sarah Collins, Maeve Sheehan, Nicola Anderson, Mark Condren, Tom Brady, Tim Healy and Olga Cronin at the *Irish Independent* and the *Sunday Independent*; Barry Roche, Lara Marlowe, Mary Carolan and Ruadhán Mac Cormaic at the *Irish Times*; Eddie Cassidy, Eoin English, Michael Clifford and Noel Baker at the *Irish Examiner*; and Siobhan Gaffney, Paschal Sheehy, Tom MacSweeney, Jennie O'Sullivan, Philip Boucher-Hayes, Órla O'Donnell and Geraldine Harney at RTÉ.

Thanks to Gill Books for first suggesting this project. I am very grateful to Sarah Liddy and Catherine Gough for all their support. Special mention to Aoibheann Molumby for her incredible work on editing and strengthening the manuscript, to Seán Hayes for fine-tuning my grammar and to Ellen Monnelly, Laura King and Teresa Daly for all their work in supporting the project. It was a great honour to work with you all again.

Special thanks to Kieran Kelly for his expert legal advice and suggestions on the manuscript.

This project would not have been possible without the help, support and understanding of my colleagues at Independent News & Media. Special mention to Gareth Morgan, Claire Murphy, Rory Tevlin, Breda Heffernan, Kirsty Blake Knox, Eimear Rabbitte, Paul Sheridan, Fionnan Sheahan, Denise Calnan, Cormac Bourke and Alan Steenson.

On a personal note, my wife, Mary, and children, Rachel, Rebecca and Ralph, as well as my mother, Nora, were staunch supporters, as always. I am very grateful for their help and understanding as I vanished for days on end to research and write material for this book.

There are no winners in this story. The killer of Sophie Toscan du Plantier – an individual responsible for one of the most brutal murders in the history of the State – was never identified and brought to justice in Ireland. A French family, who placed their trust in the Irish justice system, is still waiting for that trust to be repaid. Ian Bailey, a man entirely innocent under Irish law, has endured a twenty-three-year nightmare that shows absolutely no sign of ending. Having moved to Ireland to forge a bright new life, Mr Bailey has, in his own words, been 'bonfired' since 1997, and believes that the 'torture' of being wrongly associated with the crime will only end with his death.

It is my sincere hope that those still haunted by the awful pain inflicted on that Christmas evening, on a dark, lonely west Cork hillside in 1996, will eventually find the peace they deserve.

CONTENTS

INTRODUCTION xi

1. Murder 1

2. Investigation 10

3. Sophie Toscan du Plantier 43

4. Ian Bailey 55

5. Media 67

6. Libel Hearing 79

7. Marie Farrell 101

8. French Investigation 114

9. Extradition Bid 127

10. Wrongful Arrest 138

11. Build-up to Paris Trial 168

12. GSOC 183

13. Paris Trial 197

14. Aftermath 219

TIMELINE 234

BIBLIOGRAPHY 243

A Dream of Death

I dreamed that one had died in a strange place

Near no accustomed hand,

And they had nailed the boards above her face,

The peasants of that land,

Wondering to lay her in that solitude,

And raised above her mound

A cross they had made out of two bits of wood,

And planted cypress round;

And left her to the indifferent stars above

Until I carved these words:

She was more beautiful than thy first love,

But now lies under boards.

— WILLIAM BUTLER YEATS

INTRODUCTION

The poetry book lay open in the cottage precisely as she had left it, on the short poem by William Butler Yeats.

Shocked by the savage injuries inflicted on the murdered woman lying in the laneway nearby, the detectives realised that, in the minutes before the attack in which she was battered to death, Sophie Toscan du Plantier had been reading a poem that opened with the lines 'I dreamed that one had died in a strange place / Near no accustomed hand'.

It struck gardaí as an eerie coincidence that the woman could have been reading these words as her killer walked towards the beautiful isolated cottage on the hillside, illuminated against the dark December sky by the light from the hearth.

***

The brutal killing of Sophie Toscan du Plantier, a beautiful French mother of one, at her holiday home in Toormore, west Cork, just days before Christmas in 1996 has proved to be Ireland's highest-profile, most baffling and controversy-stalked murder mystery.

Sophie was attacked at her holiday home just hours before she was due to fly back to France, chased as she tried to flee for her life across a dark mountainside and then viciously battered to death when her killer finally caught her less than 100 metres from her cottage. Her blood-soaked body was left by the roadside. It was a killing almost unique in its brutality, its apparent lack of motive and, crucially, its subsequent lack of eyewitnesses and forensic evidence to identify the killer.

The investigation initially seemed to offer the hope of an early resolution, but it ultimately came to frustrate both the Garda Síochána and Irish prosecutors, not least because of failings and problems with the original probe. Detectives were hampered by the failure to secure any significant breakthrough in terms of key evidence – and were also plagued by what can politely be described as bad luck.

Over time, the case threatened to put Ireland and France on a judicial and diplomatic collision course over the failure to prosecute anyone for the murder of the high-profile French film executive. Twenty-three years after her battered body was discovered lying by the Toormore roadside, the investigation into the murder of Sophie Toscan du Plantier remains open.

The killing committed in west Cork resulted in a French investigation, a Paris trial, and ultimately a high-profile prosecution and conviction. Ireland and France again face the minefield of a looming extradition battle and major questions over judicial procedures and the rights of the innocent.

The individual convicted by the non-jury Paris court in May 2019 was British poet and journalist Ian Bailey, who had been twice arrested by gardaí in connection with the du Plantier investigation despite his vehement protestations of innocence. On both occasions, the journalist was released without charge.

Because of his Paris conviction and an outstanding European Arrest Warrant issued by the French authorities, Mr Bailey has been described by his solicitor as a 'prisoner in a country called Ireland'.

Sophie Toscan du Plantier was an intelligent, vivacious and independent woman who felt a deep attraction to the wild, rugged and windswept landscape of west Cork. It was a place she came to describe as her 'dream home', and she insisted on sharing the beauty of the Toormore, Schull and Goleen landscape and culture with her family, friends and teenage son.

This is Sophie's story.

1

MURDER

Shortly after 10 a.m. on Monday, 23 December 1996, Shirley Foster was setting off from her home at Toormore in order do some last-minute Christmas shopping in Schull. It was a typical Irish winter morning – there was a hint of frost on the ground and, while the morning had been bright and clear, cloud cover threatened rain showers later in the day.

Ms Foster lived on a hillside that boasted dramatic views, with Roaringwater Bay in the distance. Behind the property were spectacular views west towards Dunmanus Bay. All around the house, gorse-covered hills – interspersed with rock-studded fields carved over generations – tumbled down towards the coast. In summer, Toormore was beautiful and idyllic. In winter, it could be desolate and forbidding.

West Cork communities are used to isolation, but even by local standards this tiny Toormore community was some distance removed from the hubbub of local habitation. At the base of the hill, at the side of the laneway leading from her home towards the main road, Ms Foster noticed what she thought was a bundle of clothes. It was unusual enough to catch her attention. As she slowed to take the left-hand turn, something made her look again – and she realised that the object wasn't a bundle of clothes. Rather, it appeared to be a human form lying prone by the gate.

Horrified, she looked again to make sure and was appalled to see that it was a body with obvious bloodstains. She raced back to her home to raise the alarm and notify the gardaí. She also informed her partner, Alfie

Lyons, of the grim discovery. Together, they began a quick check of their neighbours to ensure that everyone was safe and accounted for.

Despite the fact that Clonakilty, Bantry and Skibbereen garda stations were closer, the alert was handled by Bandon Garda Station, the divisional headquarters for west Cork. The sergeant on duty dispatched two uniformed gardaí to the scene while also alerting detectives and the local superintendent to the serious nature of the call that had just been received.

The first garda patrol car arrived at the isolated scene shortly before 10.40 a.m. The two officers in attendance, Sergeant Ger Prendeville and Garda Bill Byrne, were careful not to contaminate the scene, but they were able to confirm that the alert did involve a dead body. One look was enough to see what a post-mortem would later verify: the individual was female and had been subjected to a brutal and savage attack. This did not look like a tragic road traffic accident or even a livestock incident. Neither garda recognised the deceased on sight.

A careful inspection of the scene indicated that the woman involved had likely died after a desperate struggle. So horrific were the wounds to the body and head that it was not immediately apparent what type of weapon had been used. But a concrete block was lying just two metres away. Both gardaí noticed, to their horror, what looked like bloodstains on its edges.

The gardaí also came across apparent bloodstains on a nearby gate and a piece of clothing caught on a barbed-wire fence. They could see that the woman lying in front of them was wearing walking boots. However, she also appeared to be wearing a dressing gown, as if she had been preparing for bed – something that many people who later attended the scene thought highly unusual given the distance the body was found from the house. Gardaí wondered whether the woman had been chased from her home by an intruder. She had probably been living locally because she could not have run or walked very far, dressed as she was on that cold December night.

A local GP, Dr Larry O'Connor, attended Toormore shortly after 11 a.m. and pronounced the woman dead at the scene. It was clear to Dr O'Connor, from his preliminary examination, that the woman had been dead for a number of hours. However, he could not speculate as to the time of death.

The Office of the State Pathologist had been contacted shortly before 11 a.m. that Monday. At the time, Ireland had just a single state pathologist, Professor John Harbison, who was based in Dublin. It was an almost five-hour drive from Dublin to Toormore, with the Dublin–Cork motorway a development still far in the future. But it was hoped he might be able to attend the scene that evening in order to conduct a preliminary examination that would then allow the body to be transferred to Cork Regional Hospital.

A short time later, a local priest arrived and administered the last rites, with all gardaí present joining in the murmured prayers. Shocked neighbours gathered some distance from the gateway, warned to stay back by gardaí, who were determined to preserve the entire scene. Until Professor Harbison arrived and the forensic experts were able to complete their work, the scene would have to remain carefully cordoned off.

Locals were baffled about who the person could be, although rumours were already circulating that a house on the hill, thought to have been empty for Christmas, may have had a single occupant over recent days. For a time, a rumour spread that the deceased may have come from a New Age encampment 15 kilometres away. Neighbours checking with each other had already made sure that everyone permanently resident in the area was accounted for. There was some local speculation that the death may have resulted from a road traffic incident, but gardaí already suspected a far darker cause.

Gardaí making inquiries around Toormore became aware that Sophie Toscan du Plantier had arrived at her holiday home the previous Friday evening. This was confirmed by the presence outside the Toormore property of a 1996 Ford Fiesta bearing a sticker for the car-hire company,

Avis. Gardaí were informed that Josephine Hellen acted as a caretaker for the property of her French friend. Contact was made with the Hellen family, and it was confirmed that the French woman had indeed arrived three days earlier for a pre-Christmas break and had been due to depart from Cork Airport that very day.

Because of the gruesome nature of the discovery, it was agreed that Josephine's husband, Finbarr, rather than his wife, would attend the scene. He knew Sophie by sight and would be able to identify her. Minutes after his arrival, he confirmed that the bloodstained body lying by the roadside was that of the French mother of one. Gardaí quickly realised that the international dimension of the case would make it particularly challenging.

A forensics team from the Garda Technical Bureau in Dublin were dispatched to west Cork as soon as it was confirmed that the death was being treated as suspicious. But they wouldn't arrive until late that Monday evening. Until then, uniformed gardaí were tasked with preserving the scene and any evidence that might be spotted.

By lunchtime, word had spread across west Cork about the discovery of a body and a possible murder investigation being launched by gardaí. *The Examiner*'s west Cork correspondent, Eddie Cassidy, was the first journalist to be alerted to the grim news.

I was working for *The Examiner* (later to become the *Irish Examiner*) that December. It would prove to be my last Christmas with the newspaper as I would leave the following year to take up the role of southern correspondent with the *Irish Independent*. The news from west Cork dominated the conversation in the newsroom that day. Newspapers, just like many other businesses, wind down for the Christmas period and *The Examiner* was no different. There would be reduced staff numbers on duty until early January and many older reporters timed holidays for the festive season. Everyone was horrified by the details emerging from west Cork. I remember there was sympathy for Eddie, as he would be spending his Christmas break reporting on this grim discovery.

Unlike Eddie, I would be off for Christmas and, like other reporters, would take up elements of the story in early 1997. I remember hearing the news of the Toormore death in the newsroom that day from Pat Brosnan, one of *The Examiner*'s most experienced operators and an accomplished columnist. We sat just metres apart in the newsroom in the paper's historic premises, now demolished, on Academy Street in Cork city centre. Pat briefly commented that Eddie had a major breaking story on his hands – little did we suspect that, almost a quarter of a century later, the events of that December day would still be making headlines.

Cork had witnessed its share of murders over the years – I had reported on a number of them – but there seemed an early realisation that there was something truly shocking about what had happened outside Schull.

Not long afterwards, other members of the Cork media would begin trying to determine precisely what was involved in the grim Toormore discovery and whether, as feared, the death might prove suspicious. Among those making calls about the discovery, as well as Eddie, were Tom McSweeney, southern correspondent for RTÉ; Dick Cross, southern correspondent for the *Irish Independent*, whose retirement would shortly trigger my move; Dick Hogan, southern correspondent for the *Irish Times*; and a Cork-based freelance news agency called Newsline, operated by Ann Cahill and Barry Roche. Within hours, members of the Dublin media would also be en route to west Cork. Years later, Mr Roche would succeed Mr Hogan as southern correspondent for the *Irish Times* and become the journalist to cover the du Plantier case for the longest continuous period, also breaking many of the major developments in the case.

Eddie Cassidy immediately began to make calls to local 'stringers', or news contacts, to determine if anyone had heard anything about developments in Toormore. At around 1.40 p.m., he made contact with a Schull-based freelance journalist named Ian Bailey. The exact details of that conversation would prove to be of enormous importance over the years to come.

The net result of the conversation was that Mr Bailey – accompanied by his partner, the Welsh artist Jules Thomas – decided to drive to the nearby scene to see what they could discover. The couple lived in a house called The Prairie, at Liscaha, roughly on the other side of the mountain. Ms Thomas brought a 35mm camera in case there was an opportunity to take photographs. These would be useful for any articles her partner might submit.

Mr Bailey later said he arrived at Toormore around 2.20 p.m. He approached the scene and was met by two gardaí, who immediately asked him who he was and what he was doing there. When informed that Mr Bailey was a journalist, one garda asked the couple to step back from the scene and to contact the Garda Press Office with any specific queries they might have.

The journalist said he left the scene but returned sometime between 3.30 p.m. and 4 p.m., by which time other members of the media, most from Cork city, had started to appear. Later, television crews would arrive to broadcast the first images of the scene to a national audience, who were horrified that something so appalling could happen just 48 hours before Christmas.

In churches across west Cork, from Schull to Goleen, Masses in preparation for the Christmas ceremonies now included a prayer for the unidentified individual whose body had been found at Toormore. As the afternoon began to grow dark, rumours swirled around the community that gardaí were dealing with a brutal murder and that the dead woman was a French national who had been on a pre-Christmas holiday.

By mid-afternoon gardaí had learned that the earliest Professor Harbison could attend the Toormore scene was Tuesday morning – Christmas Eve. An officer would have to be on duty throughout the night to secure the scene pending the arrival of the state pathologist. Only then could the remains be transferred to Cork for a post-mortem examination. This delay meant that the body, now covered with a protective plastic sheet, would remain outdoors for a second night. The tragedy was not lost on those present – the body of a brutally murdered French mother would leave her holiday home for the last time on Christmas Eve, en route to Cork Regional Hospital amid the twinkling Christmas lights decorating homes across west Cork.

Having confirmed the identity of the deceased, west Cork gardaí notified their Dublin superiors who, in turn, used diplomatic and police channels to pass the information to their French counterparts so that family members could be notified. That took time and, inevitably, the media, particularly the broadcast journalists, moved faster. Bulletins about the discovery of a body in west Cork were on national radio by midday.

By late afternoon, word was filtering out that the deceased was a French woman, information that was immediately picked up by the news wire services and media in Paris. The first broadcast in France was aired in the early evening of 23 December and, although it did not include the name of the victim or where in France she was from, it did include the location where the body was found and the gender of the victim. As in Ireland, news cycles in France had begun to slow in anticipation of the festive break. But this only served to ensure that this news story, which might not have made news bulletins in other circumstances, attained significant prominence in France at this early stage.

In Ireland, the murder featured in every bulletin on RTÉ as well as receiving blanket coverage in Irish newspapers from 24 December onwards. Because the Irish courts and the Dáil were now shut for Christmas, the Toormore killing remained the major daily news story over Christmas and into the new year.

***

Sophie Toscan du Plantier's extended family in Paris heard a news bulletin that Monday evening about a French national having been the victim of a suspected murder in west Cork – before they had been alerted through official police channels. The news of the discovery of the body in west Cork prompted alarm within the family. Many relatives knew that Sophie was in Ireland, but they thought she had been due to leave west Cork and return to France for the Christmas festivities. If Sophie had already left Ireland, surely it could not be her?

But Sophie's mother, Marguerite Bouniol, instinctively feared the worst. It proved to be a tragic example of accurate maternal intuition. Although she hadn't received any official confirmation that her daughter was indeed the victim, Marguerite was absolutely convinced that something terrible had happened to her beloved Sophie. Her husband, Georges, tried to console her, but Marguerite was adamant that something awful was about to engulf their family.

Incredibly, the French liaison officers had not yet managed to contact the Bouniols or du Plantiers. The family were forced to resort to getting relatives and friends who spoke English to contact every person they knew in west Cork by telephone to try to confirm Sophie's safety and whereabouts. But the family's fears were mounting by the minute. Sophie had not arrived in France on her scheduled flight, no one in the family had heard anything from her since 10 p.m. on the evening of 22 December and all attempts to contact Sophie in west Cork had proved fruitless.

By this time, the family were desperate for news, and everyone had been enlisted to ring every number they could possibly locate in west Cork for any piece of information. Finally, late on Monday evening, the family learned from one heartbreaking call to west Cork that the body found on the Toormore laneway was indeed that of their beloved Sophie.

The heartbreak for Marguerite and Georges was compounded by the realisation that someone would have to tell Sophie's son, Pierre-Louis Baudey, who was only 15 years old, that his mother had been found dead in the most violent of circumstances. The tight-knit French family were devastated by their grief, made all the worse by the inability of officials to answer their question of what exactly had happened to Sophie.

In west Cork, gardaí were about to launch a murder probe that would utterly transform lives, make Irish judicial history, test Franco-Irish political and policing links – and would remain unsolved over two decades later.

2

INVESTIGATION

From the very beginning, the investigation into the murder of Sophie Toscan du Plantier was critically hampered. A combination of unforeseen circumstances, unfortunate human error and simple bad luck for investigators meant that what initially appeared to be a case likely to see an early breakthrough proved anything but straightforward or easily resolved.

Despite initial indications that the investigation might prove fast-moving and forensics-led, gardaí found themselves coping with an increasingly complex and frustrating case marked by an almost unbelievable lack of hard evidence. During the first month, detectives would be frustrated to see every single strand of potential forensic evidence vanish into thin air or prove to be nothing more than a red herring.

There were no witnesses to the crime itself. No one locally had seen or heard anything suspicious along the laneway to the holiday home on either 22 or 23 December, or even on the days leading up to the murder. There was no security camera footage for any of the houses in the Toormore area or the key approach routes to the townland and therefore no vehicular or human movements to track. In 1996, the use of CCTV was rare in businesses in the surrounding villages of Schull, Ballydehob, Goleen and Crookhaven.

Gardaí were, almost from the very beginning, deprived of their single greatest asset – an eyewitness who could furnish information about the crime, the movements of a suspicious individual or even an unknown vehicle spotted around the area. In Toormore, no one had seen or heard anything untoward.

While detectives were initially confident that DNA or fingerprint evidence might hold the key to identifying the killer, gardaí would ultimately be left disappointed – and baffled – by the total lack of forensic evidence yielded from the crime scene. This was extraordinary given the level of violence Sophie had been subjected to.

There were nearly 50 injuries detected on Sophie's body. Most gruesome were the injuries to her head and face, which, one garda later told me, could only have been inflicted by a frenzied, prolonged attack. But gardaí would later catalogue numerous scratches and cuts consistent with having been inflicted by the thorns of briars and brambles. It suggested that the French woman had tried to flee from her attacker and, in the darkness, had stumbled through a patch of briars while being chased.

Garda Denis Harrington, who attended the scene, said it was clear Sophie had tried to flee from her attacker. 'It would appear she had tried to get away from her assailant as best she could. [Her] dressing gown was [caught] in briars. She had actually tried to climb in through the briars – [they] were the kind that would cut you, with spikes as thick as your finger.'

Strips of clothing snagged on a barbed-wire fence nearby indicated that the wire, in combination with the briars, may have slowed Sophie sufficiently to allow her assailant to catch up with her by the gate and then kill her in a brutal, unrelenting assault. Whoever killed Sophie had done so in an attack that lasted well beyond two or three blows.

Garda technical officers examined everything at the scene, from the concrete block found near the body to the apparent blood spatters on the nearby gate. Particular care was paid to Sophie's body and clothing. Given how the French woman had apparently fought desperately for her life, detectives hoped a key piece of DNA or forensic evidence might have been left behind to identify the killer or killers.

The painstaking examination of the scene yielded one development that detectives initially believed would offer their sought-after breakthrough – Sophie had strands of hair clasped in her clenched hand. The initial belief was that these must have come from her killer, perhaps ripped from their head as the young woman fought desperately for her life. The hairs were carefully removed and placed in sealed plastic sample bags for forensic analysis at the state laboratory in Dublin.

In what would, however, prove to be another major setback for the investigation, the hair strands were analysed and found to be from Sophie herself. Detectives leading the investigation were stunned at the result. The logical reasoning had been that the hairs were most likely to have come from the killer. The only explanation that could be offered now was that the strands had somehow got caught in Sophie's fist during her fight to defend herself or, more heartbreakingly, during her final dying moments as she sought to shield her head – the focus of the savage blows by her attacker.

Forensics officers also took scrapings from under Sophie's fingernails. In a significant number of such assaults, a victim fighting desperately for their life can often scratch their attacker, leaving a critical clue to the identity of the assailant. But, just like the hair strands in Sophie's clenched fist, the nail scrapings failed to deliver any significant DNA leads despite three separate sets of tests conducted over a decade.

The crime scene itself proved equally frustrating for forensic officers. So violent was the attack on the young mother that there were blood spatters almost everywhere in the laneway beside where the body was found. There was an urgency to examine and sample the area because the winter weather would destroy any such forensic evidence within a matter of hours.

But when forensic laboratory tests returned, they revealed that all bar one of the blood samples were from the deceased woman. One sample yielded unknown or 'alien' DNA. To this day that sample, which was recovered from the back door of the Toormore property, has never been identified, despite a painstaking cross-examination with all samples submitted locally as part of the investigation.

The location of the scene was also problematic for investigators. The body was found on a laneway at the foot of the hill leading to Sophie's holiday home. But the lane was also the only possible access point for those living in the homes above the holiday cottage. It was just 24 hours before Christmas Eve and locals had travel and shopping plans, resulting in a logistical nightmare for local gardaí, who had to cope with the movements of vehicles and people along a narrow laneway while trying to preserve the crime scene.

The interior of Sophie's house also proved baffling. Everything seemed to be in order, so detectives came to the belief that the French woman was confronted when outside, before being chased and fatally attacked. One theory that came to the forefront was that Sophie had heard a noise outside or had perhaps gone to answer a knock on the door just as she was preparing to go to bed. This would explain why she was dressed for bed but wearing a pair of walking boots.

Detectives wondered whether, having gone outside, Sophie had been confronted, realised her predicament and then attempted to flee downhill. But gardaí wondered why Sophie would run downhill and not towards the house at the top of the hill, which was occupied by her neighbours Alfie Lyons and Shirley Foster. Had she been cut off by her attacker? Or, in the split-second panic of realising she was in mortal danger, had she made a fatal wrong choice in her direction of flight?

There was no sign of a break-in or forced entry at any of the doors or windows. Similarly, there was no damage to furnishings inside the house and no indication that any type of disturbance had occurred inside the property. The house was in pristine condition, down to the Christmas decorations. No fingerprint or DNA evidence of any significance was ever found inside the property. Importance was initially attached to a washed pair of wine glasses on the countertop but, like all the other leads gardaí obtained, ultimately led nowhere. There was nothing to indicate that anyone had been in the house with Sophie when the fatal attack began.

As if that wasn't enough to complicate matters for investigators, there was an unexpected delay in having the body examined at the scene due to the inability of Professor Harbison to get there before Tuesday morning.

To the horror of her already devastated French family, Sophie's body remained in the laneway where she had been killed for two successive nights. The body could not be moved until the preliminary examination was conducted at the scene by the pathologist the following day.

A plastic sheet had been placed over the body in a bid to protect it and the immediate scene from the inclement December weather. The site would be protected by a uniformed garda on duty throughout the night. It had already turned exceptionally cold and hoar frost was on most areas of higher ground across west Cork. The delay had another consequence: an accurate body-temperature reading could not now be taken. A body-temperature reading can narrow time of death down to a specific period, perhaps to within two or three hours, by analysing the rate at which the remains have cooled. However, body-temperature readings are controversial in the world of forensic pathology. Some experts, such as Dr Craig Nelson of the North Carolina Chief Medical Examiner's Office, believe the multiple variable factors involved mean it is impossible to use body temperature to accurately indicate a precise time of death. All that such readings can indicate is a broader timeframe – and this was something that gardaí desperately needed. But they would now be deprived of even that.

In the case of the French mother, it would be impossible to narrow down the time of death from when she received her last phone call, shortly after 10 p.m. on 22 December, to when her body was discovered by Ms Foster at 10.10 a.m. – a timeframe of almost 12 hours. This would be yet another problem for detectives: finding anyone with a 12-hour hole in their alibi would be highly unlikely.

***

Professor Harbison arrived at the crime scene shortly before 2 p.m. on 24 December, Christmas Eve.

Professor Harbison found that Sophie had died from horrific head injuries sustained from blunt force trauma, including 'laceration and swelling of the brain, fracture of the skull, and multiple blunt head injuries'. His 13-page report – which did not enter the public domain in full detail via the media for almost a decade – made for gruesome reading:

> It was obvious that she had severe head injuries, because there were gaping wounds on the right side of the forehead and the right ear was severely lacerated at its lower edge. Beside the deceased's left shoulder and head was a flat slate, like a stone, which was heavily bloodstained. Between the deceased's body and the wire fence and within nine inches of her left hand was a nine-inch cavity block. The dead woman had long hair which had become entangled in vegetation.

He also noted a series of lacerations or marks on Sophie's neck. These could, it was suggested, have been inflicted by the heel of a boot – raising the chilling prospect that, having battered the mother with a flat stone and a concrete block, the killer then stamped on Sophie's neck, face and shoulders. The level of violence involved shocked even veteran gardaí. Professor Harbison noted an impression or indentation on the ground where Sophie's head had lain – indicating that the fatal blow, most likely from the concrete block being dropped on her head, was inflicted when the young mother was lying prone on the ground, probably unconscious: 'I was able to look at the ground when the body had been moved to note that there was a slight depression with blood on it where the head had lain. This indicated to me that the body had been in that position when the blows were struck.'

An analysis of the crime scene and the likely sequence of events led gardaí to believe that, from when Sophie was first confronted outside her Toormore home to the final blow she suffered at the bottom of the laneway, the attack had lasted a matter of minutes. It was entirely possible that her killer had been at the scene for as little as 15 minutes. The inability to narrow that timeframe down from a period of around 12 hours was a huge setback for detectives, and although they believed the killing occurred sometime between 11 p.m. and 2 a.m., they couldn't prove it.

Over the following days, gardaí would consult with the people who knew Sophie best to determine her movements, her habits while in Toormore and, above all, if anyone might have any motive to harm her. Detectives would piece together Sophie's every movement from when she first arrived at Cork Airport through to when she finished a social call on Sunday evening and returned to the Toormore property to prepare for her flight back to France the following day. It was also known that she had made a number of telephone calls to friends and family around 10 p.m. on 22 December. This would be the last time they would hear her voice.

***

The person in west Cork who arguably knew Sophie best was her housekeeper and friend, Josephine Hellen, who was also a French national. She had met Sophie shortly after she had purchased the Toormore property in 1993. Later, she had agreed to help Sophie with the property, checking on it when she was back in Paris and, when Sophie was due to arrive in west Cork, making sure the house was always ready for her arrival. Mrs Hellen was a trusted friend to Sophie – and went to exceptional lengths to look after her whenever Sophie arrived in Toormore.

On 20 December, Mrs Hellen had checked the Toormore property and lit fires so it would be warm and cosy for when Sophie arrived for her short Christmas visit. In a festive gesture, she had even gone to the trouble of decorating the house with sprigs of holly with red berries to give it a Yuletide feel for her French friend on her arrival. Sophie loved the traditional style of the festive decorations – with the holly, a roaring fire and candles making the Toormore cottage all the more welcoming.

In her subsequent statement to gardaí, Mrs Hellen said she had noticed nothing unusual at the property either before Sophie arrived or when she was there that December weekend. There simply wasn't anything out of the ordinary. The details of the gardaí statements first entered the public domain in a story by Maeve Sheehan for the *Sunday Independent* almost 15 years later.

Mrs Hellen outlined her routine for when Sophie would ring her and indicate she was travelling to west Cork. 'I would do the usual: put on the heat, do the beds and get food for the house and she would always pay me. As regards friends in this area, apart from ourselves and her two neighbours living near her and the odd workman coming to the house, she was not friendly with [anybody] else.'

Mrs Hellen explained that although Sophie would often travel to the property on her own, she also occasionally brought friends and family members, including her son, from France to stay. 'When I first became acquainted with Sophie, she used to bring a friend by the name of Bruno [Carbonnet],' Mrs Hellen explained. On occasions, she even allowed friends to use the property when she was not there.

Mrs Hellen did indicate to gardaí that, some years earlier, Sophie had suspected someone was breaking into the house to use the bathroom facilities while she was away in France and the property was empty. This became apparent when she arrived with her friend, Bruno Carbonnet, and he complained that the bath had not been properly cleaned.

> I went upstairs to check it and straight away I saw it was used. I cleaned it on the Thursday [before their arrival] and this was the Friday when they came, so it was used on Thursday night. We checked the house to see where he came in, and the window of the porch was open, so this was the only place [the intruder] could have got in and used the bath.

Sophie decided to have all the locks at the Toormore house changed. Mrs Hellen and Sophie discussed setting up a trap to determine who was breaking into the property, but there was never another incident.

Mrs Hellen told gardaí that, on 22 December, the evening before Sophie's killing, she had telephoned the property to check on her friend's planned departure the following day back to France. Sophie had still been up when the phone call was made at 10 p.m. According to Mrs Hellen, Sophie had displayed no signs of concern.

> I knew Sophie, in all probability, was up on the Sunday night because, number one, Sophie never went upstairs with her boots on. To me, her boots would never have been tied in bed. And her dressing gown was on, as far as I know. I think Sophie was sitting where the wine glass was, by the open fire, as she loved the open fire, when someone could have walked in, so she came out. Maybe she thought it was me, but we had an agreement for Monday morning.

One of the last things Sophie had done on 22 December, before she returned to her Toormore home for her last night in Ireland, was to call in to O'Sullivan's pub in Crookhaven. It was one of her favourite places in west Cork and she visited on almost every occasion she was in Ireland. Owner Dermot O'Sullivan greeted her, but little did he realise he would be one of the last people to see her alive. The French woman ordered a pot of tea and chatted happily to locals in the pub, who were eagerly anticipating the Christmas festivities. 'She seemed happy and relaxed,' Mr O'Sullivan recalled years later. 'She stayed for an hour and went away. She was a very quiet lady, and I think she loved the area because she found her own peace here.'

A careful garda inspection of the property revealed that nothing was missing. Sophie's passport, purse, bank cards and cash were all accounted for. The keys to her rental car were also found in the property. The house was not furnished with items of obvious value, given its use as a holiday home, but, even still, nothing was missing, and all the furnishings were accounted for. There was no sign of a break-in and no indication of a disturbance within the property itself. Detectives instinctively believed robbery was not the motive in the killing. In a somewhat unsettling discovery, Sophie had been reading a book of collected poems by the

Irish poet William Butler Yeats. The gardaí discovered the book, lying inside the house where Sophie had left it, open at the page of the poem 'A Dream of Death'.

While the full results of the post-mortem would not be known for 24 to 48 hours, there was an early indication – subsequently proved to be correct – that the mother of one had not been subjected to any type of sexual assault. But that did not entirely rule out the possibility that the killer may have had a sexual motive, which had been ultimately frustrated.

Initially, gardaí had more than 50 different lines of inquiry. They also had around a dozen persons of interest. But the number was whittled down very quickly as those questioned had alibis or were clearly not involved. At first, gardaí focused on whether anyone might have held a grudge against the French woman. It quickly became apparent that Sophie had a very limited circle of acquaintances in west Cork, undermining that theory. Those she knew locally were all devoted friends. Detectives realised that she simply had not spent sufficient time in west Cork to make enemies or give anyone an obvious reason to attack her. Gardaí also wondered about the timing of the attack. Very few people knew Sophie was planning on spending a few days in west Cork before Christmas – so it was practically impossible for anyone locally to have targeted her in advance. Far more likely, one garda told me years later, was that it was simply a crime of opportunity.

Detectives needed to ensure that it was a similar situation in France and that no one there had any obvious motive to harm the young woman. At the request of the gardaí, Paris gendarmes took several statements from Sophie's family and close friends to determine if anyone had a grudge against her or if she had confided in them about having been worried about anything in the days before her murder. They were also eager to ascertain how Sophie had sounded in her last conversations with her family and friends between 20 and 22 December.

Sophie's husband, Daniel Toscan du Plantier, gave a detailed statement to Paris police at the request of the gardaí. His statement, given to Police

Commandant Jean-Louis Chaumet, outlined his life with Sophie, her visit to Ireland and his last conversation with her. He revealed he had been planning to collect Sophie from Toulouse Airport on Christmas Eve after she had flown back to France from west Cork for the festive season, with the couple planning a trip overseas to Dakar early in the new year.

I am the husband of Sophie Bouniol. She was my associate, but, from 1988, she left her work and our relationship became more intimate, we began to share a life and some years later, I married her.

Sophie was very dynamic. She was a young impulsive woman, sometimes to the point of being aggressive and would not be in the habit of letting herself be walked on. In effect, she was more than a tough character, with a strict moral code, who feared nothing.

She rather avoided the world of society and gossip and preferred the chic and popular quarters where she felt more at ease. She was passionate about African art and had produced a programme on African bondage, which was transmitted at the beginning of December 1996.

I have to say, that like all couples, disputes arose, because Sophie was not an easy person to live with. In those moments she would not hesitate to leave our home and go to her close confidante, her cousin Alexandra, who lives in Geneva.

She was equally very close to Agnes Thomas [a work colleague and friend], who was indeed a confidante. If our life as a couple was sometimes not without hitches, she still decided to have a child and had ceased to use any form of contraceptive.

She expressed the desire about four years ago to purchase a house in Ireland, in a wild and isolated area, in keeping with her character. I therefore bought, at her request and in her name, for I think 400,000 francs [IR£50,000], a house situated in the immediate proximity to Fastnet lighthouse.

Personally, I only went there once, about three or four years ago, and I was able to appreciate the beauty of the place. Sophie has told me how she loved long walks in the Irish countryside, with her books, it was her favourite pastime when she holidayed there. She used to go there three or four times a year, to holiday for a week with friends, relatives or children.

She was the mother of a boy from a previous marriage, Pierre Baudey, aged about 15 years. During her absences, the house was maintained by a woman from the village, who was called Josie [Hellen]. Because of her professional life, Sophie had only been able to go to her Irish house once [that year], in the spring, much to her regret. She had therefore decided to holiday there at the end of December, during a slack period in her work.

However, beginning on 25 December, she had to return to France to accompany me to Dakar to visit friends. She left Paris on 20 December, about 9.30 a.m., for Dublin or Cork, I am not exactly sure. I did not accompany her to the airport.

During her holidays in Ireland, she would call me every day and often very late in the evening. She did not [break] that habit and called me every day and even several times a day, without ever, for one moment, intimating any problem.

On 22 December, I was in my second home in Ambax, in Haute-Garonne, and between 11.30 p.m. and midnight, French time, I had a call from Sophie. I was, however, in a work meeting with my associates in UniFrance and I indicated to Sophie that I would call her, which I did about 12 minutes later.

When I made contact, I immediately noticed in her voice that she was on the point of falling asleep and that she was in bed. I think that during the conversation, she told me that. The conversation lasted a few minutes and dealt with trivialities and the visit she had made during the day to Mr and Mrs Ungerer, who live a few kilometres from her house.

Tomi Ungerer, who hailed from Strasbourg in France, lived in Goleen in west Cork with his wife, Yvonne. Mr Ungerer, who passed away in February 2019 at the age of 87, was an internationally renowned author and illustrator. He had written and illustrated a total of 140 books, which were published in 28 different languages. He was awarded the prestigious Legion of Honour by France in 1990 and later given the title Commander of the Legion of Honour in 2018. Tomi Ungerer also boasted arguably the highest honour an illustrator can receive, the Hans Christian Andersen Award. He was also exceptionally politically minded and had campaigned against the Vietnam War, racial segregation and social exclusion – all of which made him on obvious ally and potential work collaborator for Sophie, who held similar views. Since they first met in west Cork as proud Francophiles, Sophie became firm friends with Tomi and Yvonne Ungerer. Mr du Plantier added:

She got to know Mr Ungerer last April and had been won over by his personality and his talents as a cartoonist. I think that he is the author of cartoons for children, but with a style more suited to adults. According to what she told me, she had returned home about 9.30 p.m. I suppose the Ungerers had kept her for dinner. If not, she would have gone to a pub for a sandwich or would have had a piece of cheese and a glass of red wine.

Clearly, she was very happy with this visit and had been very 'taken' by Mr Ungerer, to such an extent that they formed a work project together. I am saying that in a telephone call that I received on the morning, my wife had told me she had finally intended to return to France on 24 December and that she had been able to get a seat on a flight arriving in Toulouse at 8 p.m., though she had initially anticipated returning on 25 December.

There was no particular reason for this change of plan and it was agreed that I would meet her at Toulouse–Blagnac, on the arrival of the Aer Lingus flight. During the last telephone conversation, Sophie did not make any reference to any particular plan.

I felt she was already in her bed and was tired. I say that, to my knowledge, she did not take sleeping pills. In her Irish house, Sophie would sleep wearing a nightdress, T-shirt, pyjamas or other such [clothes]. I know that she had communication with the occupants of two other houses.

There was no history with the English people who lived there. In the case of any altercation, Sophie had such a temperament that she could fly into a rage and was not the type to offer no resistance. Equally, and in the same vein, I'm saying that, because of her character, my wife would not hide from any noise outside but would rather go out to investigate. I had been able to verify that several times.

She used to frequent the local pub, whose ambience was agreeable to her, as in Paris, where she used to frequent the popular cafés. I learned on 23 December, from a news bulletin on television, that the body of my wife was found close to the house. A few hours later I was informed by the Irish authorities.

I have absolutely no idea as to the perpetrator of the crime and do not see any possible motive for such an act, other than it being an act of violence. At no moment did she speak of receiving or inviting anybody after my telephone call.

I do not at the minute wish to say anything more. I do not have it in mind to return to Ireland. I am ready to receive, here in Paris, police officers dealing with the case, if they deem it necessary.

Statements were also taken from Sophie's other family members as well as friends and colleagues. Gardaí also sought a statement, via French police, from Bruno Carbonnet, the artist and friend who had travelled with Sophie to west Cork several years before. The statement was given to Rouen police on 28 December 1996, five days after the murder.

Mr Carbonnet, who also worked as a teacher, had been attending an art function in France from 22 to 23 December 1996 and was also heavily involved in planning for an exhibition of his artworks the following month. He told Rouen police that he first learned of Sophie's death from a friend who had telephoned him with the shocking news on Christmas Day. On the basis of his statement and watertight alibi, gardaí eliminated him from their inquiries. No garda document on record refers to him as ever being a suspect.

In his statement, Mr Carbonnet supported Daniel du Plantier's view that Sophie was a strong-willed, independent woman who was 'tough but fragile' and who drew an instinctive link between her home in Toormore and her creative pursuits. He knew of no one who would have wanted to harm Sophie or anyone who harboured a grudge against her.

Sophie and Mr Carbonnet first met in 1992. Sophie had attended an art gallery in the centre of Paris and was introduced to him by his aunt. Shortly afterwards, the pair commenced a clandestine affair. When Sophie purchased her Toormore holiday home, with funds provided by her husband, it was Mr Carbonnet who had helped her refurbish and decorate the mountainside cottage.

Madame Toscan du Plantier was for me an intimate friend during the years 1992 and 1993. In fact, I have known her since the spring of 1992, when she was introduced to me after a work meeting at the workshop of the art centre of the Ephemeral Hospital in Paris.

We afterwards became lovers. We went to Goleen in Ireland together, to the small house where I stayed and helped her to set herself up. The first time I went over there was in the Easter of 1993, when I stayed for about a fortnight. I went there on two or three occasions and we spent the holidays there together.

When asked by Rouen police about his relationship with Sophie, Mr Carbonnet said he suspected her husband knew of their affair despite Sophie being 'very discreet' and 'secretive' about her various meetings with him in 1992 and 1993.

The last time that I went to this house in Ireland was during the summer of 1993. My affair with Sophie finished in Christmas 1993, a date on which she finished it without any warning. This end was very difficult for me.

The last occasion that I have seen her again was at a burial [of a friend] in Père Lachaise Cemetery in Paris in March 1994. We had by then finished [our] relationship.

Mr Carbonnet said that, while he found the end of the relationship difficult, they had remained friendly and he had contacted Sophie by telephone in November 1996 to ask for a favour. He needed the temporary return of one of his paintings, which she had purchased during their time together. The artist was planning a special exhibition in January 1997 and required the painting for inclusion in the event. Sophie readily agreed.

The artist said it was clear that west Cork held a very special place in Sophie's heart and that she drew inspiration from the wild landscape and nature there. He told police that she always spoke of how happy she was at Toormore, even if she planned to visit on her own. It was a special place for her and seemed to stimulate her creativity and artistic instincts.

> She was a writer herself. She was secretive. The motivation for the acquisition of this house in Ireland was linked with her writing. She was someone who was tough but fragile at the same time. She sought to isolate herself from the world of the mundane because of [the] personality of her husband. Between Sophie and her husband there was in existence a type of a contract of luck for each other [a relationship based on an understanding of the career needs of the other] – she would have to be present for certain occasions defined in advance. Sophie was a woman of many facets.

***

By now gardaí were satisfied that the focus of their investigation rested in Ireland and not in France. A number of preliminary lines of inquiry in Ireland had been examined and ruled out. One was any link to a series of petty thefts from holiday homes in the west Cork area, which largely involved gas canisters being taken from properties that lay empty over the winter months. The petty thefts were believed to have been carried out by an Irish national living an almost hermit-like life in west Cork, but that individual was not around Toormore on 23 December.

Another line of inquiry examined but eventually ruled out was whether there was any link to a foreign national, a German man, who had been resident in west Cork but who had left the area in early 1997. The man later died in tragic circumstances overseas, having taken his own life. But gardaí were satisfied there was no apparent link to the Toormore killing.

Detectives intensified their focus on west Cork and a special public appeal for information was issued on RTÉ television at the request of Superintendent J.P. Twomey of Bantry Garda Station. The appeal was broadcast via RTÉ's *Crimeline* programme on 20 January 1997 for maximum reach and impact. In it, Chief Superintendent Noel Smith appealed for anyone with information to help west Cork gardaí with their inquiries. Specifically, he asked a female caller who had used the name 'Fíona' to contact gardaí again as she had potentially important information they wished to clarify.

This referred to a call received at Bandon Garda Station nine days earlier on 11 January. In the call – made from a public payphone in Cork city – the caller, named Fíona, explained that she had seen a suspicious-looking man near Kealfadda Bridge, just outside Schull and not far from Toormore, in the early hours of 23 December 1996. Fíona had been driving and had spotted the man by the roadside and noticed his unusual gait and strange appearance. She emphatically refused to give any personal details to the garda she was speaking with and ended the call.

The contact was immediately given top priority by gardaí. It was the only major piece of eyewitness testimony of anything unusual near Toormore in the hours surrounding the killing. Furthermore, if the motorist had deemed the individual sufficiently suspicious to take careful note of him, who was he and what was he doing in the area at such an early hour of the morning?

Less than 24 hours after the garda appeal on *Crimeline*, a second call was received at Bandon Garda Station from Fíona. This call again lasted just a matter of minutes before ending. But Fíona repeated what she had previously said about seeing a strange man at Kealfadda Bridge. She also confirmed the time as being in the early hours of 23 December. Gardaí traced the call to a public payphone, but this time it was in Leap, 35 kilometres from Schull. Again, Fíona refused to give any personal details. But gardaí began to suspect that the woman lived in the general west

Cork area and may have been travelling home when she passed Kealfadda Bridge that December evening. The use of public payphones was clearly designed to protect her identity.

A third phone call was received from Fíona three days later, on 24 January. This time she made the call from a private number. Gardaí had by now deemed tracing and identifying Fíona critical to their investigation. As a result, they took careful precautions in case she made contact again. They were now working with Telecom Éireann technicians and were able to trace the call to a property just outside Schull. Gardaí, in follow-up investigations, confirmed that Fíona was in fact a Schull shopkeeper called Marie Farrell. Detectives believed they had just received the stroke of luck they needed for this investigation.

Mrs Farrell was originally from Longford but had been running a clothes shop in Schull for some time. She lived in Schull with her husband, Chris, and their five children. For a time, the family had lived and worked in London, but they had decided to move back to Ireland for a better life for their children. The couple were hard-working and operated two adjacent stores in Schull – a clothes shop and a combined ice-cream parlour and sweet shop. They also maintained a street stall in Cork, close to the city's famous Coal Quay.

Gardaí conducted multiple interviews with Mrs Farrell about what precisely she had seen at Kealfadda Bridge in the early hours of 23 December. It emerged that Sophie had entered Mrs Farrell's shop during that final weekend. The French woman had gone shopping in Schull on Saturday, 21 December and, sometime between 2 p.m. and 3 p.m., had strolled into the Farrells' shop. After browsing around, she left. Sophie did not make a purchase, and at the time Mrs Farrell did not know who the elegant foreign woman was. Only subsequently did she realise the woman must have been Sophie Toscan du Plantier.

What made Sophie's brief shopping trip of interest to gardaí was the fact that Mrs Farrell recalled a man hanging around outside her shop at roughly the same time. The man stood out because of his strange appearance. He was wearing a long, dark overcoat, had short, dark hair, a sallow complexion and a generally dishevelled appearance. The man was spotted standing on the road across from the Farrells' shop, apparently hanging around aimlessly. The question immediately arose – who was this man?

***

Gardaí had carefully noted all those who had attended the general area around the crime scene on 23 December. Detective Garda Bart O'Leary spotted what appeared to be scratches on the hands of Ian Bailey, the freelance journalist, who had attended the scene to report on the crime for Irish, British and French media outlets. He was the first member of the media at the Toormore scene. The scratches were reported to the detectives leading the investigation.

After 23 December, Mr Bailey had been contributing material to various Irish, French and UK publications on an almost daily basis about the murder. His work largely appeared in the *Irish Star*, *Sunday Tribune* and several French newspapers. Gardaí began to carefully study these articles. Detectives also began to cross-reference witness statements about the timing and circumstances of Mr Bailey's arrival at the crime scene.

On 27 December, four days after the murder and just 24 hours before Mr Carbonnet was interviewed by French police in Rouen, Mr Bailey was formally nominated as a suspect in the case by gardaí. This was noted in Job Book No. 166 at Bandon Garda Station, a formal garda reporting document assigned to the incident room where the murder was being investigated.

The garda decision to nominate Mr Bailey as a suspect was largely based on the timing of Mr Bailey's arrival at the scene and the fact that he had scratches on his hands.

Days later, on 31 December 1996, Garda Denis Harrington and Garda John Paul Culligan were sent to question Mr Bailey about his movements on 22 and 23 December. Both observed the scratches on his hands. Mr Bailey explained that the scratches had resulted from killing several turkeys for Christmas and cutting the family's Christmas tree from the top of a nearby evergreen. Garda Harrington, years later, would recall the scratches as looking like 'briar-cuts'.

Gardaí were also aware of Mr Bailey's past and the fact that there had been two incidents of domestic violence during his relationship with his partner, Jules Thomas, in 1993 and in 1996. One of the gardaí now involved in the du Plantier investigation was the same officer Ms Thomas had informed she wished to formally withdraw an assault complaint previously levelled against Mr Bailey.

The most serious of the domestic violence incidents occurred on 15 May 1996, when Ms Thomas had sought a protection order against Mr Bailey. The journalist had been drinking when the assault against Ms Thomas occurred. It was so serious that Ms Thomas's daughter, Virginia, had called a family friend and neighbour, Peter Bielecki, and asked him to check on her mother. The Welsh artist was found with a swollen eye, scratches to her face, what appeared to be bite marks on her hands and a clump of her hair torn out.

When she was discovered by Mr Bielecki, Ms Thomas was lying on the bedroom floor of her home, curled into a foetal position. An appalled Mr Bielecki, who was a west Cork-based sculptor, later described the whimpering noises she was making as almost 'animal-like'. Years later, he would describe the scene of Ms Thomas lying on the floor crying like someone who 'had their soul ripped out'.

After a brief separation, Mr Bailey and Ms Thomas reconciled and resumed their relationship. Both were adamant that all was well in their home and their entire family was looking forward to a happy Christmas in December 1996.

As is usual in such cases, gardaí distributed questionnaires throughout the area to determine if anyone had seen or heard anything suspicious around Toormore or the surrounding area. They were given to neighbours, people who worked in the area and anyone who attended the scene or may have known the deceased. In the days immediately following the murder, Mr Bailey received a visit from investigating gardaí and readily agreed to complete one of the questionnaires.

On a separate occasion, shortly afterwards, he voluntarily provided fingerprints and hair samples to gardaí – a level of voluntary cooperation with the garda investigation that would later have enormous importance attached to it by officials in the Director of Public Prosecutions (DPP) office. One legal officer would note that Mr Bailey had gone to great lengths to assist and cooperate with the garda investigation – behaviour usually consistent with an innocent person who is eager to eliminate themselves from a police inquiry.

Having studied all the questionnaires and witness statements, gardaí noted discrepancies between Mr Bailey's and others' accounts of his movements that day.

Central to their queries was the timing of when Mr Bailey first learned that the deceased was a female French national. Mr Bailey was adamant that a phone call he received from Eddie Cassidy, the west Cork correspondent for *The Examiner*, included speculation that the dead person was a foreign national and possibly French. But Mr Cassidy had already denied to gardaí that he had told Mr Bailey, at 1.40 p.m. on 23 December, that there was a possible French link to the killing. Mr Cassidy was adamant he did not know at that point it was a murder, let alone that it involved a French woman. At that early stage, all he knew was that a body had been found. He said he initially believed the body could be that of a New Age traveller who had died in a hit-and-run.

Other statements also contradicted elements of Mr Bailey's precise timeline of events on 23 December. One photographer, Michael McSweeney of the Cork-based photographic agency Provision, said Mr Bailey had told him that photos of the crime scene were taken at 11 a.m. – some two hours before Mr Bailey said he had first learned of the killing. Mr Bailey flatly denied this. Another witness contradicted Mr Bailey's statement that he had never met Sophie. Goleen shopkeeper James Camier said he learned of the murder of a French woman from Ms Thomas around 11 a.m. on 23 December – something Ms Thomas would emphatically deny, insisting the shopkeeper had confused events with a meeting some 24 hours later on Christmas Eve.

A further piece of information came from a neighbour in Liscaha, who reported that a bonfire had been lit in the back garden of The Prairie on St Stephen's Day. The timing of the fire and what precisely had been burned in it would become the source of major contention between Mr Bailey and the gardaí in the weeks and months ahead.

Mr Bailey strenuously denied that any such bonfire had ever been lit over Christmas. Statements were later given to gardaí by two neighbours, Brian and Ursula Jackson, about the fire. Mrs Jackson, who had cancer, died before she could offer evidence in Mr Bailey's 2003 libel case against eight Irish and UK newspapers. Her husband, Brian, did offer evidence and said he believed Mr Bailey was tending a fire in the back of the Liscaha property on 26 December 1996. He said he had heard Mr Bailey's voice calling out and recognised who it was. Mr Bailey remained adamant that no such fire ever occurred on St Stephen's Day. 'I did not have a fire. Jules did not have a fire. I have no knowledge of a [St Stephen's Day] fire.'

Also in doubt were the contents of the disputed fire. While gardaí investigated whether clothing may have been burned, the judge in the 2003 libel case would say that even if there had been a bonfire, it was possible that nothing more than branches could have been burned.

On 30 January 1997, Ian Bailey received another visit from gardaí involved in the murder investigation. This time, they were accompanied by a senior officer. This officer stayed out of the general conversation until the very end when, Mr Bailey later claimed, he leaned forward and told the journalist that he could place him at or near the scene of the murder early on 23 December.

Another reason for the garda visit that day related to concerns raised by one detective over a Sunday newspaper article written by Mr Bailey. This article, according to the detective, contained a lot of details about Ms du Plantier's family and the French investigation. The level of detail struck the detective as odd – and gardaí were tasked with clarifying where such information had come from.

In all his statements to gardaí, Mr Bailey maintained that he had never left the home he shared in Liscaha with Ms Thomas once they had returned home from a social evening out on 22 December. On their way home, they had briefly stopped the car to admire the winter scene and the twinkling Christmas lights across the valley near Liscaha.

Once they had parked their car back at Liscaha, Mr Bailey said he went to his workroom to complete an article he was writing and never left the property until after he received the phone call from *The Examiner* the following day about the grim discovery at Toormore. It was a watertight alibi. He also maintained he had never met Sophie Toscan du Plantier over her previous four years in west Cork, only having her pointed out to him from a distance through the window of a local house.

Ms Thomas told gardaí she had gone to bed that evening and left her partner writing in the workroom. She said she vaguely recalled him getting into bed but could not specify a precise time. When she got up for breakfast the following morning, on 23 December, there was a handwritten article on the table, indicating that her partner had worked for a major portion of the previous evening. The first time both left the house on 23 December was to travel the four kilometres to Toormore in respect to the phone call Mr Bailey had received from *The Examiner*.

But gardaí received a number of statements from people in west Cork in relation to comments Mr Bailey had allegedly passed about the crime in the days after 23 December. Detectives took statements from members of the media, both Irish and foreign, in respect of conversations with Mr

Bailey. These statements led detectives to further scrutinise his version of the timeline of events on 23 December.

By this stage, a detailed statement had been taken from Mrs Farrell about what precisely she had seen at Kealfadda Bridge in the early hours of 23 December. Her account varied somewhat between her initial statement and follow-on statements taken by gardaí in respect of the exact description of the suspicious individual she claimed she saw at Kealfadda Bridge. These variations in the physical descriptions of the strange man on the road would, years later, assume enormous importance. The number of statements taken from Mrs Farrell indicated just how much weight gardaí attached to this evidence.

Gardaí believed the focus of their investigation was narrowing. A case conference was called and gardaí reviewed all the statements and evidence they had so far. The decision was made to arrest Ian Bailey and question him at Bandon Garda Station. This was despite his alibi and the fact that none of the forensic evidence linked him to the scene. But, for gardaí, Mr Bailey was emerging as a key suspect in the case. It would soon become apparent that, from February 1997, the sole focus for gardaí in west Cork was on this journalist and poet.

At 10.45 a.m. on 10 February 1997, gardaí arrested Mr Bailey at The Prairie and brought him to Bandon Garda Station for questioning. Mr Bailey was horrified that gardaí now clearly believed him to be a suspect, despite his vehement protestations of innocence and full cooperation with their inquiry from its very early stages. His partner, Jules Thomas, to the distress of her children, was also arrested and taken to Bandon Garda Station. Mr Bailey repeatedly warned gardaí that they were making a mistake.

This major development in the case did not escape media attention. There was already a media presence when Mr Bailey arrived at Bandon Garda Station in a garda car at 11.55 a.m. Despite his best efforts to shield his face, Mr Bailey was photographed being led into the station for questioning. Later in the day, a large group of reporters and photographers would assemble outside the garda station to await developments. Years later, Mr Bailey claimed he had been warned by gardaí that there was 'a hanging mob' outside the station.

Mr Bailey and Ms Thomas were separately met at the garda station by Chief Superintendent Dermot Dwyer, one of the most experienced detectives in Cork and a veteran of multiple murder investigations in both Cork city and county. According to Ms Thomas, he told her that the case would now be resolved by forensic evidence. Both had been arrested under Section 4 of the Criminal Justice Act, 1984, which meant they could be questioned for an initial period of six hours that could then be extended to 12 hours. Ms Thomas was arrested around 90 minutes after her partner.

Mr Bailey was read his rights and, three minutes after arriving at the station, he requested to see a solicitor. Bandon-based solicitor Con Murphy arrived at the station at 12.26 p.m. Mr Bailey was, throughout his period of questioning, allowed toilet breaks and provided with food and drinks as well as cigarettes. A superintendent authorised the taking of blood, fingerprints, palm prints and photographs. At 4.37 p.m. Mr Bailey was medically examined by a local GP before his period of detention was extended for another six hours. Then, at 10.44 p.m., he was released without charge.

Ms Thomas was likewise released without charge after questioning, and both returned to The Prairie. Journalists and photographers called repeatedly to their front door, asking if they wished to make any comment on the dramatic development. They later admitted that they were in a state of total shock over what had just happened and were appalled to discover that they were now under siege from the media.

***

Despite the public perception that the garda investigation was progressing rapidly, nothing happened for weeks, to the consternation of everyone.

On 17 April, the inquest into the killing was held in Bantry. The usual procedure was for the cause of death to be given so that the bereaved family could be issued with a death certificate. However, given the fact that the death was the focus of an ongoing garda murder investigation, the inquest would then be adjourned. In many murder cases, the inquest is never resumed.

State Pathologist Professor John Harbison offered very brief evidence, essentially just outlining the cause of death. He explained that Sophie Toscan du Plantier had suffered multiple injuries, but her death was due to a fractured skull and laceration of the brain. He found, from his post-mortem examination, that the skull fracture had been caused by trauma or impact from a blunt, rather than a sharp, object. No other evidence was offered before the inquest was adjourned.

On 27 January 1998 Ian Bailey was arrested a second time by gardaí. He was taken to Bandon Garda Station for questioning. Again, after almost 12 hours, he was released without charge. I was in Bandon that dark winter evening for the *Irish Independent* and I will always remember the bewilderment within the media over what was happening.

It is exceptionally rare for a person to be interviewed under arrest a second time without a charge being planned. So when Mr Bailey was released without charge and went the short distance from Bandon Garda Station to the office of his solicitor, Con Murphy, for a legal consultation, there was a palpable sense of confusion amongst the reporters gathered as to exactly what was going on and what would happen next.

Under Irish law, a person cannot be arrested a third time for questioning about the same matter unless there is an intention by gardaí to level a charge. It slowly became apparent that nothing of the sort was likely in the du Plantier investigation without further evidence coming to light.

Ultimately there were court proceedings, but they turned out to be civil rather than criminal. Mr Bailey commenced libel proceedings against eight Irish and British newspapers in 2001, before suing the State for wrongful arrest. The battle lines had been firmly drawn and Mr Bailey was now determined to use the law to underline his innocence in relation to the matter.

***

Shortly after Mr Bailey's second arrest, gardaí concluded their investigation and a case file was ready for the DPP. When submitted on 12 February 1998, it amounted to more than 2,000 pages of witness statements, interviews and a summary of the evidence gathered by investigators. Gardaí involved in the probe believed that sanction for a charge would be forthcoming. But, instead, an official in the DPP's office, Robert Sheehan, wrote back with a series of detailed questions for gardaí about the case file.

These questions were duly answered by gardaí. A second case file was submitted in March 2001, but the DPP again would not sanction a charge. Later a chasm would open between gardaí and the DPP over the relative strength of the case file submitted. In particular, the DPP had raised concerns over the reliability of one of the key witnesses interviewed by the gardaí, whose evidence was absolutely central to the garda case. There was no forensic evidence, so this witness assumed paramount importance in the garda case.

On 7 November 2001, the DPP formally ruled out the possibility of any charge being levelled against Mr Bailey. The decision was taken on the basis that any prosecution would simply not be sustainable on the evidence presented in the case file. The DPP found that there were major concerns about the reliability of the witness to whom the gardaí had attached so much importance – Mrs Farrell.

Central to these DPP concerns were the variations in the descriptions of what the Longford woman had seen at Kealfadda Bridge. In her first statement to gardaí, the peculiar man spotted walking with the distinctive gait was described as being of medium height, around five foot eight inches tall. This description was later revised upwards to around five foot ten inches in height. Later, Mrs Farrell would tell gardaí that the man was 'very tall'. It was clear the DPP was concerned by the disparity between the original height description and Mr Bailey's physical stature. The original description of the strange man at Kealfadda Bridge has him standing five foot eight inches in height, whereas Mr Bailey stands at six foot three inches in height. If the first description, rather that the subsequent statements, was accurate, it was apparent to the DPP that the individual could not have been the Manchester-born journalist who insisted he had never left the home he shared with Ms Thomas on that evening.

It was a similar situation with the peculiar individual seen outside the Schull shop, with initial statements indicating he was between five foot eight inches and five foot ten inches in height, substantially shorter than Mr Bailey, whose height is one of his most distinctive physical characteristics.

Gardaí continued their investigation in the fading hope of getting the forensic or evidential breakthrough they so desperately needed. There were pieces of intriguing information that came to light, but nothing that represented the breakthrough they needed. One of the most bizarre developments was the discovery of a bottle of wine behind a ditch in Toormore some weeks after the murder.

The bottle of wine was discovered, almost by accident, lying in a ditch just off the laneway that led to Sophie's holiday home. It was discovered in March 1997, some three months after the murder, and had clearly been exposed to the weather for some time. What intrigued detectives was that the wine bottle was unopened and that it was a French vintage not stocked by any pub or off-licence in the west Cork area. Where had it come from? And who would deliberately throw away an expensive bottle of wine without having drunk it? Those were questions that subsequent forensic tests were unfortunately unable to answer for gardaí.

It was found that the bottle of wine was worth around IR£70 (around €100 in 2020 values) and was stocked by various duty-free stores at airports around Europe. It would have been impossible for anyone to have purchased it in late 1996 in west Cork. What intrigued detectives was whether the wine had any link to Sophie's murder and, more important, to her killer and their actions immediately after the crime.

Sophie was known to love sitting by an open fire reading or writing while enjoying a glass of wine and some cheese. Had the wine come from her house? Was it taken by the killer on 23 December only for them to think better of it and, having carefully wiped the bottle clean, cast it into a bramble ditch, where, it was hoped, no one would ever find it? Gardaí had also carefully considered the washed wine glasses by the kitchen sink – had Sophie used two different glasses that day? Or had the second glass been linked to someone who visited her? Gardaí discounted the second theory given the extreme violence used in the killing and the absence of any sign of disturbance in the house.

***

Gardaí were at times swamped with information that, while initially tantalising, they couldn't match with their overall murder investigation. One such piece of information came from Galway travel agent Maurice Sweeney. His information was revealed 12 years after the killing in an article by Shane Phelan in the *Irish Independent*.

Mr Sweeney operated a travel business in Loughrea, Co. Galway. He said that, around 2.30 p.m. on 23 December 1996, a man with a French accent came into his premises enquiring about accommodation for the night.

'He came in looking for a hotel near Dublin Airport and also inquired about numbers for bed and breakfasts in west Cork. He had been in a bed and breakfast there and had left without paying. I assume he wanted their number so he could send on the money. It was two days before Christmas, which I thought was a little bit odd,' he explained.

The unknown Frenchman had come into the Galway travel agency around four and a half hours after Sophie's body had been found. Mr

Sweeney described the man as being of medium height and medium build, with sallow skin.

When Mr Sweeney saw the garda appeal for information about the Toormore killing weeks later, the mystery Frenchman immediately sprang to his mind, and he contacted gardaí. Mr Sweeney made several further contacts. However, the Galway businessman later claimed he felt his information was not being treated seriously by gardaí. He felt so strongly about this that he later took the trouble to write to Minister for Justice Michael McDowell querying what action gardaí had taken on the basis of his information.

Ten years after the murder, Mr Sweeney was interviewed by gardaí as part of a formal case review. It was apparent that investigating detectives were unable to make any link between the mystery Frenchman in Galway and the murder in west Cork. Significantly, gardaí were never contacted by any west Cork bed and breakfast owner about a French national who had stayed locally between 19 and 23 December 1996 and who had left without paying for their accommodation.

Another piece of information that came to gardaí weeks after the killing was as equally mysterious. One person said they had seen a blue-coloured car driving at speed on the Goleen–Skibbereen road on 22 or 23 December. But that was it. Nothing to indicate that the vehicle had ever been even near the turn-off for Sophie's Toormore home. No indication of the licence-plate number or even the car's specific make or model. Years later, information of this type would be the basis for a number of conspiracy theories put forward about the case, including that a now-deceased garda member was somehow involved.

Detectives were also plagued by misleading information, which was either well-intentioned or provided by people who had become obsessed by the sensational nature of the crime. I wrote about one such individual who contacted gardaí and the *Irish Independent*. He claimed to have information about the killing and, specifically, what he alleged had happened to the murder weapon. I reported on the fact that an individual had come forward with new information and had been interviewed by gardaí. There had been speculation for some time that the killer used two blunt objects, not just the concrete block found at the scene. The man alleged he knew where the supposed second weapon had been disposed of. However, gardaí treated his claims with scepticism from the very start. They subsequently came to the conclusion that the man, while well-intentioned, was a fantasist; he had a history of mental health problems.

The problems with the murder investigation in Ireland were met with increasing incredulity by Sophie's family in France. Some were decidedly diplomatic towards the Irish authorities. Paul Haennig, solicitor for Mr du Plantier, said in 2002, 'We are not critical of the investigators – we are just patient.'

However, Daniel Toscan du Plantier, in the 18 months before his death in 2003, was increasingly critical of the Irish handling of his wife's murder investigation and incredulous that no court action had resulted. 'We have rarely seen police as sure of their suspicion and incapable of finding proof. Three days after the murder the police said, "We know who the killer is." But five years later we are still at this stage,' he said.

Sophie's parents, Georges and Marguerite Bouniol, accompanied by Sophie's aunt, Marie-Madeleine Opalka, made the painful trip each December or January to west Cork to attend an anniversary Mass in Goleen parish church for their daughter, usually celebrated by Father John O'Donovan. I covered those trips each year and, without fail, the couple would appeal for public help for the gardaí while steadfastly refusing to attack the Irish authorities for the failure to bring Sophie's killer to justice.

As the years passed it became increasingly heartbreaking to see the elderly couple clinging to the forlorn hope that somehow, somewhere, new information would emerge, which would allow Sophie's killer to be identified and then face justice. Each time, after the anniversary Mass, a handful of west Cork locals would gather in the winter gloom and embrace the couple, expressing their personal sorrow and sympathy for what the French parents were enduring.

On one occasion, standing with other Cork-based reporters outside Goleen parish church, I listened as Marie-Madeleine, whose flawless English meant that she acted as a translator for Georges and Marguerite during each visit, explained that their greatest fear was that they would not live to see justice done for their daughter.

'The policemen we meet [each year] are very kind people,' Marguerite explained, as Marie-Madeleine translated for her. 'But I have to say that I could not understand the way that the Anglo-Saxon judicial system was working. We come back to west Cork every year. It is very, very difficult for us. But we hope and we pray that justice will be done someday for Sophie. She was viciously killed. Her face was smashed. But we can do absolutely nothing. We can do nothing for her except fight for justice. She was murdered in terrible circumstances. The fact that she was left like that – it is terrible. Would you do it to a dog?'

The French media, however, was far less forgiving or understanding of the Irish authorities and the problems faced by gardaí. Paris-based newspapers and magazines frequently wrote that the Irish authorities had bungled the case from the very beginning and that a litany of errors had effectively ruined any chance of a prosecution being levelled. On the fifth anniversary of Sophie's death, one French newspaper carried an in-depth review of the case. It declared that, had the killing occurred in France, the killer would already be several years into a sentence.

3

SOPHIE TOSCAN DU PLANTIER

Sophie Andrée Jacqueline Bouniol was born on 28 July 1957, 14 days after France had celebrated its national Bastille Day holiday. She was the first child of Georges Bouniol and Marguerite Gazeau. The couple were from families whose roots were in the Lozère area of France, though both grew up in Paris, where they would later live and work.

The couple met in 1951 and were married three years later. Georges, like other young French men his age, had completed his compulsory military service. He had attended university and qualified as a dentist. He initially worked as a junior partner in a busy city practice before taking over the business, located in a Paris building that also had comfortable living quarters attached. Sophie was almost two when the couple welcomed their second child, Bertrand. Years later, they would have another son, Stéphane.

Georges and Marguerite were devoted parents, and their lives were centred on their young family. They lived in an apartment just a couple of hundred metres from the River Seine and central Paris, which Marguerite had transformed into a beautiful home. Staunch Catholics, they attended local religious services, often in Notre-Dame. Like other French families, they had holidays both in France and abroad. Products of their era, and grateful for the way France had been rebuilt after World War II to emerge once again as a prosperous European nation, the couple were conservative, worked hard and saved for their children's education. The children were the focus of Georges and Marguerite's world, with care taken over their education, social life and sporting activities.

Sophie was a precocious child. Beautiful, confident and intelligent, she was the centre of almost every event she became involved in. Friends would later recall how Sophie would 'illuminate a room just by walking into it'. Even as a child she knew her own mind and displayed early signs of a strongly independent personality.

The Bouniols maintained close contact with their extended family. So much so that Sophie drew some of her closest friends from within her wide circle of cousins, including Alexandra and Patricia. She was also particularly close to her aunt, Marie-Madeleine Gazeau. Marie-Madeleine would marry the acclaimed French–Polish artist, Roman Opalka.

Roman Opalka was born on 27 August 1931 at Hocquincourt, northern France. His parents were from Poland, and they returned to Poland in 1935. However, they were deported following the invasion by Nazi Germany. Roman was lucky to survive the war, and he went back to Poland after 1945, where he made his name as a pioneering conceptual artist. He returned to France in 1977 and eventually became a French citizen, splitting his time with Marie-Madeleine between their homes in Paris and Venice until his death at the age of 79 in 2011. His influence on Sophie's early life would deepen Sophie's interest in and exposure to the arts and underpin her future career as a filmmaker, writer and passionate fan of poetry and music

In school, Sophie's intelligence ensured she always scored close to the top of her class. While she was strong in most subjects, it was within the spheres of art and literature that she thrived. She became an avid reader and, like most French teens, was absolutely devoted to the cinema, in particular French cinema, which was entering its golden era.

It also became apparent as she grew into her teens that Sophie was not only intelligent but determined and increasingly independent. Although exceptionally close to her parents, she was also single-minded once she had made a decision, whether it was to do with her studies, her personal life or her political beliefs.

Not surprisingly, Sophie attracted the admiring glances of teenage boys. Strikingly good-looking, her blonde hair framed a pretty, freckled face, lit up by magnetic eyes. Combined with a confident, bubbly personality, it meant Sophie had to cope with besotted young admirers.

But for Sophie and her parents, nothing was to divert her from her education. She attended a school in Italy to focus on arts and language skills, which she was determined to hone. It was the latter that brought her to Ireland for the first time. Seeking to improve her English, Sophie signed up for a language skills programme that involved staying with a family in Dublin for a month in 1971. The following year she returned to Ireland for another one-month stint.

While the other Bouniol siblings travelled to Ireland for similar language skills programmes, the visit had the greatest impact on Sophie, and not just in terms of her enhanced English. Ireland had a far greater impact on Sophie than on her brothers. The country and its culture seemed to make a connection with her that would, rather than fade over time, become more intense and persistent.

Twenty years later, Sophie would seek to renew that connection on a more permanent basis with a holiday home in west Cork.

Her parents were taken aback when, despite her passion for the arts, Sophie told them she wanted to study law at the prestigious University of Paris. Friends and family had anticipated her seeking to forge some kind of career in the arts, but Sophie had made her mind up. It was while in college that she first met Pierre-Jean Baudey.

Tall, dark and with film-star good looks, Pierre-Jean was quiet, personable and easy company. Sophie seemed totally at ease in his company. Everyone noted what a lovely couple they made. But Sophie's happiness with Pierre-Jean was increasingly in contrast to her studies. As her friends had feared, legal studies hadn't captivated Sophie's heart and she struggled to maintain interest in her courses. She easily passed her exams but was now openly questioning whether this was the field she wanted to devote the rest of her life to.

Ultimately, despite the misgivings of her family, she left university.

Not long afterwards, she married Pierre-Jean. They opened their own shop and worked in retail for a time. In spite of the fact that they never had a lot of money, both were very happy. That helped to ease any concerns her friends may have had at her decision to abandon her studies.

Their wedding took place on 21 June 1980. Sophie was 22. She had opted for a simple, elegant Victorian-style wedding gown. Its high collar, short train and understated design placed all the focus on Sophie's striking features and golden-blonde hair, which was pulled back in a simple ponytail. Everyone agreed that she made a beautiful bride.

Ten months after the wedding, Sophie's son, Pierre-Louis, was born. Sophie was absolutely devoted to her little son who, in appearance, shared more with his dark-haired father than his blonde mother. Sadly, too much had happened too fast in the relationship between Sophie and Pierre-Jean. The idyllic romance of the previous year was lost in a struggle of different priorities, financial pressures, the demands of raising a baby, and arguments about what their goals should be.

A short time after the birth of Pierre-Louis, Sophie and Pierre-Jean separated. While their friends hoped there would be a reconciliation within a few weeks, none occurred, and in 1983 the couple made the decision to divorce. They had been married and living together for less than a year.

Sophie moved back to the area where her parents lived, where they were delighted to offer active support in raising little Pierre-Louis. There was just over a decade in age between Pierre-Louis and Sophie's youngest brother, Stéphane, so it was hardly surprising that there were times when Pierre-Louis almost seemed like a much younger sibling rather than a nephew.

Pierre-Louis spent a substantial amount of time with his extended family as Sophie sought to reorganise her life and serve as her little family's main breadwinner. She held a number of jobs, was never out of work and was thrifty in managing her finances. Sophie eventually focused on the media as a career that suited both her interests and her disposition.

With her bubbly personality, intelligence and good looks, Sophie was a natural in the public relations sector. Eventually she secured a job working for UniFrance. Founded in 1949, UniFrance worked to promote French films overseas and, in particular, in French-speaking countries and the United States. Managed by the Centre National de la Cinématographie, it boasted hundreds of members ranging from film directors to studio officials and from screenwriters to agents.

Because of the perceived cultural importance of French cinema, UniFrance could call on significant political and economic support when required. French cinema was seen as a critical method of promoting France itself, and successive governments – from Charles de Gaulle to François Mitterrand to Jacques Chirac – were staunch in their support of the agency and its work. French-owned firms were also keen to be associated with such a promotion of Gallic culture and major French film releases.

For Sophie, UniFrance marked a turning point in her life. She had suddenly found what she had been looking for and what her legal studies had failed to provide. It combined her passion for the arts with the challenge of using her work to make a difference in the world as she saw it. Cinema also offered her a way of combining her work with her strong political views. Fascinated by African art, Sophie was eventually able to get involved in a film project dealing with African art and the exploitation of women in the African continent. She also pursued projects ranging from the importance of cinema in French society to the role of women in modern post-war Europe.

One woman she met through her new work, Agnes Thomas, became one of her closest friends and confidantes. For the remainder of her life, Sophie treated Agnes like a sister. She trusted Agnes implicitly, and the two women were in almost daily contact right up until the time of Sophie's death.

Another person she met through UniFrance was Daniel Toscan du Plantier. For a time, Sophie worked for Daniel, who was elected to the prestigious role of chairman of UniFrance in 1988. Daniel was 47 years old, while Sophie was 31 years old. He already ranked as one of the most influential people in French cinema and was a hugely respected producer. Among his film credits were Peter Greenaway's acclaimed film *The Cook, the Thief, His Wife & Her Lover*.

Daniel du Plantier had originally worked for the publisher of the prestigious French newspaper *France-Soir*, but then pursued a career in the film industry. From 1975 he served as the director general of the Gaumont Film Company, the oldest in the world. It was a period of tremendous success for Gaumont, which had the backing of multimillionaire French media tycoon Nicolas Seydoux. The firm was so successful it forged collaborations with international film giants such as Disney and Sony.

When Sophie joined UniFrance, Daniel had just divorced his second wife, having been married first to Marie-Christine Barrault and then Francesca Comencini. Ms Comencini was a well-known Italian actor in the European film industry.

After Sophie's death in 1996, Daniel would marry again. In 1998 he married Melita Nikolic, who had moved to France from the former Yugoslavia with her parents. He was 57, while she was 29. Just as with Sophie, Daniel met Melita through UniFrance, where she was pursuing a career in the film industry.

In their five years together before his death, they would have two children, Tosca and Maxime. Melita had become involved in a Moroccan film festival through her husband and, after his death, continued her involvement in the Marrakech event in his memory.

The late 1980s marked the pinnacle of Daniel du Plantier's career and, at the time, he ranked as one of the most powerful men in the influential French cinema industry. He rubbed shoulders with the great and the good in French society and was known to be quite friendly with Jacques Chirac, then the mayor of Paris, who would go on to become the president of France. But he also boasted links across French industries such as car manufacturing, petrochemicals and telecommunications. Executives in these industries were only too happy to support high-profile French films and film events.

Over this period, Sophie had been involved in a number of relationships, but they were brief and never threatened to rival the romance she had previously had with Pierre-Jean. Her devotion was entirely focused on little Pierre-Louis. Mother and son spent a lot of time together in Paris and Sophie insisted on taking her son with her on family holidays abroad.

Sophie was already setting her sights beyond UniFrance. Daniel, whom she had grown to know and trust, encouraged her to follow her professional dreams. Working at the agency had helped her focus on what she wanted for her career – and had helped build her confidence in her ability to achieve it.

She used Daniel as a sounding board for her plans to work in the film industry, with little intention of getting involved in a relationship with the older man whom she considered more of an ally and an advisor. However, over time, they grew closer. Initially regarding him as a trusted industry friend, Sophie was wary: the older film executive was known for his dalliances.

Sophie and Daniel became involved, and, in 1990, just over two years after they met, they married. It was a marriage that was greeted with some reservations by her family and friends. Her new husband was almost 17 years her senior and had already been divorced twice. But Sophie was adamant, and both her friends and family had learned that, once convinced of something, she was nothing if not single-minded.

The couple were highly visible in French society, appearing at major film and cultural events in Paris as well as the annual Cannes Film Festival. They made for a dashing pair – Daniel was sophisticated and elegant, Sophie was young, beautiful and had a personality that made her stand out from the crowd.

But Sophie was determined she would be regarded for her own work rather than for working with her second husband. She pursued independent film projects and became friendly with some of the most ambitious and talented people in the French film sector, including Jérôme Clément, who was the driving force behind the highly regarded ARTE television channel.

It was an exciting period within the French film industry, with a whole new generation of French stars helping to broaden the appeal of indigenous films, particularly in English-speaking markets such as the UK and US. That, in turn, led to opportunities for smaller film projects and, in particular, for documentaries, which were becoming a hugely popular genre of their own.

Daniel was wealthy and, as well as a beautiful home in Paris, he had a holiday villa in Ambax, located in the Haute-Garonne region. It was a beautiful area of France and Sophie became very fond of the home in Ambax. The couple would spend a lot of their time together there. She began to find more and more time for writing. Her poetry was very much influenced by nature, and she found her muse in the countryside of both her parents' native Lozère as well as Ambax. But she increasingly found herself thinking about the wild countryside she had seen in Ireland as a teenager almost two decades earlier.

With financial support from Daniel, she began to consider the possibility of buying a holiday home in Ireland. Her enthusiasm was infectious, and she quickly enlisted her friends, fully briefing them on precisely what she was looking for. Her cousin Alexandra was particularly supportive and was trusted by Sophie to select and view potential properties. Her priorities were a location in a wild, isolated area, with, if possible, either a view of the sea or easy access to the coast. Sophie looked in west Cork, Kerry and even Wicklow during her search, using various Irish bed and breakfasts as bases for property exploration. At one point, she even considered a house on an island off the west Cork coast but rejected this on the basis of practicalities and ease of access.

Having considered numerous options, she finally settled on a well-maintained cottage at Toormore, located off the Skibbereen–Schull road. It fit the bill. Isolated, with astounding views over the rugged local countryside, it was located about 100 metres from another property – but so far from the main road as to offer a sense of total peace and seclusion.

Author and screenplay writer Michael Sheridan was the first to outline the circumstances of Sophie's choice of Irish getaway in his 2002 book, *Death in December*. He revealed that although Sophie was enchanted with the Toormore house she eventually selected, her cousin was less enthusiastic. Alexandra had an uneasy feeling about the house – a sense of dread. She favoured a different property, but Sophie had her mind made up. Alexandra's foreboding about Toormore was something that would be noted in the years after the tragedy.

The Toormore house quickly became Sophie's special place – her refuge. She proudly brought her family to her new Irish holiday home, and it became a favourite summer holiday location for Pierre-Louis and his school friends. She also brought work friends and her cousins for short visits. Georges and Marguerite were brought to Toormore and given a tour of their daughter's favourite local shops and restaurants, often choosing to have their evening meal on the small flagged terrace in front of the property, with its views south over the hills and fields to the sea.

Her friend Agnes Thomas visited Toormore once with Sophie and noted how her friend loved the west Cork area. 'She loved being by the sea and she was fascinated by the beautiful view outside her house,' Agnes recalled years later. Poignantly, Sophie had wanted Agnes to travel with her to Toormore between 20 and 23 December 1996, but Agnes was unable to travel because of a commitment to a birthday celebration in France. 'I wanted to go, but because of a birthday could not. Perhaps if I had been there, Sophie would still be alive. I had lost my best friend. It was very shocking.'

Sophie's repeated visits led to her forging some friendships in the area. She became friendly with her close neighbours, Shirley Foster and Alfie Lyons, French expats Yvonne and Thomas 'Tomi' Ungerer, publicans

Billy and Angela O'Sullivan, Josephine Hellen and US-born cheesemaker Bill Hogan.

The wildness of the countryside surrounding her new holiday home proved everything that she had hoped for. She adored the desolate, rugged coastline, with pathways leading to headlands and cliffs battered by the Atlantic. Sophie would carefully plan her walks to the headlands between Roaringwater Bay and Dunmanus Bay, and these would then inspire her writing and poetry. One of her favourite walks was to Three Castle Head, wedged between Mizen Head and the entrance to Dunmanus Bay. Years later, her friends would recall that when Sophie returned to France from her west Cork holiday home, she immediately seemed to be planning her next trip back. 'She loved this place – it was very special to her,' Marie-Madeleine explained.

Daniel never shared his wife's enthusiasm for the isolation and rugged beauty of Toormore. He considered the house too remote, too difficult to access and too far from the social hubs around which their lives now revolved. One friend recalled that the French film executive considered the house 'cold and draughty'. He never needed the sense of isolation that Toormore offered Sophie.

His view was apparently that, if they needed a quiet period away from their frenetic work and social scene in Paris, didn't they have the house in Ambax? They both loved the Haute-Garonne property, and it was far easier to access from Paris. Toormore never held any magic for him, unlike the attraction it offered to Sophie.

Daniel would ever only make one visit to Toormore with Sophie. After her death he would return to Toormore just once more.

In the early years of their marriage, there were strains, mostly linked to their career demands and strong personalities. Often, Sophie would seek a little time away from the apartment they shared, usually just a matter of hours or, on rare occasions, a few days. Toormore became the place Sophie went to think, to write and to consider where her life was going. Sometimes the differences between the couple would lead Sophie to seek time alone, either in west Cork or at a flat she had in Paris. Now in her mid-30s, Sophie didn't hesitate to opt for time alone when her relationship with Daniel became fraught or complicated. On occasions, these separations were only for a matter of days. At one time, she stayed away from Daniel's apartment for two weeks. But these short periods apart all occurred in the early part of their marriage, roughly around the time of her relationship with Bruno Carbonnet, from whom the police had sought a statement after her murder.

A relationship between Sophie and Bruno developed in 1991, which saw Sophie bring the artist with her to Toormore – something that, for her, carried great significance. Their relationship continued for slightly over a year before Sophie ended it in 1993.

From 1993 onwards Sophie and Daniel's marriage slowly adapted to the demands of their strong personalities and hectic careers. The couple had forged an understanding of each other and a very close bond. There were no more extended periods apart and, as Daniel du Plantier told French police after Sophie's death, they were in 1996 discussing having a child together. Years later, Agnes Thomas would verify this. The tragedy was that, at the end of 1996, Sophie and Daniel were enjoying the happiest period of their married life.

If Daniel du Plantier knew about the relationship with Bruno Carbonnet, he never publicly commented on it. The confirmation of the relationship came in statements made by the artist to French police in the immediate aftermath of Sophie's death and at the request of gardaí, who wanted to eliminate him from their inquiries.

What is known is that, when Sophie arrived alone at Cork Airport shortly before 2.30 p.m. on Friday, 20 December 1996, her relationship with Bruno Carbonnet had been over for more than three years. She planned to spend a short break at Toormore before flying back to Paris to spend Christmas with her husband. She then planned to fly to Dakar for a New Year's break with Daniel. The following year, 1997, was when the couple hoped to have a child together.

Sophie was planning to fly back to Paris on the Aer Lingus flight from Cork Airport on Monday 23 December for onward transfer to Toulouse, where she would meet her husband. She would be murdered roughly 12 hours before her scheduled departure time.

4

IAN BAILEY

Ian Bailey was born just outside Manchester, England, to middle-class parents in 1957, just 12 years since the end of World War II. Manchester, one of the great industrial hubs of the UK, had suffered severe damage from German bombing, along with its outlying industrial outposts including Salford, Bolton and Stockport, where the Bailey family lived.

Even football clubs had suffered at the hands of the Luftwaffe. Manchester United had, for a time, been forced to use the stadium of their fierce opponents, Manchester City, while bomb damage to their own facilities was repaired. The post-war years had been difficult in Manchester, as in all other parts of the UK, with vast areas of damage to be repaired and shortages of many goods, especially luxuries, until well into the 1950s. Food rationing had only ended in the UK, having been introduced in 1940, just three years before Mr Bailey's birth.

But with the rebuilding of the city and suburbs came optimism and opportunity. By the 1960s, when Mr Bailey was a schoolboy, Manchester had become not just an economic hub for the UK but also a cultural and artistic centre, just like its near neighbour and great rival Liverpool.

Intelligent, outgoing and with a passion for the arts, Ian Bailey couldn't have picked a more vibrant place to spend his early childhood, possibly with the exception of London. A good student, he tested towards the top of his school classes and had a particular flair for literature.

In 1966, when Ian was nine years old, his father and mother decided to relocate their young family, which now included a daughter, Kay, to the south. The Baileys were set on a move to Gloucester, some 217 kilometres south of Stockport. Ian's father worked as a craft butcher, and employment opportunities were better in Gloucestershire than in Lancashire. It was also thought that the area might offer a better lifestyle for the two children. Years later, Ian Bailey would recall his parents as hard-working people who were utterly devoted to their young family.

Mr Bailey was enrolled in a religious-run school called The Crypt, and the move south, if anything, saw his grades improve. The Crypt traces its history back to 1539 and it ranks as one of the oldest schools in England. The UK at the time had a tiered education system, with the very best students guided towards grammar schools. These schools boasted a record of academic excellence with an exceptionally high proportion of students going on to university.

In this environment, the teen's interests in literature, poetry and the arts were further encouraged. By his late teens Ian had decided on a career in journalism, which offered not only the variety to indulge his interests, such as archaeology and history, but also the flexibility for him to pursue his interest in writing and poetry.

A key moment for his choice of career was when he stumbled across a copy of *All the President's Men*, the acclaimed investigative book by Washington journalists Carl Bernstein and Bob Woodward that detailed their work on the Watergate scandal. He admitted that the book captivated him and sparked what would become a lifelong fascination with journalism and, in particular, with investigative reporting.

Almost half a century later, and in very different circumstances, Mr Bailey would explain the impact the book had on the course of his life. 'I thought, that is what I want to do. You are trying to discover things.'

Like many other journalists, his budding career started by reporting on local community events. He submitted articles to the local paper in Gloucester on events he came across and incidents at his school. Some were relatively mundane, such as reports on school rugby matches, community appeals or local festivals. Others were more dramatic – such as an attack by a swarm of bees on a group of locals. He had taken a part-time job on a fish stall at the popular Gloucester market, and this helped to deliver stories through local tittle-tattle.

Filing such reports taught him how to properly present news copy and, even more usefully, gave him an introduction to key figures within the local journalism industry. This was instrumental in helping to secure him a trainee placement with a local news agency. Provincial papers and agencies provided some of the very best training for young journalists, with some of the top journalists in both the UK and Ireland tracing their beginnings to a local newspaper or radio station. As a result, Ian's burgeoning portfolio of published work secured him a place on a journalism course in Wales.

It was in 1978 that Mr Bailey first met fellow English journalist Sarah Limbrick. She was a talented young reporter working on the *Gloucester Gazette*. She would go on to work for a number of national newspapers and TV stations, as well as working on television scripts. A relationship quickly developed between the pair, and in late 1979 the couple married. However, the whirlwind romance didn't last. The marriage soon ran into difficulties, eventually ending after just four years. Ms Limbrick would later go to work in London while Mr Bailey remained in Gloucestershire.

By 1980, having successfully completed the journalism training course, and with the experience of the Gloucester news agency safely under his belt, Mr Bailey moved to Cheltenham, where there was freelance work available. A busy town, Cheltenham-based journalists benefited from its famous racecourse and its associations with both the military and intelligence communities. Cheltenham had a famous military academy, several army and RAF bases and was also home to one of the most secretive elements of the British defence network, General Communications Headquarters. Mr Bailey's innate confidence, striking good looks and determination to make a success of his career quickly began to pay dividends. Having supplied stories on a freelance basis to a number of leading UK national and provincial papers, he subsequently secured work with the *Sunday Times* and their respected Insight investigative team.

While there was prestige in filing for titles such as the *Sunday Times*, the *Daily Telegraph* and *The Guardian*, the nature of the UK newspaper industry of the early 1980s meant that the very best money was always to be made from selling salacious stories to the tabloids, including *The Sun*, *Daily Star*, *News of the World*, *Mirror* and *Sunday Mirror*. A strong story for one of the tabloids could pay two or three times as much as a story in the broadsheets. Hence, it was usually work supplying the London-based tabloids that became the bread and butter for every provincial news agency.

Financially, Mr Bailey was doing very well, and for most of the 1980s he was as busy as he wanted to be. It helped that this was still the heyday of the newspaper industry in the UK and most titles had very generous budgets for freelance work in the provinces. From working with one freelance agency, Mr Bailey eventually set up his own operation and increased the number of titles he was supplying from his Cheltenham base.

***

In 2016, recalling that period of his life, Mr Bailey noted how he had gone from writing simple stories about school events for his local paper to supplying articles for some of the most prestigious news organisations in the world. 'I acted as a news correspondent for local, regional and national newspapers as well as television,' he said. 'I was an occasional member of the *Sunday Times* Insight team and I also worked in-house for BBC local television in Bristol and for HTV West. Over the years, I authored thousands of news items.'

However, while working on a story in 1986, he made a trip that would radically alter the course of his life. That year, he made a short visit to Ireland and visited west Cork for the first time. It made a lasting impression on the 29-year-old. The laid-back lifestyle he witnessed in west Cork shone an unflattering light on his chosen life in Cheltenham.

In describing his work in Cheltenham, Mr Bailey would later refer to the articles that proved most profitable for his agency as 'frivolous'. After the breakdown of his marriage, he grew increasingly unhappy with his work in Gloucester, Cheltenham, Bristol, and even London. Almost unbeknownst to himself, the trip to Ireland had lit the spark of a desire to start a new life and focus more on his artistic interests, such as music and poetry.

His 1986 visit to Ireland prompted Mr Bailey to re-evaluate where his life was going. He would ultimately make a total of three visits to Ireland before deciding, to the astonishment of his friends, family and colleagues in both Gloucester and Cheltenham, to abandon his career in England and permanently relocate to west Cork.

A significant element in his decision to move to Ireland, as he would acknowledge in court proceedings to come, was his growing disillusionment with journalism, and the demands of his freelance job. Working as a freelancer can be a profitable option, but it is also one of the toughest fields in the industry, particularly when dealing with tabloid papers, which have an insatiable appetite for lurid stories. Operating a freelance agency can be even more demanding. A freelance is only as good as their last major story, they can never afford to be off-duty and they are constantly defending their market from other freelancers who are only too eager to poach work from them.

While getting work published was one thing, getting subsequent payment for it was another matter; it meant a huge amount of administration in submitting and then chasing invoices. For someone who loved poetry, who adored the reflective, almost mystical aspect of nature and who was also very sociable in terms of his fondness for music, art and cultural events, operating a successful UK news agency would inevitably prove to be a draining experience.

In 1991 Mr Bailey said goodbye to his Cheltenham and Gloucester friends and moved to Ireland. He initially stayed in Waterford with some acquaintances to give him time to decide on his next move. He was able to secure some casual farm work in the south-east to earn an income, before he decided, after a brief interlude in Wicklow, to move west to the Mizen Head area of Cork. Wild, rugged, and with a bohemian feel, thanks to its thriving population of migrants from all over Europe, North America and Asia, west Cork had long been a haven for artists, film stars, musicians, industrialists and even drop-outs.

West Cork would eventually boast resident celebrities such as Jeremy Irons, Sinéad Cusack, Neil Jordan, Jeremy Paxman, Roy Disney, David Puttnam, Graham Norton and Carol Vorderman. The area became so fashionable that former British Prime Minister Tony Blair and his wife, Cherie, briefly holidayed in west Cork with the Puttnams. But it wasn't just celebrities who were attracted to the place. An area near Dunmanway became home to one of the biggest New Age encampments in Ireland. Organic and vegan foods were commonplace in west Cork years before becoming popular in Irish cities. The region even boasted its own Buddhist retreat.

Mr Bailey secured a job working part-time at a fish factory in Schull and became a regular on the social scene in Schull, Skibbereen, Bantry and even smaller villages like Goleen and Ballydehob. The tall Englishman with an avid interest in all things Irish soon became a well-known figure in west Cork.

It was while working at the Schull fish factory that he first met Welsh artist Jules Thomas. She had gone to buy fish as part of her weekly family shopping and struck up a conversation with the former journalist. Given his own time studying in Wales, it was natural that they quickly became friends.

Initially he rented a room from Jules Thomas at her property at Liscaha, a short distance outside Schull. This was where she had her art studio and was raising her daughters. Not long afterwards, they began a relationship. 'We became friendly and then we became lovers,' Mr Bailey explained. As the relationship developed, he would work around the

Liscaha property, help Ms Thomas's children with their homework and attend cultural events with her across west Cork.

Ms Thomas was an accomplished and successful artist. Born in Wales, she would later confirm that she had wanted to be an artist from the tender age of just three. She had studied at Dartington College of Arts in Devon. Dartington was founded in 1961 on the estate established by Leonard Knight Elmhirst, one of the Bloomsbury set of 1920s London. For a time, Dartington served as one of the most prestigious arts-focused colleges in England and boasted connections with George Bernard Shaw, Virginia Woolf and Julian Bell.

The Welsh artist then graduated from the prestigious Kingston College in London with a qualification in art and three-dimensional design. It was her search for artistic inspiration in landscape that eventually led her to Ireland in 1973. She based herself in west Cork, where she raised her three daughters, Saffron, Virginia and Fenella. When Ms Thomas first met Mr Bailey, her daughters were aged between ten and seventeen.

Her art – gorgeous landscapes and seascapes – was inspired by the rugged west Cork countryside, which she would call home for the next 40 years. From her Liscaha studio – a dedicated art room at the pretty cottage outside Schull named The Prairie – she sold works both in Ireland and overseas. Ms Thomas secured prestigious commissions, including a display of wildlife murals for the Mizen Head Visitor Centre and works for the Jameson Heritage Centre, the Skellig Experience Visitor Centre, the Killaloe Visitor Centre and the Kenmare Heritage Centre. She would also supply a wildlife mural to Lulworth Cove Wildlife Centre in Dorset in the UK. Her work was exhibited at the Lavit Gallery and at various other arts events in Cork. Many of her artworks evoking the magic of the Irish landscape have been exported to Irish-Americans in the US.

Their shared love of the arts would underpin a relationship that would prove, by their own admission, to be both a loving union and an emotional, occasionally volatile rollercoaster. But despite this, almost 30 years later the couple are still together and still living at The Prairie in Liscaha.

Fascinated by Irish history and the Gaelic language, Mr Bailey avidly read everything he could about Ireland and west Cork. The local landscape, folklore and culture slowly began to infuse his writing, both in his poetry and in the diary he maintained daily. What he originally intended to be lyrics for songs and ballads eventually emerged as poetry reflecting rich Irish themes including nature, farming, history and the landscape. Some were also incredibly personal, dealing with the question of how someone might fit in with this history-soaked land.

Like many other Englishmen before him who had moved to Ireland and fallen in love with the local culture, Mr Bailey even decided for a time to go by the Gaelic version of his name – Eoin O'Baille. His musical instrument of choice at parties and arts events even became the bodhrán.

Many of his new Irish friends were sufficiently impressed with his poetry to suggest that he show his works to the famous west Cork-based poet John Montague. Mr Bailey had undertaken some gardening work for the New York-born poet and his American partner, the author Elizabeth Wassell, so it was easy to arrange for some of his poetry to be submitted to them for an expert opinion. The literary couple, who had fallen in love in the US despite a 28-year age difference, had relocated to west Cork in 1993, and they readily agreed to offer the Englishman whatever help and advice they could.

Mr Montague – who died in the south of France in December 2016 – was sufficiently impressed by Mr Bailey's work to encourage him to continue with his writing. He also made a number of suggestions about how the young Englishman could hone his craft. Later, the poet made the aspiring younger writer the gift of an old typewriter. In return, Mr Bailey would submit his poems to the couple with such affectionate handwritten notes as 'To the Bard, John, and to the Lady Elizabeth'.

It was a fledgling friendship that would not last, with contact effectively easing after Mr Bailey's 1996 assault on Ms Thomas, and then ceasing after his arrest by gardaí as part of the Sophie Toscan du Plantier murder investigation. In an interview with Emily Hourican for the *Sunday Independent* in June 2010, Ms Wassell said the couple were appalled when they learned about the full details of Mr Bailey's assault on Ms Thomas – an attack that required hospitalisation.

For the next few months, the couple continued to offer Mr Bailey gardening work at their west Cork home. He had spoken of his remorse about the domestic violence incident and his determination to change his life. Both felt they could best help him by providing work and supporting his attempt to address his own personal issues. But they began to slowly reduce the number of occasions on which he would be invited into their kitchen to discuss his poetry or to local literary events. Contact ended after Mr Bailey's first arrest by gardaí in February 1997 in connection with the du Plantier investigation.

On 10 January 2000, Mr Montague wrote an article about the murder of Sophie Toscan du Plantier for the prestigious *New Yorker* magazine. The piece was headlined 'A Devil in the Hills' and it brought the already high-profile Toormore killing to the attention of an even greater global audience.

It immediately became apparent that the article had greatly offended Mr Bailey, in particular the references to his poetry and the newspaper articles he had submitted about the killing in December 1996 and January 1997. One reference in the magazine article was to the fact that Mr Bailey had submitted 'scraps of songs and poem ballads' for consideration. Mr Montague wrote that 'there was a glimmer of talent there but it needed a level of discipline which he seemed unprepared to give'. The article also contained a line that claimed the Manchester-born journalist was effectively 'unruffled by his [new-found] notoriety'.

While he has steadfastly refused over the years to comment on the *New Yorker* article, it is abundantly evident that Mr Bailey considered the piece a personal betrayal by a poet he held in high esteem – not just of his relationship with the poet but also of the writings of which he was so intensely proud.

Mr Montague later became extremely wary about the aftermath of the article and claimed he had received a message from Mr Bailey that informed him, 'Don't bother coming back to west Cork.' Mr Montague, who spent time in the US and France each year before returning to his home in west Cork, was sufficiently concerned to contact gardaí to let them know to when he would be away for any extended period of time.

Afterwards, Mr Montague rarely spoke of his former protégé. One of the few remarks he passed publicly about Mr Bailey was to say: 'I don't think anyone knew Ian really well, even himself.' Ms Wassell would go on to describe Mr Bailey to *The Scotsman* newspaper as 'a lost soul' who had clearly come to Ireland to rediscover himself.

'I always felt Ian was a man who didn't seem to have his own moorings, so he overcompensated with a great show of narcissism. The way he refashioned himself into Eoin O'Baille made him seem, at least to some people in the community, a little unstable,' Montague said.

***

Earlier, in 1993, Mr Bailey had signed up for a community employment project in west Cork but began to feel the itch to get back into journalism. His first ventures involved submissions to a publication operated by the environmental campaign group Earthwatch. He also got involved in working on a script for a film that was being shot locally, which was shown to both former Minister for Arts Michael D. Higgins and Academy Award-winning producer David Puttnam, who lived locally and was hugely supportive of local arts events.

As well as learning the bodhrán, Mr Bailey's fascination with all things Irish led him to study the Irish language and, in particular, the meaning of ancient Gaelic place names across west Cork. He became a member of local storytelling groups and offered to read his poetry at various local events and festivals. On one occasion, he proudly displayed his new-found talent on the bodhrán at a summer festival on Cape Clear, an island just a short ferry ride off the coast from Schull.

His interest in all things Gaelic was apparent to all. For a time, even articles he submitted used the by-line 'Eoin O'Baille' rather than his English name. He also began to sign off conversations to friends and neighbours with 'Slán', a departure from his usual 'Cheers' or 'Good luck'.

Mr Bailey made for a colourful figure in west Cork, a place famed for never suffering from a shortage of bohemian characters. His height and good looks had always made him stand out from the crowd, but now his dress sense added to the impression he made. The journalist at one point favoured rustic fisherman-style jumpers and could easily have passed for an extra in *Ryan's Daughter*. In later years he would wear hats decorated with pheasant feathers, brightly coloured scarves and walking boots.

Some revelled in Mr Bailey's company, charmed by his flair for the dramatic and his love of both music and poetry. He became a familiar face on the west Cork arts and festival scenes, often proving the heart and soul of the party. Others, however, were less enamoured and found him a strange character. A former neighbour, Brian Jackson, would comment years later that some considered him a 'strange man'. Mr Jackson said he had heard Mr Bailey's hobby was 'destroying religious artefacts'.

Others felt his propensity for walking alone late at night and into the early hours of the morning with a large tree branch he called his 'thinking stick' was highly unusual, even by the eccentric behaviours of some in west Cork.

As he worked to build up his journalistic contacts in west Cork, Mr Bailey also undertook a range of casual jobs. He did gardening work around Schull, which, for a time, led locals to describe his craft as 'New Age gardening' because of his preference for using natural west Cork materials in his work, such as driftwood, bog timber, wildflowers and locally excavated rocks. He also did odd jobs for friends and neighbours to earn a little extra cash. At Liscaha, he helped with the vegetable garden, raised chickens and turkeys, and chopped firewood for the winter. In years to follow he would develop a successful market-stall business, offering organic vegetables and homemade pizza at farmers' markets across west Cork.

***

After five years in Ireland, by 1996 Mr Bailey was expanding his journalism to the point where he was now ready to submit material to the two biggest media outlets in the area: the *Southern Star* and *The Examiner*, both of which would pay for acceptable material. The money involved may not have been substantial, but any such commissions or freelance earnings would be a welcome supplement to the family income at Liscaha.

Many of the articles he submitted reflected his interests, such as stories involving nature, wildlife, the arts and local festivals. His aim was to establish himself as a 'stringer' or local freelancer for *The Examiner* – a position that could lead to further opportunities. Just when Mr Bailey seemed to have found the life he was looking for in a place that offered itself as a muse to his art, his entire world was thrown into chaos by a journalistic assignment that, at the outset, looked like a long-awaited opportunity to make a name for himself and earn paid work, not only from Cork-based publications but also national titles based in Dublin, including the *Irish Independent*, where my predecessor as southern correspondent, Dick Cross, was now dealing with the horrific discovery at Toormore.

Around lunchtime on 23 December 1996, Mr Bailey received a telephone call from *The Examiner* while he was in the middle of last-minute preparations with his partner and her children for Christmas in less than 48 hours' time. He was cutting a tree to help decorate The Prairie and assisting with killing and plucking turkeys for Christmas dinner. The call relayed the shocking news about the discovery of a body in nearby Toormore. Mr Bailey was the closest journalist to the area and the newspaper wanted to know if he had heard anything locally. He decided to go to the scene – with fateful consequences.

5

MEDIA

One of the great ironies of the du Plantier murder investigation is that Ian Bailey, an experienced and talented journalist, would later argue that some of the most anguished moments of his life were inflicted by the very industry in which he had worked for over 20 years.

Mr Bailey's first arrest by gardaí was on 10 February 1997. As he walked into Bandon Garda Station that lunchtime, a photographer waiting at the station, Mike Browne, managed to get a picture of him, flanked by two officers, before he vanished through the doorway. Within a couple of hours, Bandon Garda Station was surrounded by a large number of photographers, reporters and TV crews from the national media. The following day, 11 February, the *Irish Sun* splashed this development in the du Plantier investigation across its front page. Critically, it not only used the photograph taken at the station but also identified Mr Bailey by name.

This was a significant decision. By tradition, newspapers – and particularly tabloid newspapers – usually only identify someone by name if they believe there is a likelihood of a court charge to follow. The Irish media is, as a rule, very wary of publicly identifying someone in an ongoing criminal investigation, for several reasons, the most powerful of which is the potential for them to be sued. There have been exceptions, but usually a person is only named if they have somehow already identified themselves or if the media has very good reason for doing so. The presumption of innocence is taken extremely seriously.

In the case of Mr Bailey's arrest and subsequent questioning at Bandon Garda Station, it was never apparent that any charge was likely. Hence, the decision to publicly identify Mr Bailey at such an early point was highly unusual. At the time, many of us wondered whether the decision was linked to the fact that he was a journalist who had been reporting on the murder investigation. While it was highly unusual to see a journalist who had been working on a criminal case suddenly get arrested for the crime, it hardly amounted to grounds for naming him – particularly at the time when social media didn't exist and the Irish media were, by and large, far more conservative than they are today.

I was amazed at the decision to identify Mr Bailey at such an early stage – and I wasn't alone. The conversation in *The Examiner* newsroom at the time was whether the *Irish Sun* knew something about likely developments that no one else did.

The stance of the *Irish Sun* sparked a lemming-like reaction from many other newspapers and radio stations. Once one newspaper had identified him, some others, but not all, felt compelled to do the same. Years later, Mr Bailey would describe what happened to him from 10 February as akin to being caught in a feeding frenzy. Despite there being no indication of any imminent court proceedings and his vehement protestations of innocence to gardaí, his name was now being publicly associated with the du Plantier investigation by the media.

Part of the problem was that, having worked for some of the bestselling and most news-driven tabloids in the UK, Mr Bailey understood like few others the *modus operandi* of the so-called 'red tops'. One of the oldest maxims in the industry was that a newspaper never refused ink. Now that he had been publicly identified, Mr Bailey could either fill the vacuum of newspaper and broadcast space with his protestations of innocence or stay silent, in the knowledge that stories about the du Plantier investigation would be written anyway. And the majority of those stories would now include his name, whether he liked it or not.

Mr Bailey's arrest had been significant for the media in many ways. First, he had not only written about the killing but had been to the fore in delivering some of the most high-profile and contentious storylines about the case, especially about Sophie's private life in France. He had even submitted material to some of the very newspapers now considering whether to name him as the person who had been arrested by gardaí.

Second, the English journalist cut a very striking figure – tall, raven-haired and handsome, he was nothing if not photogenic. There were now multiple images of Mr Bailey available for the newspapers to use if needed. For tabloid newspapers, a striking image added yet another layer to the story.

Third, the fact that Mr Bailey is English added further to the international dimension of the case, particularly since most of the major tabloids were UK-owned. The murder of Sophie Toscan du Plantier was no longer just a Franco-Irish story. The arrest of an Englishman meant that the killing was suddenly attracting the attention of the UK press that, only a few weeks earlier, would have devoted just a few paragraphs to the story.

The Irish journalists covering the case for UK-owned tabloids found themselves dealing not only with Dublin-based news editors eager for updates on the case but with London-based news editors determined to push the story as far as they legally could for their British editions.

***

A person unversed in media operations might have gone straight to a solicitor for help and advice. They might be counselled that a stern legal cease-and-desist warning fired across the bows of the media might deter future coverage. There is nothing like a solicitor's warning letter to concentrate minds and ensure that all aspects of an article are legally tested before publication.

But Mr Bailey, having carefully considered his position, eventually decided on a different course of action, with seismic implications for both him and his life in west Cork. Rather than threaten the media with punitive legal action if they persisted in identifying him, he would instead trust them to publish his side of the story. He would attempt to counter what he saw as unfounded reports about himself with firm denials of any involvement.

Mr Bailey almost certainly took into account that he was in the process of rebuilding his freelance career in west Cork. Threatening news editors with legal action was hardly likely to further his freelance prospects with the very same media outlets going forward. As he was to repeatedly insist, he was, after all, an innocent man and this would be borne out in time, when the real killer would be identified.

Two days after his release by gardaí, Mr Bailey gave brief interviews to two journalists who had effectively camped outside his home in west Cork for the previous 48 hours – John Kierans of the *Irish Mirror* and Senan Molony of the *Irish Daily Star*. Both were talented and highly experienced operators, who had devoted hours to encouraging Mr Bailey to speak with them about the dramatic events of the previous week. Mr Kierans would go on to become editor-in-chief of the *Irish Mirror*, while Mr Molony would later become political editor of the *Irish Daily Mail*.

The interviews were painstakingly negotiated via a series of notes exchanged at The Prairie. Both journalists also had the advantage of it being their rival, the *Irish Sun*, that had first named Mr Bailey – and they could now offer him a chance to respond and get across his side of the story in their pages.

The two tabloids devoted their front-page splash to the brief interviews with Mr Bailey. Both stories were described as 'exclusives', although Mr Bailey would later take issue with this description. The articles revolved around his protestations of innocence and his vehement denials to gardaí of any involvement in the terrible crime. But, as time would tell, the greatest impact of the articles was not their overall content or Mr Bailey's protestations of innocence but the fact that Mr Bailey was again mentioned by name in association with the du Plantier investigation. He was now being consistently associated with the du Plantier investigation in the minds of the Irish public.

***

On 14 February, after four days of having large elements of the Irish and British broadcast and print media camped outside his Liscaha home, Mr Bailey again decided to break his silence on the matter. He agreed to an interview on RTÉ's flagship Radio 1 current affairs programme, *Today with Pat Kenny*. RTÉ researchers had been in continual contact with him and, given that he was being quoted in tabloid newspapers, felt the radio-listening public should hear Mr Bailey's side of the story too. In terms of impact, only *The Late Late Show* on RTÉ television had greater reach than *Today with Pat Kenny*, which boasted a daily listenership of around 300,000.

With over two decades of experience in print and broadcast journalism, Mr Bailey obviously felt he could get his side of the story across – and emphasise what a horrific mistake the gardaí had made in arresting him days earlier. He was, he maintained, an innocent man who had cooperated fully with gardaí in their bid to identify the real killer. It was also clearly hoped that, by speaking on RTÉ, he might be able to draw a line under the publicity following the events of 10 February. As it transpired, it was a forlorn hope.

Mr Bailey's telephone interview on Radio 1 that February morning would still be discussed more than 20 years later.

Throughout the Radio 1 piece, Mr Bailey protested his innocence and stressed that he had at all times denied any involvement in the matter to gardaí. He had also fully cooperated with detectives. Some elements of the interview did prove favourable to Mr Bailey. The RTÉ presenter raised the issue of why the journalist was publicly identified immediately after his arrest by one tabloid newspaper. Mr Kenny said it was not only 'highly unusual' but also 'irregular' – the norm in such cases would be for the arrested person's identity to be withheld unless there was some indication of further action about to be taken by gardaí.

However, Mr Kenny focused the interview on the reasons for Mr Bailey becoming a suspect in the first place – the scratches spotted on his arms by gardaí on 23 December 1996 at Toormore. The journalist ultimately said that it was probably reasonable for gardaí to view him as a suspect at the time.

From that day on, many newspapers would refer to Mr Bailey as 'the self-confessed suspect' in the investigation. The interview generated a raft of articles in the Irish and UK media the next day, including extensive pieces in the broadsheet newspapers.

The interviews also had the net effect of making Irish and UK publications less wary of identifying Mr Bailey than they might otherwise have been. While one tabloid had broken cover with its initial identification of him after the Bandon Garda Station questioning, it was only in the immediate aftermath of this interview that the remainder of the media appeared to become comfortable with regularly using Mr Bailey's name. From now on, almost every article published about the status of the du Plantier investigation invariably included some reference to Mr Bailey.

Some 18 years later, during his legal action for wrongful arrest, Mr Bailey acknowledged that a better course of action might have been to stay silent and not agree to the RTÉ interview. He conceded it was 'unwise' to go on radio four days after his release following the Bandon Garda Station questioning. He described Mr Kenny as a 'clever interviewer' who brought the conversation to areas that Mr Bailey had not anticipated or been prepared for. Mr Bailey had certainly not been ready for the query as to whether it was reasonable for gardaí to consider him a suspect in the matter.

He explained his decision to give interviews by saying that he had been desperately trying to defend his good name and counter the tsunami of negative publicity swirling around him. He said that at that time, in early

1997, he felt he was 'under siege' by the media. He came to believe that his silence on the matter would achieve absolutely nothing: '[Rather I was] stating my innocence and just putting the record straight.'

He forcefully rejected claims that he had actually enjoyed all the attention he was getting, particularly around west Cork, objecting to the claim that he was 'thriving on the publicity'. He said he had never wanted to be 'the centre of attention'. 'I was working as a professional journalist at the time. I enjoyed that [career]. But I was not thriving.' He pointed out that no element of what he endured after February 1997 could ever be described as enjoyable. 'It was an absolute nightmare – a torture,' he said.

He said that at times he felt like he was dealing with 'xenophobia' as a consequence of the publicity that surrounded him. Mr Bailey explained that there was nothing enjoyable in having media outlets that once published his work now decline to do so. He also pointed out that he was not the one who had brought his identity into the public domain in the first place – that was done on 11 February, without either his knowledge or his consent.

The net result of the interviews between 12 and 14 February was that, whenever an article was written about the du Plantier investigation, Mr Bailey's name was invariably referenced in some fashion. The description of himself as a 'self-confessed suspect' was something that Mr Bailey was exasperated by and would complain about in the years to follow. In 2015, he was still annoyed at the phrase, pointing out – quite accurately – that he had never actually used the term 'in the course of the entire RTÉ interview with Pat Kenny'. Yet that was the single consequence of the interview that impacted on future media coverage of the du Plantier investigation – not the vehement denials or protestations of innocence. As far as newspapers and radio stations were concerned, Mr Bailey had described himself as a suspect in the case.

***

Mr Bailey was arrested by gardaí for a second time in January 1998 and there was little hesitation among Irish and UK newspapers in confirming the identity of the person detained.

Unlike in 1997, Mr Bailey now decided to keep his own counsel, and there were no interviews when he was again released without charge. He did not speak to the media contingent gathered in Bandon that winter evening or in the days following his release. A statement issued by his solicitor asked for his privacy to be respected by the media.

Over the next three years, Mr Bailey would eventually agree to a handful of fresh interviews, one of which was for a major Sunday newspaper special on the case. The interviews were given, as the journalist would explain in 2003, on the basis of assurances that the articles would try to depict matters from his point of view – as an innocent person wrongly associated with a terrible crime – and that they would be fair and favourable to him and his plight.

Mr Bailey said he was horrified when the articles involved were finally published. One had the headline 'Investigating with the Prime Suspect'. To his shock, another headline read 'Sophie Man's Shame'. The articles were instrumental in his decision to signal defamation actions in 2001 against eight Irish and British newspapers. The action – which would ultimately be heard in December 2003 – did little to keep Mr Bailey out of newspaper headlines or TV and radio bulletins.

He grew increasingly aghast at how he was being depicted in the media. Some agreed with him. Veteran journalist Colman Doyle, who had worked on the original Sophie Toscan du Plantier murder story in December 1996, said he was shocked by some of the coverage that Mr Bailey attracted, despite the Englishman being polite and helpful to anyone he came across in his work. 'I thought he was being demonised … [I found him to be] an excellent journalist and a nice person.'

***

During this period, I had regular telephone contact with Mr Bailey. I had changed jobs in 1997, leaving *The Examiner* and joining the *Irish Independent* as southern correspondent. It meant that the ongoing du Plantier murder investigation would be one of the major cases I would be monitoring for my new employers. Twenty-three years later, it is still one of the major crime stories I write about on a regular basis.

My job regularly entailed ringing Mr Bailey for any updates or comments he might have – usually in response to the latest breaking story about developments in the garda investigation or a visit to west Cork by Sophie's family. In all the years of contacting Mr Bailey I found him to be nothing but polite and as helpful as the circumstances allowed. At the outset, Mr Bailey made it clear that everything he said was off the record and he would not be making any comment or giving any interview. But he was always unfailingly considerate and well-spoken. If I missed him at his Liscaha home and left a message, he would invariably return the call. There were times I felt sympathy for him because I believed he still held out hope of resurrecting his career as a journalist despite all that had happened. I remember one phone call in late 1998 during which he steadfastly declined to make any comment on the latest development in the case but then asked me about opportunities for photojournalists at Independent Newspapers.

Over time, Mr Bailey got to know the Cork-based reporters dealing with the du Plantier case. There were also times when I felt he was eager to hear the latest news about the case and would ask the same questions about the latest information that I had intended to table to him. Some calls would last a matter of seconds – other calls could last half an hour or more. Once, to my embarrassment, he even accepted a call and explained that he couldn't talk because he was in the Four Courts in Dublin awaiting a hearing on a European Arrest Warrant.

***

On 18 August 2001, Mr Bailey assaulted his partner, Ms Thomas, at their Liscaha home. He had damaged his leg by tearing his Achilles tendon, an exceptionally painful injury. His leg was in a cast and he was on painkillers for the discomfort. Because of the ongoing publicity surrounding him over the du Plantier investigation, he was undoubtedly also under emotional strain. Ms Thomas was sorting through the contents of her handbag that afternoon when a minor dispute broke out between the couple. She had inadvertently woken her partner from a nap he was having on the sofa and, despite the trivial nature of the row, he lashed out at her.

Mr Bailey struck the Welsh artist with his crutch, inflicting injuries to her face and left eye. The assault continued and he struck her several more times with his crutch before she was able to leave the room. She ultimately received a black eye, an inflamed cheekbone and cuts to her lip. She also suffered bruising to her arms and legs. A short time later, the journalist left the property.

The incident was sufficiently serious that local gardaí soon became aware of it. Mr Bailey was arrested on 22 August at Cork Airport. He explained to gardaí that he thought it best for him to return to the UK to allow Ms Thomas a bit of time and space so that things could calm down. Gardaí brought him back to west Cork. He appeared before a special sitting of Listowel District Court the following day, charged with assault against Ms Thomas contrary to the Non-Fatal Offences Against the Persons Act. Superintendent Frank O'Brien applied for a remand in custody, as he said that gardaí had concerns over whether Mr Bailey would answer the charge and that, when arrested, he had been in possession of a one-way ticket to the UK.

Mr Bailey was remanded in custody and appeared first before Clonakilty and then Skibbereen district courts. He was granted bail but was initially unable to meet the bail terms involved. Because of this, the journalist subsequently spent over three weeks in custody before his case was dealt with.

His arrest and appearance at various district court sittings over the next few weeks made headlines not just in Ireland but in the UK and

France. The fact that the assault involved a woman was accorded major significance by the French media. Mr Bailey's every court appearance up until his sentencing was covered by the Irish and UK media.

One of my abiding memories of that time was coming out of a west Cork court hearing, in which Mr Bailey had just been remanded with consent to bail, only to receive a call on my old Nokia phone to urgently turn on my car radio. Those were the days when mobile phones were either turned on or off – and only the really expensive models had a 'silent' function. When I did turn on the radio I heard the unfolding tragedy of the 11 September 2001 terrorist attacks on the World Trade Center in New York. The following day, Mr Bailey's court report was relegated to a distant inside page in the newspaper.

***

On 17 September Mr Bailey finally appeared before Judge James O'Connor at Skibbereen District Court. The journalist, who was by now 44 years old, admitted the assault on his partner of 10 years. Ms Thomas was not in court for the hearing.

Judge O'Connor was told that Ms Thomas feared for her safety because of the attack. Having heard an outline of the facts, and that Mr Bailey had already spent more than three weeks in custody, the judge imposed a three-month suspended prison sentence. He also ordered that Mr Bailey pay compensation of IR£2,500 and allowed him until the following February to do so. That would subsequently prove the focus of further court hearings as Mr Bailey had no regular source of income and owned no assets suitable for disposal in Ireland.

Judge O'Connor also directed that Mr Bailey be of good behaviour for a two-year period until the end of 2003 – coincidentally, the very time that his long-awaited defamation action would finally arrive before Cork Circuit Civil Court.

Not surprisingly, there was a large media presence for the Skibbereen hearing with reporters, photographers and TV crews assembled outside. Mr Bailey, who looked pale, left the courtroom without comment and was driven away by a friend. Before he left, he politely nodded to the local journalists whom he had by now come to know on a personal basis. Even with the enormous coverage devoted to the appalling aftermath of the New York, Washington and Pennsylvania terrorist attacks, his suspended prison sentence was still accorded major coverage in every Irish newspaper the following day.

Any hopes Mr Bailey had of the relentless media glare slowly fading were by now clearly abandoned. Instead he decided to challenge the media head-on with a civil action that would, if anything, dwarf the coverage that he had been accorded in the media over the preceding four years. The looming Cork Circuit Court action would also dramatically escalate public interest in the du Plantier investigation and have profound, if unexpected, consequences in France.

6

LIBEL HEARING

Two years later, Mr Bailey found himself back in the headlines. On Monday, 8 December 2003, he commenced a series of libel actions before Cork Circuit Court. The actions were taken, as he would later explain, in a bid to end 'monstrous' media reports about him both in Ireland and in his native UK in the context of the ongoing Sophie Toscan du Plantier investigation.

He complained that his life had been rendered a 'nightmare' through unfair and inaccurate media reports about the killing. Mr Bailey's barrister, Jim Duggan BL, declared that his client had been the victim of a trial by media – that he had been not only subjected to 'character assassination' but also 'demonised' to the point where he was being ostracised in his adopted west Cork community.

What quickly became apparent was that, far from ending media interest in him, the libel actions were akin to pouring petrol on an already smouldering fire. By the end of the two-week hearing, the entire country was fascinated with the du Plantier case, Ian Bailey and the dramatic revelations of the Cork libel action.

Such was the profile of the Cork Circuit Court action, it even made headlines in the UK and France. Critically, the French media became aware for the first time of key elements of the garda murder file in Ireland as a result of the material that was brought into the public domain by the newspapers' defence team during the court proceedings. They were revelations that would have far-reaching consequences.

Mr Bailey had decided to sue eight Irish and British newspapers over specific articles they had written about him over the previous years. The newspapers being sued were the *Sunday Independent*, the *Independent on Sunday*, *The Times*, the *Sunday Times*, the *Daily Telegraph*, the *Irish Mirror*, the *Irish Star* and the *Irish Sun*. The Manchester journalist was taking on some of the biggest media organisations in Ireland and the UK.

I was covering the case each day for the *Irish Independent*, the *Evening Herald* and the *Sunday Independent*, and knew from months beforehand that the libel hearing would generate huge public interest. But what none of us Cork-based journalists fully appreciated was just how dramatic the evidence would turn out to be and how all-consuming interest in the case would become.

In truth, Ireland had never experienced a libel action like it before or since. Somewhat bizarrely, the highest-profile libel action taken in Cork in modern times was heard in a former garden supplies warehouse that was being used as a temporary courthouse while the main Cork Courthouse on Washington Street was the subject of a protracted €26-million renovation programme. It was a setting totally at odds with the profile of the case at hearing.

By the end of the two-week action, curiosity about the case had grown so intense that there wasn't even standing room in the main court on the concluding day of evidence, with journalists who had covered the duration of the trial having to access the court early through a back door just to ensure they secured a seat for the judge's ruling.

Members of the public attended in unprecedented numbers. Dozens of people would queue in the morning for the court to open just to secure the best seats in the public gallery. Many brought their lunches with them. One pensioner I spoke to said it was more interesting than any daytime programme on RTÉ or TV3. At the conclusion of the trial I bumped into a Sunday's Well businessman who happened to own the building where my newspaper's Cork office was located. He, like everyone else, had become gripped by the case and wanted to watch its conclusion in person.

There were several interesting aspects to the case. First, Mr Bailey decided to take his action before the Circuit Court, not the High Court. While it is always more costly to take proceedings before the High Court, the potential damages that can be awarded are effectively unlimited. In the Circuit Court, damages were limited to €38,000 (though they have since been increased to €75,000). If Mr Bailey were to win all the actions, the most he could receive in damages was €266,000 – hardly a vast sum given the issues at stake.

Another crucial difference between such High Court and Circuit Court libel hearings is that, before the High Court, the matter must be argued before a judge and jury. In the Circuit Court, the matter would be decided solely by a judge, in this case Judge Patrick Moran.

Although the State was not a party to the proceedings, it was an interested party. It had objected to any material related to the garda murder file being entered into evidence lest it compromise potential future action. The murder case remained both open and active and the State was acutely aware of this fact. Specifically, the State did not want any of the investigating gardaí to be called as witnesses by the newspapers' defence team.

The DPP had already made it clear that, on the current basis of the garda case file, no action would be directed. This decision dated back to a major assessment of the garda file conducted in 2001 by Robert Sheehan, an official within the DPP's office. He found that there was not sufficient evidence to support a prosecution. In addition, he ruled not only that there was no tangible evidence against Mr Bailey but that the journalist's actions in offering to cooperate with investigating officers at the earliest possible stage was, if anything, likely to point towards his innocence.

The summary of Sheehan's report played no part in the libel hearing. It didn't properly enter the public domain until nine years later, during the first French attempt to have Mr Bailey extradited from Ireland. For the time being, all anyone understood was that in 2001 the DPP had emphatically ruled out any question of a prosecution in the absence of new evidence.

Few of us at the time realised the critical importance of a ruling made by Judge Moran on the opening day of the hearing that gave the newspapers' legal team access to specific material obtained by the gardaí. In granting the disclosure order, the defence received the right to examine Mr Bailey's personal diaries and writings – and to cross-examine him in evidence about them. Those diaries had been in garda possession since 1997/1998. But, at the same time, no gardaí involved in the murder investigation itself would be called to offer evidence.

Mr Bailey was represented by Bandon-based solicitor Con Murphy, who would be appointed a Cork Circuit Court judge the following year. Tragically, Mr Murphy would later die after a short illness, at the age of just 51, in August 2011. Leading Mr Bailey's legal team was barrister Jim Duggan BL.

In contrast, the newspapers were represented by four different firms of solicitors, with McAleese and Co. taking the lead. Their team was led by David Holland SC and Paul Gallagher SC, who would later become Ireland's Attorney General. Everyone realised that the newspapers were determined to fight the action tooth and nail – there would be no eleventh-hour settlement on the steps of the courthouse.

The hearing opened with Mr Duggan outlining the damage to Mr Bailey's reputation as a result of the articles. The barrister said that his client had been branded as 'the murderer' as a consequence of the articles, that Mr Bailey was now being shunned within the west Cork community he had chosen to make his home and that his life had been rendered a 'living nightmare' because of the ongoing newspaper coverage of the crime and the constant association of him with the terrible events of 23 December 1996. Mr Duggan said that Mr Bailey's primary hope was that the true culprit would be caught by gardaí and convicted of the killing.

He told the court that Mr Bailey's sole purpose in taking the libel action was to defend his good name and to demonstrate to people in west Cork not only that was he innocent, but that he had been treated dreadfully by being associated with Mrs du Plantier's death. It was further claimed that Mr Bailey had only agreed to participate in interviews with some of the journalists involved after the promise of a favourable or sympathetic article. When the articles had been published, Mr Duggan said, his client had been appalled and had felt betrayed by what was written.

Mr Duggan said that the case was not about portraying his client as a 'saint'. He said it was critical to understand that gardaí had been supplied with Mr Bailey's clothing, his hair, DNA and blood samples, but no charge had ever been levelled against him in respect of the killing. Mr Bailey, the barrister argued, had been left with no alternative but to take the libel actions in a bid to publicly underline his innocence and defend his reputation from what he termed the 'grossly defamatory slurs' cast against him.

In his opening statement, Mr Gallagher argued that the newspapers had never portrayed Mr Bailey as the killer. Rather, they had dealt with him in the context of the fact that he was the main suspect when the articles in question had been published. He argued that Mr Bailey was a 'very violent man', who had actually cooperated with many of the journalists.

Tall, composed and with a notebook in his hand, Mr Bailey, with his partner Jules Thomas by his side, listened without emotion to the opening statements, pausing occasionally to take notes. By mid-afternoon, the opening statements had concluded, and the main drama began. Mr Bailey took the witness stand to outline to his legal team the damage caused to his reputation.

What struck me most in the courtroom that day was how dramatically he had aged. I had first encountered Ian Bailey in 1997, a couple of months after his first arrest. With his raven-black hair, a tall and upright bearing and strikingly handsome features, I thought he looked more like a leading Shakespearean actor than a journalist. Six years later, I was shocked by his appearance. His temples were greying and his face was haggard and drawn. He appeared to have aged 20 years. There could be no doubt in anyone's mind that the past six years had taken a terrible toll on him. Yet, despite the obvious strain he was under, he took to the witness box with a confidence that indicated he had been eagerly waiting for this day to defend his good name. Over a total of five days, he gave evidence in what could only be described as a gruelling process.

Mr Bailey explained how he had moved to Ireland in 1991 and met Welsh artist Jules Thomas. At the time, he was working at a fish factory in Schull. They began a relationship and, after dabbling in various jobs in west Cork, he decided to try to revive his journalistic career by supplying occasional stories to the *Cork Examiner*.

He said that he received a phone call on 23 December 1996 from Eddie Cassidy, the newspaper's west Cork correspondent at the time and now a news editor with the paper. Mr Bailey said that Mr Cassidy informed him that there had been a murder outside Schull and that it was understood to involve a person who was a foreign national. There was a suggestion that the person involved might be French – details Mr Cassidy would later insist he had not been aware of at that time.

Mr Bailey was adamant that this was the first occasion he had heard anything about the murder. He also insisted it was the only reason he had decided to go to the site of the incident that day. At the time, he had been helping Ms Thomas with preparations for Christmas. His jobs were to cut down an evergreen to use as a Christmas tree for the family home and to kill turkeys that had been fattened for the festive season, both for the family's own use and for sale.

He said he used a knife to kill and prepare the turkeys but, as he did so, he was scratched by a bird's talons. He explained that he also received some abrasions to his arms when he was cutting down a seven metre-high fir tree to use as the family Christmas tree. He was assisted in cutting down the tree by Ms Thomas's daughter Saffron.

Accompanied by Ms Thomas, he made his way to Toormore after the call from Mr Cassidy and discovered a calamitous scene with a heavy garda presence.

'I could see a lot of garda activity on the hillside [below Ms du Plantier's house]. A little later, a few gardaí came up to me. I explained that I was there for the *Cork Examiner*. They told me to contact the Garda Press Office.' Mr Bailey moved a short distance back, and Ms Thomas, who had brought a single-lens reflex camera, began to take photographs of the scene and the garda activity using a telephoto lens.

Mr Bailey later submitted articles to both *The Examiner* and the *Irish Independent*, but both ran with pieces by staff reporters for the editions on 24 December. However, he secured work supplying material to a number of Irish and French publications, including the *Irish Star* and the *Sunday Tribune*. By this stage it had been confirmed locally that the victim was Sophie Toscan du Plantier.

Throughout his barrister's questioning, Mr Bailey remained focused and detailed in his answers. He explained the circumstances of his two arrests by the gardaí in February 1997 and January 1998. The decision to arrest him left him deeply shocked – and he claimed gardaí had blatantly tried to frighten him into admitting the crime. At one point he claimed that a garda told him he was 'finished in Ireland'. He also claimed that another officer warned him that if he was not convicted of the killing, he would be 'found dead with a bullet in the back of the head'.

Mr Bailey told the court that he was stunned on his arrival at Bandon Garda Station on 10 February 1997 to discover a media posse already waiting for him. He desperately tried to shield his face from the photographers, but one still managed to get a shot of him being led into the station for questioning under arrest.

He said he had consistently maintained his innocence to gardaí at the station and had agreed to supply any forensic samples requested, knowing he had nothing to hide. 'I had no fears about giving my blood or DNA,' he said. Throughout a questioning period he described as 'ferocious', Mr Bailey maintained that he had absolutely nothing to do with the crime.

Mr Bailey's name was first used by the media in connection with the du Plantier investigation the following day. The *Irish Sun* published his name and photograph in connection with the garda arrest. Shortly afterwards, other publications also identified him as the person held by gardaí.

Released without charge, he was detained again by gardaí eleven months later. In a mirror image of the first arrest, he was questioned at Bandon Garda Station before being once again released without charge, going straight from the station to the offices of his solicitor, Mr Murphy, just a couple of hundred metres away. Again, he was identified in the media as the person detained by gardaí.

Mr Bailey's subsequent release without charge made headlines not just in Ireland but in the UK and France. The newspapers published the following Sunday carried extensive articles on the latest in the garda investigation. Mr Bailey complained of the enormous impact of the coverage on his life: 'I was stripped of my presumption of innocence. Life was a struggle. Sometimes it felt like I was being eaten alive. I have been absolutely battered [by publicity]. I felt sick to the pit of [my] stomach. I was now untouchable [to west Cork locals]. There were times when I felt like a hunted animal.'

Mr Duggan concluded his questioning of his client on the second day of the hearing. Mr Gallagher, for the newspapers, then began his cross-examination after the lunch recess. Like most of the other journalists covering the case, I had worked throughout lunch to type up the gripping evidence of the morning session in a bid to ease the pressure on myself after court finished at 5 p.m. I might as well not have bothered, because in the opening two hours of Mr Gallagher's questioning that Tuesday afternoon, everything I had just written was superseded by the incredible exchanges between Mr Gallagher and the plaintiff.

The future Attorney General, like a guided missile, homed in on incidents in 1996 and 2001, when Mr Bailey was arrested by gardaí in relation to allegations of violent assaults against his partner, Ms Thomas. Mr Bailey explained that he had been under a lot of pressure in 2001, when one incident had occurred. The journalist said he had 'eternal regret' over the matters involved. He insisted that he took 'full responsibility' for them. He acknowledged he had hurt Ms Thomas and very much regretted what had happened. One incident he referred to as 'an indiscretion'.

But Mr Gallagher suggested that the injuries inflicted in some of the incidents represented 'an animal-like [attack]'. The senior counsel outlined in great detail the injuries suffered by Ms Thomas, which included a cut to her mouth that required eight stitches, bite marks, a badly bruised eye and clumps of hair being torn from her scalp.

Mr Bailey, while querying some of the details of the incidents, such as the scale, duration and circumstances, acknowledged that they were 'appalling'. But he rejected suggestions that he was prone to violence. 'I am not a violent man – this was not a premeditated attack. I did not intend to hurt her.' He insisted that the incidents, which he now deeply regretted, were sparked by alcohol consumption.

Central to the newspapers' defence were Mr Bailey's diaries, which had been seized by gardaí but were now being examined in forensic detail in court.

The diaries would provide some of the most remarkable headlines of the entire hearing. In truth, they were nothing short of sensational. Mr Gallagher would carefully question the journalist about writings in which he described himself as 'damned to hell', 'an animal on two feet' and that there was 'something badly wrong with me'. But, crucially, entries in the diaries also emphasised that the journalist and poet had nothing to do with the Toormore tragedy.

'Ultimately, there is and can be no evidence – unless it is invented – to connect me to [a] crime I did not commit.' He also used his diary to ponder why gardaí should ever have regarded him as a suspect. The diaries also documented how highly Mr Bailey regarded his writings and how frustrated he was with his lack of success with them, and with his life in general.

I write well, with confidence, fluidity and flair – and yet I find it so hard to make ends meet. I know I am a great poet, but I am frustrated at not being published.

I always seem to fuck up. There is nothing that I have touched in my life which I haven't ruined or has not fallen apart. Even here in Ireland, as well as [I] try and create something, I have fucked up more times than anybody could be expected. Why, why, why?

The overtly sexual passages in the diaries were not dealt with during cross-examination by Mr Gallagher. But newspapers would later publish extensive details of these extracts, including passages in which Mr Bailey wrote, sometimes at length and in astonishing detail, about his preferences and views on sex, which ranged across everything from sexual positions to multiple partners. In one astonishing entry, he wrote that he was 'totally obsessed with sex, I love my drugs and I adore alcohol … grass and hash are so horny … there is a direct correlation, I am sure, between the herb and sex … I think there is little hope of redemption in this life.'

On 13 May 2007, the *Irish Daily Mail* printed lengthy edited extracts from the diaries, with emphasis on the passages depicting sexual content, noting that they were 'long and rambling and … can only be described as pornographic'.

Elements of the diary entries also reflected poorly on the poet and his view of his loyal partner, such as one passage written on 10 October 1994. 'I absolutely need mental stimulation and unfortunately I cannot get it from Jules. She is fine as a sexual partner but as a soulmate I feel little in common. I am often taken by brighter young things,' he wrote.

Arguably the most dramatic diary entry was written by Mr Bailey in 1996, around the time of one of the incidents involving Ms Thomas. 'One act of whiskey-induced madness – coupled and cracked – in an awful act of violence I severely damaged you and made you feel that death was near. As I lay and write, I know there is something badly wrong with me. For through remorse-filled sentiments, disgust fills me. I am afraid for myself – a cowardly fear. For although I have damaged and made grief your life, I have damaged my own destiny and future to the point where I am seeing, in destroying you, I destroyed me. In doing what I did I am damned to hell.'

Mr Gallagher queried how he could balance such writing with the description of the injuries sustained by Ms Thomas and his own insistence that one of the incidents involved was 'an indiscretion'.

But the journalist insisted his writings had to be judged in an abstract way. He said they should not be taken literally – and that he had adopted a form of writing in the style of the Welsh poet Dylan Thomas, whom Mr Bailey admired.

The senior counsel again pointed out that Ms Thomas had been subjected to attacks by Mr Bailey in 1993, 1996 and again in 2001.

The highest-profile of the domestic violence incidents occurred in August 2001, when Mr Bailey, who had suffered a painful Achilles tendon injury, lashed out at Ms Thomas using his leg plaster and his crutch.

Mr Bailey, in one reply to Mr Gallagher, clearly attempted to draw a line under the incidents with Ms Thomas. 'There is no justification for domestic violence ... but the fact that I have committed these with Jules does not mean that I am a murderer.'

He also rejected comments attributed to him by some in west Cork, which formed a key part of the newspapers defence case – and insisted he was totally innocent in relation to the du Plantier investigation.

The journalist said, in response to allegations from some in west Cork, that he was the subject of 'lies, fabrications and untruths'. He emphatically rejected suggestions by the newspapers' legal team that he had admitted to a number of people in west Cork his involvement in the du Plantier matter over the years. Mr Bailey flatly denied this and insisted that he had discussed some hurtful local rumours with people – but had never conceded any role in the crime.

He insisted that gardaí were determined to convict him of the killing. 'There were efforts to pervert the course of justice,' he said bluntly.

Mr Bailey claimed that, at one point, a garda told him that because there had been a full moon on the night of Ms du Plantier's killing, he must have acted 'like a werewolf monster'. He told Judge Moran he was convinced that certain gardaí were trying to 'stitch [him] up' for the crime.

Mr Bailey was visibly tired at the conclusion of his cross-examination. Yet he had never lost his composure during what was, at times, incredibly intense questioning over material that, for any human being, must have been extremely upsetting to deal with.

What struck me as remarkable was that the sole occasion when Mr Bailey displayed emotion and seemed genuinely upset was when his artistic talents were queried. He was clearly unhappy when the material in relation to his treatment of his partner was put to him, but he responded to those difficult questions in a calm, measured and logical manner and never displayed emotion. But Mr Gallagher had later referred to a fisherman who said Mr Bailey was a 'bad poet and brutal bodhrán player' at a festival concert on Cape Clear Island. The reference clearly stung the journalist, and he insisted on disputing the statement – pointing out that his bodhrán performance during the island arts festival had been greeted by a positive response from the crowd.

The remainder of the plaintiff's case focused on the media coverage and its impact on those closest to Mr Bailey. Ms Thomas's mother, Beryl-Ann, an artist like her daughter, described the journalist as pleasant and a 'normal human being'.

Ms Thomas's eldest daughter, Saffron, wept as she outlined the impact the media coverage had on her extended family: 'It is like a dark cloud … a heavy weight … that just never goes away.' There were times, she told the court, her family felt like sitting inside their home outside Liscaha in darkness or with the curtains pulled because of the fear of being watched by members of the media gathered outside. She also explained that the impact the coverage of the du Plantier case was having on her mother and Mr Bailey was apparent to herself and her two siblings. The young woman slated some of the media coverage as 'disgusting' and very upsetting. 'They cried every day, my Lord. They cried every day for about two years. People did not know whether they should talk to them or not.'

Two west Cork locals were also called to offer testimony about the impact the media coverage had on Mr Bailey. Thomas Brosnan and Brendan Houlihan, both businessmen in west Cork (although their relationship to Mr Bailey was never specified), said they noticed a dramatic change in Mr Bailey following media coverage that named him in relation to the ongoing murder investigation. Mr Houlihan told the libel hearing he felt, at the time, that Mr Bailey had been 'branded'. Mr Brosnan said he believed that the media coverage of the du Plantier case had resulted in Mr Bailey already being convicted.

Jules Thomas also offered evidence. She described the violent incidents with her partner as a 'moment of alcoholic madness'. The artist insisted that she felt the media treatment of both her and her family had actually been far worse than any of the domestic disputes she had with her partner. She claimed that at one point her home had been under siege by the media, with reporters and photographers camped outside the front gate of her cottage. She said she was particularly concerned about the impact of the press coverage on her children. At times, the family would sit inside their darkened home with the lights turned off in case there were photographers outside. They would also check at the windows before answering unexpected calls to the front door lest it be reporters or photographers.

Ms Thomas flatly rejected suggestions that her partner had ever publicly admitted to any connection to the du Plantier killing. She said that she had been present at one of the occasions when Bailey was reported to have admitted to the killing; she insisted he was merely repeating what others, including gardaí, were saying locally about him.

She also took issue with elements of her own garda statements and claimed that she could not remember having said specific things that were detailed in them. Ms Thomas confirmed that she had even gone to a solicitor to formally write to gardaí to indicate that she was disputing several elements of the statements.

Ms Thomas also insisted that she trusted Mr Bailey despite the three domestic violence incidents between 1993 and 2001. She told the court that he no longer drank alcohol and that they had successfully built a life together in west Cork. In reference to how she had been treated by both the gardaí and the media since 1997, the artist said she was left feeling 'damaged'.

***

The daily arrival of Mr Bailey and Ms Thomas at the court dominated the photographic coverage of the case. During the initial part of the hearing, the couple would leave the court at lunch to go for food in the nearby city centre. Ms Thomas would sometimes arrive back to the court with shopping or flowers. However, as the hearing became more intense and the media coverage more comprehensive, the couple would often opt to remain in the court complex until the conclusion of the day's proceedings. Paul Byrne, the southern correspondent with TV3, felt sympathy for the couple as they maintained their lonely day-long wait in the temporary court premises. One day, as a gesture of kindness, he offered to bring them back coffee, a sandwich or fruit when he returned from his own lunch. They politely declined – but he brought them coffee anyhow. His act of kindness would not be forgotten by Mr Bailey. Over the years, Mr Byrne has managed to get interviews with Mr Bailey when all others failed, and two years later, the TV3 journalist would deliver one of the biggest twists in the entire case with an exclusive report about the recanting of evidence that had been central to the defamation action.

***

The second and concluding week of the libel hearing was dominated by the defence team calling various witnesses to attest to Mr Bailey's statements and behaviour in respect of the du Plantier case – all of which, the defence argued, undermined his claim that the publicity had damaged the public perception of him.

On the hearing's seventh day, a total of fourteen witnesses were called. Some of the testimony undoubtedly weakened Mr Bailey's claims about the impact of the newspaper publicity. It also painted a remarkable picture of the journalist and his social interactions with west Cork locals.

One witness was Malachi Reid, who, as a fourteen-year-old schoolboy in Schull in early 1997, got a lift home from Mr Bailey. During the short trip, Mr Reid said that the journalist, without bidding, brought up the du Plantier case. The teen, making conversation, had asked Mr Bailey how he was. The reply left him shocked. 'I was fine up until I went up and bashed her fucking brains in,' he claimed Mr Bailey told him. The schoolboy went home and told his mother, Amanda Reid, about the conversation, which he felt was a clear reference to the murder. Both were so shaken that they locked all the doors that night.

When the alleged conversation was put to him, Mr Bailey insisted that he had simply been recounting what others in west Cork were saying.

Similarly, he insisted that he had also been repeating these hurtful rumours about him during a gathering with Ritchie and Rosie Shelly at Jules Thomas's home on 31 December 1998. Mr Bailey and Ms Thomas had met the young couple in a west Cork pub that evening and began chatting with them. The Shellys were invited back to The Prairie for a drink.

Both had felt sympathy for Mr Bailey and his partner over the media focus on them. On arrival, they were taken aback that they were the only ones present at the house, having expected some type of New Year's Eve party to be taking place. Ritchie Shelly told the court that Mr Bailey's conversation was dominated by the du Plantier case. The journalist even produced what he referred to as a 'case file' about the tragedy.

Mr Shelly noticed that his wife was increasingly unhappy with the tone of the evening and he decided they would cut the night short and return to their own home. He told the libel hearing that Mr Bailey had then left the room only to return in an agitated state. '[Mr Bailey] came back into the kitchen … he was crying. [He] put his arms around me and said, "I did it, I did it. I went too far." I assumed he was talking about the murder because that is what we were talking about all night.'

Mrs Shelly said that she considered Mr Bailey to be obsessed with the murder and that he had collected articles written about the case. She was so concerned by the journalist's emotional outburst that she told her husband they should quit the house immediately, despite not having a car with them. They made a phone call to a relative asking to be collected. Mrs Shelly insisted that they walk down the road towards the person coming to collect them rather than remain at the Liscaha property. When questioned by Mr Gallagher, Mrs Shelly said that the comments that evening had felt like some 'kind of confession'.

Ceri Williams, a neighbour of Mr Bailey, told the hearing that a woman once confronted Mr Bailey at a party and told him to his face that he was a murderer. She said that while the journalist was highly intelligent and multi-talented, people were wary of him after details of the domestic violence incidents had become known. She bluntly admitted in cross-examination, 'I don't like him.'

Sculptor Peter Bielecki explained that he received a phone call in May 1996 from Ms Thomas's daughter Virginia, who, sounding distressed, asked him to call to their family home because Mr Bailey had assaulted her mother. Mr Bielecki was so upset at the recollection of Ms Thomas's physical condition that he had to pause during evidence to compose himself. 'It was absolutely the most appalling thing I have ever witnessed. [She] was curled up in a foetal position at the foot of the bed. I could hear what I can only describe as almost animal sounds. It was as if someone had their soul ripped out,' he said. He agreed, at the request of her family and because he was a close family friend, to remain at the property for three weeks. Mr Bielecki admitted that he slept with a hammer under his pillow out of concern over what would happen if Mr Bailey returned unexpectedly. Mr Bielecki ended his friendship with Mr Bailey and said he felt 'betrayed' by the journalist over the way he had treated his partner.

Another man, Bill Fuller, said he had been 'shocked and upset' by comments he claimed Mr Bailey had passed. Mr Fuller said that, sometime after the December 1996 murder, Mr Bailey, speaking in the second person, referred to seeing Ms du Plantier walking up the aisle of the Spar shop 'with her tight arse … you fancied her. You went up to see what you could get. She ran away screaming. You chased her. You went too far – you had to finish her off.' Mr Bailey flatly rejected this claim and denied ever saying anything of the sort.

Several other witnesses offered evidence that challenged Mr Bailey's insistence that he had never met Ms du Plantier during her time in west Cork. Alfie Lyons, a neighbour of Ms du Plantier, and the partner of Shirley Foster, the woman who discovered the body on the Toormore laneway on 23 December 1996 as she went to do Christmas shopping, said he believed the journalist had met the French woman some 18 months before her death. 'As far as I can recollect, I did introduce him to Sophie. I am 90 per cent certain that I did,' he said.

Paul Webster, a France-based journalist who had been working for *The Guardian* in 1996, said he had spoken with Mr Bailey about possible coverage of the du Plantier case. Mr Webster said it was made clear to him that Mr Bailey had had contact with the deceased. 'He made it absolutely clear that he had talked to her,' he said.

Other witnesses offered evidence that challenged the timeline offered by Mr Bailey, who was adamant he first learned of the killing at lunchtime when contacted by *The Examiner*. Shirley Foster said she met Mr Bailey driving up her laneway at speed. The meeting was not, she said, on the main Skibbereen–Schull road as Mr Bailey had claimed. Mike MacSweeney, a photographer for Provision Photographic Agency, said he was told by Mr Bailey that photographs of the murder scene were available. These had, he said, been taken around 11 a.m. However, this was two hours earlier than Mr Bailey had indicated that he had first learned of the killing.

Eddie Cassidy was adamant he had not told Mr Bailey during their telephone call that the Toormore incident was a murder nor that it involved a French national. He told the hearing that at the time he made the call on that December morning, he had still been trying to determine if it was a hit-and-run or whether it might have involved someone from a local New Age traveller community.

James Camier, who operated a vegetable shop in Goleen, said he recalled Ms Thomas calling in to him around 11 a.m. on 23 December 1996 and informing him that a murder had taken place and that it involved a French national. Ms Thomas would say that this meeting took place on 24 December, a full 24 hours later, but Mr Camier was insistent it was the earlier date.

It was put to Mr Bailey that he had confirmed his involvement to Helen Callanan, news editor with the *Sunday Tribune*, in a telephone conversation in early 1997. Mr Bailey insisted he merely confirmed to her what was being said locally about him. 'People were asking her who Eoin Bailey was. At one point she said that it was being said that I was the killer. I said, "Yes, that is right." I said it in jest. It was said in a light-hearted way. I had heard it from other journalists that I was supposed to have done it – I really was not taking it seriously,' he said.

Mr Bailey said it was a similar story with the comments he had made to Sophie's friend Yvonne Ungerer. He was adamant that he merely repeated to Mrs Ungerer the hurtful things being said about him – namely that he had killed Sophie with a concrete block. 'I was not in any way serious – I do not think she took it seriously,' he insisted.

Just when it appeared the libel action couldn't get any more sensational, the defence team introduced someone who would quickly become the focal point of the hearing. Schull shopkeeper Marie Farrell took to the witness stand on 17 December, the eighth day of the hearing. From then on, her evidence would dominate the newspaper coverage and the hearing itself.

Mrs Farrell said she was living in fear of Mr Bailey and was afraid to allow her children out of her sight because of him. She claimed that

Mr Bailey had effectively been 'torturing her' and that she was only reluctantly appearing at the libel hearing on foot of a subpoena issued by the newspapers' defence team.

The shopkeeper told how, in the early hours of 23 December 1996, she was driving to her home outside Schull. She said that as she passed Kealfadda Bridge she saw a 'tall man, in a dark coat, kind of distinctive-looking'. The man was walking with an unusual gait, his arms swinging by his side.

She said that, in January 1997, she spotted the same man in Schull, not far from her shop. It was at this point she notified gardaí. The man was identified to her as Ian Bailey. This statement was crucial because it contradicted Mr Bailey's assertion that he never left the Liscaha property after returning home with Ms Thomas on 22 December. Kealfadda Bridge was approximately four kilometres from the du Plantier holiday home.

Mrs Farrell then claimed she was informed that Mr Bailey wanted to meet her. When he came to her shop, she said, he checked it to see if it was 'clean' and that there were no 'bugs' or electronic recording devices. The journalist had brought a tape recorder with him and said he wanted Mrs Farrell to say that the gardaí were placing her under duress to make a false statement about him. The shopkeeper told the hushed courtroom that she had refused to make any such recorded statement. She claimed Mr Bailey's attitude towards her then changed. Later, she claimed he told her he knew things about her – and produced addresses in London and Longford she had associations with. It would subsequently emerge that Mrs Farrell had had apparent difficulties with the Department of Social Services while living in the UK.

She said she met him some weeks later and he shouted at her, 'I know you saw me ... but I did not kill Sophie.' She alleged that on another occasion Mr Bailey had been across the street and made cut-throat gestures to her. Under cross-examination by Mr Duggan, she emphatically denied she had been placed under any kind of duress by gardaí to make a statement implicating Mr Bailey. She also denied she had personally invited the journalist to her shop. 'I do not think any woman in her right frame of mind would invite Ian Bailey to her shop – especially when she is on her own,' she replied.

Direct evidence ended, and the plaintiff and defence teams then took two days to make their closing arguments. Strangely for a libel action, not one of the journalists involved in the articles in question was called to offer evidence, a fact loudly complained about by Mr Duggan, who alleged that his client had just been subjected to 'trial by ambush'. However, in a libel action the role of a plaintiff is to establish what alleged damage was caused to their reputation, and witnesses relate specifically to this task. Effectively, it was up to the defending media outlet whether to call the journalists involved to offer evidence.

Judge Moran said that, given the length of the hearing and the large amount of material that he wanted to consider, he would reserve his judgement until early in the new year. The move did not come as a surprise. Few expected a ruling within a matter of days after such an intensive two-week case, particularly with Christmas less than a fortnight away. Mr Bailey looked calm but weary after the Circuit Court experience.

***

On 19 January 2004, Cork's Camden Quay ground to a standstill as reporters, photographers, lawyers and members of the public battled to pack into the small courtroom. Dozens of people milled around outside the courthouse waiting for news of the ruling. Six different TV crews stalked the pavement, waiting for the verdict and footage of the key individuals in the case.

An inkling of which way the ruling might go came when Mr Bailey arrived with just his legal team. It was the first time throughout the entire hearing he had attended court without his partner by his side.

Just over 40 minutes after beginning his ruling address, Judge Moran dashed Mr Bailey's hopes of a landmark judgment against the media.

Far from the triumphant victory he had hoped for, the outcome of the libel case was a disaster for him. The judge said that the journalist had attempted to mislead the hearing about whether he was a violent man – and that none of the newspapers had defamed him by referring to him as the prime suspect in the du Plantier case.

The only comfort for Mr Bailey was that Judge Moran ruled against the *Irish Mirror* and the *Irish Sun* on a secondary issue to the hearing. This involved allegations by both papers that Mr Bailey had been violent towards his ex-wife, Sarah Limbrick. The judge said no evidence whatsoever had been offered for this, and he ruled that Mr Bailey had been defamed as a result.

But the judge, in a hard-hitting conclusion, said he would have 'no hesitation in describing Mr Bailey as a violent man'. He said it was apparent that Mr Bailey 'is a man who likes a certain amount of notoriety, likes to be in the limelight and likes a bit of self-publicity'.

Sitting in the courtroom, Mr Bailey showed no emotion, despite the obvious implications of the ruling. He stared stoically ahead as the judge's comments drew gasps from some in the public gallery. After Judge Moran concluded his address, Mr Bailey briefly conferred with his legal team before leaving the court. So large was the crowd of reporters, photographers, TV crews and onlookers outside the courtroom that gardaí had to clear a path for him to reach the vehicle waiting for him.

He was left facing having to pay three-fifths of the newspapers' costs in their successful defence of the action. Mr Bailey's legal team secured just half their costs against the two newspapers who were found to have defamed the journalist on the secondary issue. The total cost of the libel action was put at between €600,000 and €700,000, with Mr Bailey facing having to pay €200,000 of the newspapers' costs. The newspapers immediately moved to freeze any defamation award payable to Mr Bailey on the secondary action until he indicated how he intended to pay his share of the costs ruling.

The hearing was clearly exhausting for Mr Bailey and Ms Thomas. But they weren't the only ones. The entire Cork media were exhausted from a two-week case that, given the unrelenting daily 14-hour workload, seemed more like a six-week hearing.

I briefly spoke to a couple of the journalists whose work had been cited. It is every journalist's worst nightmare to have a defamation action taken against them and there was sympathy among their Cork colleagues for those involved. From my brief conversations with them, I realised most had been keen to offer evidence and felt frustrated at not being afforded an opportunity to do so, even though they understood the legal strategy involved.

For Mr Bailey, the ruling could not have been more damaging. He faced potentially ruinous costs and, having taken the action to defend his good name, found himself again at the centre of an unrelenting media spotlight. Had he won the action, there is little doubt but that the future media approach towards him would have been radically different.

There was no doubt in my mind that a decisive factor in the entire two-week hearing was the evidence of shopkeeper Marie Farrell, who was now being referred to as 'the star witness' of the libel action.

7

MARIE FARRELL

Ian Bailey may have maintained his calm demeanour amid the furore over his Circuit Court libel defeat, but few doubted that he was absolutely devastated by the outcome. What everyone had assumed would be a legal action with the media being put firmly on the defensive had instead resulted in Mr Bailey's life being put under the microscope for public scrutiny.

Friends of the poet would later claim that he was effectively ambushed in the court, with his supporters particularly aggrieved that none of the journalists who had penned the relevant articles was ever put in the witness box. However, under Irish defamation law, Mr Bailey's case was to set out the damage allegedly caused to his reputation – not to demand evidence from those who wrote the articles.

The newspapers' defence strategy was to put the spotlight on Mr Bailey. And it had worked.

That January day, having painstakingly made his way through the scrum of reporters, photographers, TV crews and fascinated members of the public outside the Camden Quay court premises, he wearily headed back to west Cork. The car sped away and Mr Bailey vanished from sight for several weeks.

Every newspaper, radio programme and TV station wanted to hear from the journalist to get his reaction to the hearing and its remarkable outcome. He was, in media terms, the most sought-after man in Ireland. But he was nowhere to be found. Bruised by the intensive media focus on him throughout December and January, he took comfort with good friends in west Cork who were willing to shield him from the unyielding glare of the media.

On occasions, he avoided the Liscaha property altogether because it was a magnet for reporters and photographers seeking to contact him. Sometimes he would go shopping with Jules Thomas in either Skibbereen or Clonakilty, only to realise that their old Nissan car was being followed. His every movement in west Cork seemed to attract photographers, journalists and the simply curious.

***

Later that year there were significant developments: Mr Bailey's long-standing solicitor, Con Murphy, was appointed a circuit court judge to the bench in Cork, where he would serve alongside Judge Patrick Moran, at that point the longest-serving circuit court judge in Ireland, as well as Judge Seán Ó Donnabháin. The newly appointed Judge Murphy's senior colleague was the very judge who had ruled against his client in the defamation action.

The journalist now needed a new solicitor – and the man he turned to was one of the highest-profile criminal defence solicitors in Cork, if not in Ireland. Frank Buttimer had built one of the most successful legal practices in Cork city and, since the late 1990s, had been renowned for his involvement in some of the most prominent criminal trials staged in the south, ranging from cases of armed robbery to murder.

The 2005 decision of the Central Criminal Court to resume hearing major criminal cases in Cork, Limerick and Galway, rather than every case having to be heard in Dublin, was a landmark ruling. One of the first murder trials heard in Cork after that decision involved a young man who was defended by Mr Buttimer. His client was acquitted.

A consummate criminal defence solicitor, Mr Buttimer was also a capable and articulate media performer. He was a regular on TV and radio programmes, offering his opinion about various legal issues in

Ireland. Few doubted that Mr Buttimer's involvement signalled that Mr Bailey's legal battles were likely to intensify rather than recede.

***

It had also been quickly established that Mr Bailey would be appealing the Circuit Court libel rulings to the High Court. The appeal was confirmed on 21 February 2004, just over a month after he lost six of the eight libel actions he had taken and had costs of €200,000 awarded against him.

The newspapers vowed to 'contest the appeal as vigorously as [they] contested the original Circuit Court hearing'. But, they said, the circumstances of the High Court appeal were 'further proof' of the deeply flawed and unfair libel laws in Ireland. Under Irish libel laws, Mr Bailey did not have to lodge any money in court as a preliminary to his appeal, despite having an award of almost €200,000 against him from the Circuit Court. But the appeal would progress nonetheless.

'Mr Bailey had nothing to lose by taking a gamble in the Circuit Court and now he has nothing to lose by taking another gamble in the High Court,' explained solicitor Hugh Hannigan of Simon McAleese and Co., who acted for Independent News and Media. Such a case would now take some time to prepare and to reach the hearing stage, potentially up to two years.

***

The other major development in the case happened in France. Having been briefed daily on the revelations in the Cork Circuit Court libel action, Sophie's family found encouragement that something, finally, would surely have to happen in Ireland. Alain Spilliaert, solicitor for the Bouniol family, explained in January 2004 that the family felt some kind of judicial action was now warranted in Ireland on foot of the dramatic revelations and witness testimonies. For months after the libel ruling and the costs award, the French family had held out hope that something would happen in Ireland.

They signalled a civil action against Mr Bailey. Their aim was to use this to maintain pressure for some form of prosecution to be sanctioned. I understood it was not their intention to seek any financial compensation from the Manchester journalist, who, as had already been made clear, owned no property in Ireland, had no major assets and was currently not in any form of permanent employment.

As the weeks following the 2004 ruling slowly passed, it became abundantly clear that the libel action hadn't changed anything in Ireland in prosecutorial terms. Having lodged a criminal complaint over Sophie's death with the French authorities in 1997, the family slowly began to consider whether an action in France might now be preferable to one in Ireland. If the Irish authorities would not act, despite the revelations of the libel action, the French would surely take action to see justice done for the family.

***

The Association for the Truth about the Murder of Sophie Toscan du Plantier (ASSOPH), or l'Association pour le vérité sur l'assassinat de Sophie Toscan du Plantier, drew together a powerful mix of Sophie's family, her friends and former film industry colleagues as well as associates of her husband, Daniel du Plantier. ASSOPH also ensured that the influential French media would continue to highlight key developments with the case. Although formally established in 2007, ASSOPH's existence can be dated back to a seismic development in the case in Ireland two years earlier.

In October 2005, this startling development also threatened to have implications for the gardaí, Mr Bailey's pending High Court appeal and even the Irish government. On 13 October, TV3's southern correspondent, Paul Byrne, broke the story that Marie Farrell, the so-called 'star witness' of the Circuit Court libel hearing, was now retracting all her statements.

The Schull shopkeeper, in a truly astonishing TV interview, claimed not only that her evidence was false but that it had only been offered after she had been put under extreme duress by gardaí to incriminate Mr Bailey. The interview dominated the news headlines in Ireland for days.

She was now adamant that it was not Mr Bailey she had seen at Kealfadda Bridge in the early hours of 23 December 1996. She said her subsequent statements alleging that the journalist had subjected her to a campaign of intimidation in west Cork were totally without foundation and delivered purely because of the pressure she had been put under by unnamed gardaí.

Mrs Farrell used the TV interview to publicly apologise to Mr Bailey for her statements both to gardaí as part of their original investigation and on oath during the libel hearing. She apologised for any hurt he or his family may have suffered as a result. Mrs Farrell said that while she deeply regretted what had happened, she had been under extreme pressure at the time and felt she had no other alternative.

Well, I panicked. Initially, I panicked because I had actually been out that night and I was somewhere where my husband didn't know I was. I just thought the guards know what they're talking about, there's no way they'd say it was Ian Bailey if it wasn't. And I just thought, I'll do what they're saying and that's the end of it for me.

Between 1997 and the libel trial ... I had signed numerous statements. A lot of them, I didn't even know what was in them. I was just asked to sign statements. I found out afterwards, you know, that they had been saying Ian Bailey had been harassing me and all sorts of things like that and none of that was true. But the gardaí just kept putting more and more pressure on me. I was just getting in deeper and deeper and it was just, like, getting out of control.

In the run-up to the libel hearing in December 2003, she kept praying that she would not be required to take the witness stand or even to attend. She was horrified when she was told she would have to attend and offer sworn testimony. Ultimately, she was issued with a witness subpoena.

For the whole week of that trial I kept saying, you know, that I wasn't going. There was no way I was going to court. But I had certain gardaí ringing me, sometimes three or four times a day telling me that I had to go to the court. My husband was telling me I wasn't to go. I was adamant I wasn't going. I told them there was no way I was going to court and telling lies.

But then I got a phone call the day before I appeared at the libel trial, and a garda told me that if I didn't go an application would be made to the court to have me arrested. He said, 'You'll probably be brought there in handcuffs, which is worse.' So he said I had to meet a different garda that morning and that he'd run through everything with me and that I had nothing to worry about, stick to the story and there was nothing to worry about.

So the morning that I did appear at the libel trial, I met a garda just outside Cork city. He told me what I had to say, and stick to it, and there would be no problems. When I got up on the stand I was panicking, and I was thinking, 'Will I tell the judge the truth here?'

Then I looked down to the back of the court and there was, you know, the gardaí standing there watching me with their arms folded. I thought, you know, 'I have no way out of this.' But at the same time I could not remember what I was meant to say. So it was a relief then when that was over.

The shopkeeper said she did not want to be in the Cork court and did not want to give evidence. But she said she felt under intolerable strain from the gardaí to participate and to back up the previous sworn statements she had given them in respect of the du Plantier investigation. '[It was only] because I was being put under so much pressure from the gardai,' she said.

Mrs Farrell said she finally decided to retract her statement and go public with the reasons why she had made such allegations under oath because she felt trapped by the whole saga and that she feared that it would never end.

I got a phone call from a garda, and we were just talking in general and then he said to me that Sophie's parents were taking a civil action against Ian Bailey for Sophie's wrongful death. And he said, 'You know that's going to end up in court and you're going to have to go in there again?' And I said there is no way that I would ever, ever go to court and tell lies for the guards again.

I said, 'You know, if you keep pushing me now, I'm going to go and see Frank Buttimer.' He said, 'You know, no one is going to be interested in what you have to say.' And I said, 'You know, maybe Ian Bailey will be interested?' I said, 'I am going to tell them the whole truth about what happened.' He said, 'If you go down that road you will never again have a day's peace as long as you live.' [But] I know I'm telling you the truth.

I did it because I knew it was the right thing to do. I had to come forward and tell the truth. I've gone through years of, I don't know how to say it, harassment? Hardship? Stress? Because of doing the right thing. What I did in 1996 and 1997 was stupid. I was naive. I really, really thought that the guards could do no wrong.

Over the coming months she would go on to do more detailed interviews with TV3, in an attempt to explain her statements to gardaí, her evidence during the libel hearing and why she had finally decided to offer a different narrative.

The interview caused a sensation. It was akin to throwing a stick of dynamite into an already blazing bonfire. Every Irish newspaper covered the story in the subsequent days and Mrs Farrell was inundated with pleas to appear on radio and TV programmes.

The TV3 interview marked a shift in public perceptions towards Mr Bailey and the garda investigation. In France, the news unsettled Sophie's family and their supporters, encouraging them to mobilise and form what would eventually become ASSOPH.

But if the interview had a seismic impact on the Irish media, its impact on the Irish judicial system was on an altogether greater scale.

Mrs Farrell had been as good as her word to the gardaí: six months before the TV3 interview, she had made contact with Mr Bailey's solicitor, Frank Buttimer. She had first made contact with Mr Buttimer on 18 April. Three weeks later, on 10 May, she visited Mr Buttimer's legal offices on Washington Street in Cork – just a stroll from Cork's famous eighteenth-century courthouse – and made a detailed statement about both what she had seen at Kealfadda Bridge in December 1996 and what she said had transpired between her and gardaí between 1997 and 2003.

She also made detailed statements to him about the circumstances of the Circuit Court defamation action. Mrs Farrell also consulted with her own solicitor about the legal situation she found herself in.

Frank Buttimer was clear in his assessment of the implications of what Mrs Farrell had to say. He warned that his client had been the victim of outrageous behaviour by agents of the State – Mr Bailey had consistently maintained his innocence and attempts had been made by some to 'stitch [him] up' for the crime.

Mr Bailey is greatly relieved at this development. He is grateful to Mrs Farrell for her courage [in coming forward]. I genuinely mean that – her courage in coming forward at this point in time and being satisfied to correct the wrong that she could be accused of doing. The easier option would have been to remain silent and allow the thing to stay as it was and to fester. She has now put herself back into the focus and the spotlight.

The issue was directly raised with Minister for Justice Michael McDowell as it potentially had profound consequences far beyond the gardaí for the impartiality of the entire system of administration of justice in Ireland. The government was also acutely aware of the impact such allegations would have for the French, who were still hoping that some kind of judicial action over Sophie's death would be sanctioned in Ireland.

Almost immediately it was confirmed that Assistant Commissioner Ray McAndrew would review the allegations made by Mrs Farrell and, in particular, her claims in respect of the behaviour of key officers involved in the du Plantier investigation over the previous decade. The review would involve interviews with all key players involved. But, critically, there was no indication at the outset that the report would ever be published.

Instead, the McAndrew Report would be submitted to the garda commissioner on its completion in 2007. It comprised interviews with almost 100 people, around 50 of whom were either serving or retired gardaí and detectives. The Minister for Justice would also be briefed on its findings and recommendations.

But it wasn't just the garda commissioner and Minister for Justice who examined the McAndrew Report. It was also submitted to the DPP's office for consideration. To the surprise of no one, it subsequently emerged that no prosecutorial action was recommended on the basis of the report or its findings.

That report has never been made available to the public – and has never been fully referenced in any of the court proceedings either in Ireland or France. The McAndrew Report was not even discussed in detail in the Garda Síochána Ombudsman Commission (GSOC) report, which would be painstakingly compiled over eight years following formal complaints about their treatment at the hands of gardaí by Mr Bailey, Ms Thomas and Mrs Farrell.

It was obvious that Mrs Farrell's complaint about alleged garda duress would have enormous implications, not least for future legal actions. In the meantime, Mrs Farrell and her family moved out of west Cork and back to Longford, where they had previously been based, but she would not be able to retreat from the media spotlight.

***

The next step in Mr Bailey's legal battle came in 2007, with the arrival of his appeal against the Cork Circuit Court libel rulings before the High Court. On 13 February, the long-awaited case opened in the Washington Street court complex in Cork city centre before Mr Justice Brian McGovern. The temporary Camden Quay courthouse had been abandoned now that the historic Washington Street premises was ready following a lavish revamp.

A large media presence was on hand for what many expected to prove a very high-profile, if fraught, hearing that could last at least twice as long as the two-week Circuit Court proceedings. What dominated the thoughts, including my own, of every journalist present was the role Marie Farrell would now play in the court action. The pundits were correct about the appeal proving both high-profile and fraught, but the action lasted less than four days at hearing and ended with a whimper rather than any searing legal oratory or dramatic ruling. As for Mrs Farrell, she didn't feature in the hearing at all.

The High Court appeal opened in stuttering fashion amid consultations and clarifications between the opposing legal sides. Mr Bailey once again opened proceedings in the witness box to set out the damage he had suffered as a result of the newspaper articles published between 1997 and 2001.

His evidence was nothing if not headline-grabbing. One west Cork individual was described by Mr Bailey as having a penchant for marijuana. Another unrelated comment by Mr Bailey resulted in proceedings being temporarily halted before the appellant's legal team issued clarifications to mollify members of the legal team for six of the newspapers who were perceived to have been the possible target of the remark.

Another lengthy adjournment then prompted speculation that talks were under way to reach a settlement. The speculation proved to be correct. Shane Phelan, at the time a senior reporter with the *Irish Daily Star*, approached me as we waited in the courtroom for the case to resume hearing evidence and whispered that a deal was now in the offing. Instead of a marathon libel appeal we would instead be dealing with a High Court 'sprint'.

To the astonishment of many, it was announced that the case had collapsed on its fourth day at hearing. The High Court was informed that Mr Bailey was withdrawing his appeal. He would not be paid any damages by the six newspapers that had successfully defended the 2003 action. The publications in question had, however, agreed to make an undisclosed contribution to his legal costs. Additionally, the newspapers agreed to waive the legal costs that had arisen from their Circuit Court libel victory and would not pursue Mr Bailey for the estimated €200,000 involved.

Over the following days, legal analysts would speculate that the newspapers had carefully calculated the cost of fighting and winning a lengthy High Court libel battle and judged that it would effectively equate to a defeat. Better, it seemed, to negotiate an early route out of the action that suited everyone involved. But the newspapers went to great pains after the action ended to stress that no damages had been paid to Mr Bailey.

Solicitor Paula Mullooly, acting for Independent News and Media, said it was a full and final settlement of the matter and represented a clear victory for the industry. 'No damages will be paid to Mr Bailey,' she emphasised.

But Mr Bailey and his legal team also hailed the settlement as a victory – and an outcome that would allow him to now focus on the bigger legal battles looming on his horizon. His legal team also highlighted the newspapers' comment that nothing in the articles cited was intended to suggest that Mr Bailey was a murderer and that it was accepted Mr Bailey had at all times maintained his innocence.

'Now he can concentrate on battles to come,' Frank Buttimer said. 'We are initiating proceedings against the State. [Mr Bailey] has cooperated with the garda inquiry, which is ongoing, and about to report in relation to garda misbehaviour to do with this case.

'Claims for damages will certainly proceed to full hearing in relation to what was done to him by the State and by agents of the State – with regard to why he was selected as the offender in this case, the reason for it, the background to it [and] the consequences he suffered as a result of being falsely labelled as the offender. Lest anybody think that these matters will not proceed [to a hearing], they absolutely will,' the Cork solicitor vowed.

Mr Bailey's counsel, Brendan Nix SC, told Mr Justice McGovern the matter had ended following talks. 'The defendant newspapers confirm that nothing in any of these articles was ever intended to suggest that Ian Bailey murdered Sophie Toscan du Plantier. The defendants are not saying now nor did they ever say he was a murderer,' he said.

The 2007 High Court action would not mark the end of Mr Bailey's legal battles over what he complained had been done to him in west Cork between 1997 and 2003. However, his next High Court action, rather than lasting four days, would make Irish legal history.

***

His ongoing legal battles had one positive side-effect for Mr Bailey – it revived a long-standing interest in the law that brought him back to university. In 2006, just as his High Court libel appeal was rumbling towards a hearing, he decided to pursue a law degree at University College Cork. He began his studies and lived for a time in a small rented flat just off Cork's Coal Quay. Mr Bailey became a regular at UCC Law Society events.

The journalist loved his studies and, on 7 December 2010, he graduated with a Bachelor of Civil Law degree. At his graduation, he spoke to Cork journalist Olivia Kelleher for several newspapers and took pains to insist that he had had a great interest in the law since his days as a journalist in Cheltenham and Gloucester and that his studies were not a direct result of his Circuit Court and High Court experiences in Ireland.

The irony was lost on no one that Mr Bailey and the landmark court actions he had triggered would likely feature in the study programmes of future students in the university.

8

FRENCH INVESTIGATION

Frustrated by events in Ireland and increasingly worried that no one would ever be prosecuted over the murder, the French decided to change tactics.

In the immediate aftermath of the 2003 libel hearing a civil lawsuit had been flagged by the Bouniol family that had made headlines across Ireland. The lawsuit was signalled with the apparent intention that it might persuade the Irish authorities to review the garda case file once again and reconsider the decision not to take further action.

While two reviews of the garda case file were indeed ordered, one before the defamation action and one subsequent to it, the DPP's stance on the matter did not change. There would be no prosecution as the DPP did not consider there was sufficient evidence to justify a charge. So much had now happened with the case and so much had been brought into the public domain that there was an increasing belief that any prosecution in Ireland would be impossible.

By 2007 it had become apparent that the civil action, even if it proceeded, offered limited scope to achieve the goals of the French family. The Irish authorities showed no sign of sanctioning action on the basis of the garda case file and, as the libel action revealed with its cost award, Mr Bailey had no assets, wealth or income to pursue as part of any civil litigation process. Instead, the family and their supporters turned to the French law.

***

In early 1997 a formal complaint had been lodged with the French authorities over the killing in Ireland. Although the complaint had been made just weeks after the killing, the family had not yet lost hope in the Irish criminal justice system at that point. Rather, it was a procedure often used by French families for a loved one who died overseas. It effectively involved the French authorities in the process and, at the very least, ensured judicial and diplomatic weight was added to their search for answers and justice.

The complaint was lodged by Daniel du Plantier as well as Georges and Marguerite Bouniol before the Tribunal de Grande Instance in Paris on 17 January 1997, just 25 days after Sophie's death. Such complaints can serve another long-term purpose: under France's Napoleonic Code, it was possible for French authorities to conduct a domestic investigation into a crime that had occurred outside their jurisdiction. All that was required was that the crime involved a French citizen.

It did not matter that the suspect was not on French soil or that the bulk of witnesses were outside French jurisdiction. It also did not matter that the original investigation was not carried out by French police. The Napoleonic Code – amended under further French statutes in the 1960s – provided France with all the legal powers required to conduct a full investigation and, if necessary, a prosecution.

Such a legal option is totally alien in both Ireland and the UK, where a very different legal system, tracing its roots back to Anglo-Saxon times, is in place. Whereas Ireland and the UK have an adversarial judicial system, in which there are very strict rules in place over evidence, jurisdiction and testimony, France operates an entirely different system, in which prosecutors had much greater freedom.

***

In 2007 ASSOPH, in consultation with Sophie's family and solicitors, Alain Spilliaert and Eric Dupond-Moretti, came to the realisation that, if Ireland wouldn't sanction a prosecution for its own legal reasons, a French-led investigation could potentially lead to criminal proceedings against Mr Bailey in Paris. The association's campaign was boosted by the calibre of the people involved.

Sophie's uncle, Jean-Pierre Gazeau, was the president of ASSOPH and a driving force in both its foundation and subsequent work. Mr Gazeau was a mathematician and physicist who specialised in quantum physics and came to rank as one of France's top academics. Quiet, polite and fluent in English and Spanish, he brought the logic, planning and determination of an academic to the work of ASSOPH. It also helped that Mr Gazeau was well versed in international negotiations. As one of the top physicists in France, he was a visiting consultant and researcher with science foundations and universities in the United States, Japan, Canada, China, and even Iran.

Mr Gazeau was joined by Julien Cros, Jean-Antoine Bloc, Michel Puechavy and a number of others. Those who were either actively involved with ASSOPH or quietly supported its work included some of the top journalists, film executives, justice campaigners, women's rights activists and politicians in France. The association also had a Dublin-based solicitor, James McGuill, representing their legal interests in Ireland.

The campaign launched by ASSOPH was hugely effective from the very start. It focused on legal submissions and galvanising public and political opinion in France. Its campaign was methodical and unrelenting. The case had captivated public interest in France for years, and there was widespread sympathy for the Bouniol and du Plantier families for what they had endured since 1996.

A number of articles were written in French newspapers about Sophie's killing and the fact that her family had been denied justice in Ireland. While the French family were careful not to alienate Irish interests by being overly critical of the west Cork investigation or Irish state agencies, the French media were less forgiving of how Ireland had handled the case and, in particular, the failings of the garda

A delighted seven-year-old Sophie poses outside Notre-Dame Cathedral after her First Holy Communion. The lady adjusting her veil is her adored aunt, Marie-Madeleine Opalka, who would later play a crucial role in supporting Sophie's parents after her brutal murder. (© *Shutterstock*)

Beautiful, intelligent and fiercely independent, Sophie Bouniol strikes a pensive pose. (© *Daragh McSweeney/Provision*)

Sophie cuts a striking figure as she poses by the window of her Paris apartment. (© *Daragh McSweeney/Provision*)

A youthful Sophie demonstrates the natural warmth and happiness that captivated everyone she met. (© *Shutterstock*)

Sophie poses for the camera as she is hugged by her nine-year-old son during a family holiday. The focus of Sophie's world was her beloved son, Pierre-Louis. (© *Shutterstock*)

Sophie smiles happily in 1995, flanked by the two beloved men in her life: her husband, Daniel Toscan du Plantier, and her son, Pierre-Louis Baudey-Vignaud. (© *Pool BENAINOUS/HIRES/Getty Images*)

Daniel Toscan du Plantier and Pierre-Louis Baudey-Vignaud follow Sophie's coffin out of the church after her requiem Mass in France in January 1997. Her parents, Georges and Marguerite Bouniol, and her first husband, Pierre-Jean Baudey, are partially obscured in the background. (© *Gilles Bouquillon/Getty Images*)

The laneway leading to Sophie's Toormore property. Sophie's body was found by a gate in the far left of the photo, where the laneway curves uphill towards her house. (© *STR/AFP via Getty Images*)

Tall, raven-haired and handsome, Manchester-born journalist Ian Bailey in west Cork in February 1997. (© *Daragh McSweeney/Provision*)

The simple stone Celtic cross that marks the spot where Sophie's body was found. The cross is inscribed 'Sophie'. (© *Daragh McSweeney/Provision*)

Georges and Marguerite Bouniol lovingly place white lilies at the cross. For 15 years, Sophie's parents visited Toormore for her anniversary. (© *Daragh McSweeney/Provision*)

Daniel Toscan du Plantier and his solicitor, Paul Haennig, right, address the media at a Cork hotel in July 2000 during his single visit to Ireland after the murder of his wife. (© *Daragh McSweeney/ Provision*)

Paul Gallagher SC, who was lead counsel for the Irish and UK newspapers in the libel action. He would go on to become Ireland's Attorney General. (© *Daragh McSweeney/ Provision*)

Ian Bailey and his partner, Jules Thomas, walk back into the Camden Quay court premises carrying flowers and Christmas presents during a lunchtime break in his December 2003 libel action against eight Irish and UK newspapers. (© *Daragh McSweeney/ Provision*)

Schull shopkeeper Marie Farrell leaves the Cork Circuit Court premises on Camden Quay during the 2003 libel action. She was dubbed the 'star witness' of the two-week hearing. (© *Daragh McSweeney/Provision*)

Senior gardaí greet members of the French detective unit working with Magistrate Patrick Gachon during their investigative trip to west Cork in 2011. (© *Daragh McSweeney/Provision*)

French detectives and forensic experts conduct a site visit at Toormore as part of their Irish investigation. (© *Daragh McSweeney/Provision*)

Georges and Marguerite Bouniol leave Goleen church after a memorial Mass for Sophie in 2012. Marie-Madeleine Opalka can be seen in the background. (© *Daragh McSweeney/Provision*)

Jules Thomas, Ian Bailey and his solicitor, Frank Buttimer, speak to the assembled media outside the Four Courts in Dublin in 2012 after his landmark Supreme Court victory against a French extradition bid. That's my hand coming in from the left with a tape recorder. (© *Peter Muhly/AFP via Getty Images*)

Jules Thomas gazes proudly up at her partner, Ian Bailey, as he displays his UCC law thesis on 'Policing the Police – Garda Accountability in Ireland'. (© *Daragh McSweeney/Provision*)

Ian Bailey poses for the camera as he delivers a special lecture for the West Cork Debating Society in Skibbereen in 2013. (*Courtesy of Niall Duffy*)

Jean-Pierre Gazeau, left, and Jean-Antoine Bloc of ASSOPH at a 2014 press conference to urge the Irish authorities to continue cooperation with the French investigation into the murder of Sophie Toscan du Plantier. They hold copies of a book about the murder, entitled *A Denial of Justice*. (© *Daragh McSweeney/Provision*)

Pierre-Louis Baudey-Vignaud pictured in west Cork during one of his trips to his mother's Toormore home. He refused to sell Sophie's beloved property and retained it for holidays with his family and friends. (© *Daragh McSweeney/Provision*)

Pierre-Louis Baudey-Vignaud photographed attending the May 2019 opening of the Paris trial over his mother's murder. (© *Alain Jocard/AFP via Getty Images*)

Jean-Antoine Bloc, a key figure in ASSOPH's decade-long campaign for justice for Sophie, attending the Paris trial. (© *Eric Feferberg/AFP via Getty Images*)

Pierre-Jean Baudey, right, talks to the Bouniol family's long-standing lawyer, Alain Spilliaert, during a break in proceedings at the Paris trial. (© *Eric Feferberg/AFP via Getty Images*)

Ian Bailey works on a wood carving at a west Cork farmers' market.
(© *aphperspective/ Alamy*)

A remarkable image of Ian Bailey surrounded by wildflowers in the garden of his Liscaha home on 31 May 2019, the day he learned he had been convicted *in absentia* of Sophie's murder at the Paris trial.
(© *Mark Condren/Irish Independent*)

A sombre Ian Bailey leaves the Four Courts in Dublin in December 2019 after a judge endorsed a third French extradition warrant and listed it for a full hearing before the High Court in 2020. (© *Damien Eagers/AFP via Getty Images*)

investigation. Numerous articles claimed that the original investigation had been bungled.

In March 2008, a hugely influential piece was written by Marie-Victoire Louis entitled 'The Murder of Sophie Toscan du Plantier née Bouniol – eleven years of failure and denial of justice'. A sociologist and a researcher with the French National Centre for Scientific Research, she was one of France's most respected experts on violence against women. Journalists such as Guy Girard, who had worked with Sophie, and Pascale Gérin of *Le Parisien* also raised the plight facing the du Plantier and Bouniol families now that little or nothing appeared likely to happen in Ireland. The articles had a significant impact on French public opinion and bolstered the case for something to be done in France to help the family.

President Nicolas Sarkozy had taken office in the Élysée Palace in 2007, and it was made clear that French support and political influence would be fully behind the family – as it had been during the term of President Jacques Chirac, who had been in office at the time of the murder and who was a good friend of Daniel du Plantier, who had died in 2003, just months before the Cork libel action opened. His death was a significant setback for the French campaigners as he wielded enormous influence and, had he lived, he would have been in a position to galvanise political, business and societal support for the fledgling ASSOPH campaign. However, others had influence which could be brought to bear. Mr Gazeau had also acted as a science advisor to several campaigns and events led by President Chirac, all of which lent weight to the investigation now about to get under way.

Within 12 months of the foundation of ASSOPH, the French authorities had agreed to appoint a special magistrate to investigate the circumstances of Sophie's death. Magistrate Patrick Gachon was appointed to the role in November 2007. He was given access to the full resources of the French police and would be assisted by fellow magistrate Nathalie Dutartre. Both were experienced legal officers and were given the resources and time to conduct the type of investigation they saw fit over the 23 December 1996 killing. They had the full support of Sophie's family – and the resources of the French state. The two magistrates also had access to some of the most experienced police detectives in Paris, some of whom had spent years dealing with homicide cases.

Many of the Paris-based detectives who would assist the investigation by Magistrates Gachon and Dutartre also had experience of so-called 'cold case' reviews. Such long-unsolved cases, many of which dated back years or even decades, required a specialist police approach and a forensic ability to review old evidence. They also required time and vast reserves of patience.

Critically, the French investigative team would also be given whatever support they required in Ireland, including full access to the original garda murder file. This ensured that the French investigators would have access to all witness statements, forensic reports, the crime scene photographs and the post-mortem examination file of State Pathologist Professor John Harbison. If the French police team had not had access to the Irish files, an investigation would be fatally compromised from the outset.

This granting of access was unprecedented. It also confirmed, beyond any doubt, that no action would ever be taken by the DPP over the garda case file in Ireland. Any such action would be critically undermined from the very start by the fact that access to the file had been given to someone outside the Irish judicial process – and would open any future prosecution, even one taken on the basis of new evidence, to an immediate legal challenge based on a breach of process.

While it was never confirmed, the astonishing level of access granted to Magistrate Gachon and his police team was clearly the result of consultations between Paris and Dublin at the very highest levels. Even allowing for existing European judicial and police cooperation protocols, journalists covering the case – including myself – felt the level of access given to the French was astonishing.

The Irish authorities were clearly eager to facilitate the French police and avoid potential fallout from any perceived failings of the domestic investigation. It was a sensitive issue for successive Irish governments, who were clearly determined to do everything within their power not to alienate the French authorities, while carefully negotiating Irish legal requirements.

***

The first move in Magistrate Gachon's investigation would prove one of its most shocking – the exhumation of Sophie's body. On 26 June 2008, it emerged that Magistrate Gachon had applied to a French judge for permission to exhume the body for the purpose of conducting a fresh battery of forensic tests. Permission was granted within a matter of weeks. While forensic science and, in particular, DNA sampling had developed dramatically in the 12 years since the killing, there was still major doubt over the benefits of such an action.

One garda source I spoke to at the time was incredulous at the decision, pointing out that after a post-mortem examination in Ireland and such a lengthy period of time, not to mention two burials, the chance of obtaining critical new evidence was remote at the very best. Sophie's body had been subjected to a full post-mortem examination in Ireland on 24 December 1996 before being released to her family and brought back to France. It had already been exhumed once before. That exhumation in 2004 was done for the purpose of moving her body to a family plot in a different part of France. Sophie was initially buried in Mauvezin, near Ambax in the Haute-Garonne region of south-west France. This was close to where her husband, Daniel, maintained a beautiful country retreat and where Sophie had spent glorious holidays. If Toormore was her special place, Ambax was the place outside Paris closest to her husband's heart.

However, Mr du Plantier had been buried in Paris, not interred beside Sophie at her Mauvezin resting place. A year after he died, Sophie's family decided to have her buried closer to a property they owned in the Lozère region, not far from Combret, a beautiful mountain town in south central

France. It meant her plot could be visited more easily and frequently by her family and friends. It was also intended that, in future years, family members would be interred beside Sophie. Their exhumation request was granted, and the body was quietly moved.

On 1 July 2008, Sophie's remains were exhumed for a second time in an operation that began shortly before dawn at 5.30 a.m. The entire procedure was tightly controlled by French police. The exhumation took just over an hour and a half to complete. A number of Irish journalists and photographers had travelled to France to report on the major development in the case but were kept well back from the scene by gendarmes who gruffly refused to engage with the foreign press. French journalists were likewise not permitted access close to the area where the exhumation was being conducted. The French police were adamant that nothing would be allowed to interfere with the operation or potentially cause upset for the family.

None of Sophie's family chose to attend the scene. ASSOPH founder and Sophie's uncle Jean-Pierre Gazeau said it would be too upsetting and the family did not want to distract investigators from their painstaking work. 'The family will not be there,' he said on the eve of the exhumation. 'There will be some officials but that will be it. The remains will be taken to Paris and we hope that some new evidence can be found.'

Following the exhumation, Sophie's body was transferred by police escort to a specialist Paris forensic facility, where a second post-mortem examination was conducted. Given that it had been 12 years since the killing, the post-mortem examination and the forensic sampling process required almost a week to complete. The bulk of the tests focused on DNA sampling to determine if any unexplained genetic profiles were present. Other tests, including fibre, hair and organic material sampling, were also conducted.

In December 2008, Magistrate Gachon formally received the full case file from gardaí. This allowed the French investigation team to review all the garda interviews and case notes to determine what their next move would be. By early 2009 it was confirmed that French police would travel to Ireland to conduct interviews with the key individuals spoken to by gardaí 12 years earlier.

***

On 12 June 2009, Magistrates Gachon and Dutartre flew into Ireland and travelled to west Cork to view the key sites of the investigation for themselves. They were briefed by senior gardaí in west Cork and were offered the Irish force's full cooperation. They visited the Toormore site where Sophie's body had been discovered and they had access to her holiday home. Magistrate Gachon did not offer any media interviews while in west Cork, and it was clear that his visit was preparatory to a major French investigative operation.

Having carefully consulted with gardaí in west Cork, Magistrate Gachon asked two senior officers to follow up that meeting by travelling to Paris for further consultations. Permission was given by the government and Garda Síochána chiefs for both officers to travel to Paris, a development revealed by Barry Roche in the *Irish Times*.

The pace of developments in France accelerated and Magistrate Gachon, in early 2010, moved to issue a European Arrest Warrant for Mr Bailey – a decision that stunned most Irish observers, but which had been expected by the French family and their supporters. The warrant was issued on the basis that the French wanted to formally question Mr Bailey in Paris as part of their investigation.

***

Just nine days after Mr Bailey's UCC graduation in December 2010, the French extradition bid was listed for preliminary High Court hearing. Under various European judicial and police cooperation agreements, there are strict protocols to be followed in respect of EAWs. In the case of the French warrant, it had to be listed before the High Court and then considered at a full hearing. If the warrant was valid and if there weren't any glaring errors in it, it had to be considered on its merits before the Supreme Court if challenged or appealed. For Mr Bailey, this news was hardly the ideal backdrop against which to celebrate a major academic achievement.

'It certainly was not made easier but I have had great support [from family and friends] – I would like to say that the standard of tuition in the academic fraternity here is exceptionally high.'

Mr Bailey said that he now hoped to pursue his law studies towards a master's degree but realised that in post-recession Ireland securing work in the legal world would not be easy or straightforward. 'In the present climate, [for] journalists, lawyers, engineers, mechanics … it is going to be very difficult. We are heading into unknown territory.'

At the time, many of us wondered whether his 'unknown territory' comment was more about judicial than economic matters. In terms of the French extradition warrant, few doubted but that Ireland and France were now heading into uncharted legal waters.

***

Sophie's family were determined to play their part and keep the case in the headlines. On 15 December 2010, Georges and Marguerite Bouniol flew into Cork. The purpose of their visit was to mark the fourteenth anniversary of their daughter's death. The visit made headlines across the Irish media as a result of the extradition proceedings that had just been triggered.

Together with other Cork-based reporters, I met Georges and Marguerite during their visit, which once again revolved around staying at Sophie's Toormore house, the laying of a wreath of white lilies at the stone Celtic cross that marks the spot where she died, and attending Mass in Goleen parish church. Marguerite was adamant they were not in Ireland because of the Paris investigation or the extradition proceedings.

We are old now, so we will not suffer for many years more. We do not wish what we are living for anyone. We suffer a lot. We do not come here for what will happen tomorrow. That is not our problem. We do not come for that. That is the job of the justice system.

We could not come to Ireland last year [2009] but we are happy to come back this year because we owe it to our daughter. She suffered so much when she tried to escape and then she was hunted down. She suffered so much that we want to suffer as well. I have had to be twice as strong as anyone – but it is natural, is it not, that I should want my daughter's murderer to be behind bars?

There are moments I do not believe at all. There is something totally unjust and abnormal about parents surviving their children. I know you will say I am biased because I was her mother, but Sophie really did have all the [best] qualities. She loved life, she was gay and pretty. She loved meeting people and loved nature. She spoke to everyone. In Ireland, the people we met told us, 'She was like one of us.' But it is still very difficult to talk about.

There were times it was difficult to witness at close hand the obvious grief and pain etched on the faces of the elderly couple. Over the years, many members of the Cork media had got to know them and were touched by their kindness and generosity. The couple also went to great pains to thank the gardaí locally for the support they had shown them during their various trips, especially Superintendent Liam Horgan of Bantry Garda Station, who invariably met Georges and Marguerite Bouniol each time they visited and ensured they had whatever liaison support they required.

A few years earlier, after a press conference with the family at Cork Airport, I had decided it would be worth attending a special candlelit vigil at Toormore that had been planned by the family. That evening was dark, damp and grim. Standing on the bleak hillside at Toormore, waiting for the event to begin around 8 p.m., I was surprised to be approached by Mr Gazeau, Sophie's uncle. It was, he said, a cold evening and he asked if I would like to come into the house for a hot drink and a seat by the fire.

I politely declined, not wanting to intrude on a private family gathering, at which point I was told that if I didn't walk up the hill to the property, the elderly Mrs Bouniol had promised she would walk down to the gate to bring me a hot drink. Accompanied by a photographer who had been shivering beside me in the December cold, I walked up to Sophie's old house. Inside, we were made to sit by the roaring fire and offered rum and cheese. When we both declined the rum, hot mugs of coffee were then pressed into our hands. Some 30 minutes later, and just a short time before the candlelit ceremony was due to start, we offered our thanks, shook hands with our hosts and left the house. It was a kindness I have never forgotten.

Every time there is a development in the long-running investigation, I remember that, while for those of us in the media it is a news item, for Sophie's family and her elderly parents the search for justice has effectively become their life. More than once I've wondered why such evil befalls the kindest and most decent of people.

***

Two years after their first meeting with senior garda officers, the French investigation team were finally ready for witness interviews in Ireland. On 3 October 2011, a five-man team of experienced Paris detectives and forensic experts flew to Ireland to conduct an exhaustive series of interviews in west Cork with those who had been interviewed by gardaí as part of their original Irish investigation between 1996 and 1998.

Gardaí confirmed that the French team was being assisted under European mutual assistance agreements:

Following a request through the Central Authority for Mutual Assistance at the Department of Justice and Equality, a team of French investigators comprising of three police detectives and two scientists will arrive in Cork this afternoon [3 October]. The purpose of their visit is to interview witnesses and conduct an examination of a number of exhibits seized by An Garda Síochána as part of its investigation into the murder of Ms du Plantier. Throughout their stay, the French investigators will be assisted by members of An Garda Síochána from the west Cork Garda division under the direction of Chief Superintendent Tom Hayes.

During their time in Ireland, a garda spokesperson said, the Paris police team would be assisted by officials from the French embassies in Dublin and London. A special press conference was facilitated at Bandon Garda Station on 4 October.

The press briefing was conducted with the assistance of Eric Battesti, a senior official at the French embassy in London, who was acting as liaison between the gardaí and the Paris detectives and forensic officers during their time in west Cork. The briefing was notable for a number of reasons.

First, Mr Battesti said the French investigation team were confident of making progress during their fortnight of work in Ireland. There was no attempt to downplay the importance of the work of the Paris detectives. Mr Battesti said it was hoped there would be sufficient evidence gathered to facilitate a future prosecution in France. However, it was also admitted that no new witnesses had come forward, despite the recent appeals in both the Irish and French media. That meant the French team would be entirely reliant on the garda case file – the same file that the DPP had ruled was not sufficient to justify any prosecution in Ireland. The French authorities also confirmed that Mr Bailey remained a suspect in their investigation.

Critically, all the interviews proposed by the French police team had to be conducted on a voluntary basis – the French could not compel anyone to participate in the planned question-and-answer sessions in Ireland. The interviews would also be videotaped in case they were required for any future court proceedings. Over two weeks, the French team interviewed a total of 30 people. Among those interviewed were Jules Thomas and two of her daughters. Mr Bailey had offered to be interviewed but his offer was not taken up by the French investigators.

The French forensic experts focused on the garda murder file itself. Their priority was the 200 exhibits gathered by detectives between 1996 and 1998, which were still in storage at Bandon Garda Station. Unfortunately, there were problems over the preservation of that evidence that would later become painfully apparent.

***

Since their first arrest, both Ian Bailey and Jules Thomas had complained about their treatment at the hands of certain gardaí in west Cork. Ultimately, these complaints crystallised into two forms of action – the High Court civil action for alleged wrongful arrest and a more detailed complaint to the Garda Síochána Ombudsman Commission over the alleged behaviour of some officers involved in the du Plantier investigation. As 2011 drew to a close, at the same time that the French investigative team were assessing the murder file, Mr Bailey formally lodged this complaint to GSOC. He clearly hoped that a GSOC probe would be a major plank in his defence against a French prosecution. If GSOC found any corroboration of his claims that the original garda investigation against him was flawed, it would dramatically undermine a French action, which would be largely based on the same garda file.

9

EXTRADITION BID

The cramped confines of the Supreme Court provided one of the most clear-cut legal victories Mr Bailey ever enjoyed in Ireland. Watching him arrive at the Four Courts that damp morning of 1 March 2012, flanked by Jules Thomas and Frank Buttimer, I was struck by how his entire life had been consumed by the legal battle over Sophie's death.

Minutes later, Mr Bailey had closed his eyes and a faint smile crossed his face as the Supreme Court rejected the French bid for his extradition. It was a unanimous ruling – and some of the commentary by the judges was devastating in their assessment of the investigation and, in its turn, the decision by the French to pursue a European Arrest Warrant for the British journalist.

Outside the Four Courts complex, Mr Bailey gave a brief press conference. The poet's first public reaction to his Supreme Court victory was poignant – he paid an emotional tribute to Ms Thomas, who had stood beside him despite the tumult of the previous 16 years. Immaculately dressed in a blue blazer, white shirt and paisley tie, Mr Bailey looked tired and drawn – but relieved that he would not face extradition to France. Facing a crowd of reporters, photographers and TV crews, he insisted on paying tribute to her before referencing the importance of the Supreme Court ruling.

I want to stress my appreciation to Jules, who has stood by me through thick and thin, and to our family, friends and supporters in west Cork and further afield. This has obviously been a very trying time for me [and

Jules] – I would like to thank the Supreme Court for their considered and prompt determination of this matter. On a personal note I am obviously relieved that this part of the proceedings is over – there are many stages and matters still to be dealt with and for that reason I won't be making any further statement.

Ms Thomas declined to make any comment to the assembled reporters. She studiously ignored the cameras of the photographers and TV crews. Similarly, she had remained silent through the hour-long hearing before the Supreme Court, when the extradition dismissal had been delivered.

Mr Bailey stressed to the reporters just how difficult the EAW proceedings had been for him. 'It has been hell,' he said bluntly. 'It has been very hard, very hard – on Jules in particular. You wouldn't be able to believe the hell we have been put through by this awfulness. We are now going to talk about where we go from here.'

Asked by one journalist whether he had any comment to make for the family of Ms du Plantier in France, Mr Bailey declined: 'I do not at this stage, no.' Mr Buttimer urged the assembled media to consider what his client had endured. 'You have absolutely no idea the kind of life Mr Bailey and his partner Jules Thomas have had to lead, not just because of the extradition but because of the fifteen-year period during which he has been wrongly associated with this crime. His life has been intolerably difficult.'

Mr Buttimer pointedly confirmed that Mr Bailey would now be pressing ahead with his High Court action against the State for wrongful arrest. That action had been unavoidably delayed while the French extradition request was dealt with by the High Court and then the Supreme Court. Mr Buttimer also said that answers now needed to be provided over some of the disturbing elements of the investigation highlighted just minutes earlier by the Supreme Court. 'There have been inquiries into this case heretofore – those inquiries have been, in my humble opinion, non-productive. What has surprised me is the political silence to events which have been clearly laid out in the court and which are now in the public domain. I don't think it is for citizens to make calls in circumstances like this – this is a matter for those in authority to take stock of what has happened and take a serious look at the various issues concerning this case.'

Mr Buttimer was pointedly referencing the original 44-page report of the garda investigation into Sophie's killing that, in 2001, was central to ruling out a prosecution in Ireland. That report by the DPP had clearly carried enormous weight with the Supreme Court judges. Prepared by a solicitor in the DPP's office, Robert Sheehan, the report didn't just criticise the garda investigation as much as demolish it – and erase any suggestion that Mr Bailey might be charged. In a hammer blow to the original garda investigation, it had described the west Cork probe as 'thoroughly flawed and prejudiced'.

It detailed a total lack of forensic evidence against the Englishman and what one DPP official called the 'unsafe practices' that some gardaí engaged in during the high-profile murder inquiry – including a claim that at least one garda offered cash, clothes and drugs to a vulnerable drug user in exchange for information about Mr Bailey. The report also criticised garda for arresting Jules Thomas despite a specific instruction from the DPP not to do so.

Mr Buttimer considered the report, which had been disclosed to Mr Bailey's legal team on the instructions of the Attorney General in advance of the Supreme Court hearing, to be of paramount importance. This was because it was so critical of the garda case file. Crucially, that report also singled out the actions of Mr Bailey as consistent with those of an innocent party and that there was effectively no evidence against him in relation to the matter. Mr Bailey's legal team also believed that the report added weight to their consistent claim that there had been a conspiracy against their client.

That DPP report would be a catalyst for Mr Bailey's long-signalled action against the State for wrongful arrest. While he had indicated the action as early as 2007, the case had been mired in logistical delays and postponements. Based on what had been disclosed as part of the Supreme Court extradition process, that High Court action would now be prioritised.

The Supreme Court didn't pull its punches over the implications of the internal DPP report. It was described as 'dramatic and shocking'. Supreme Court Judge Adrian Hardiman said it was now open to the new DPP, Claire Loftus, to decide what criminal charges, if any, should be brought against the unnamed gardaí who allegedly tried to apply political pressure to the DPP to bring about a murder prosecution.

The five judges of the Supreme Court, led by Chief Justice Mrs Justice Susan Denham, unanimously overturned the earlier High Court decision to allow Mr Bailey's extradition through the enforcement of the French EAW. The Supreme Court ruled that Mr Bailey should not be surrendered to France. The court pointed out that no decision to put Mr Bailey on trial had been taken by the French authorities in 2011 or 2012 – such a decision by French authorities was required under Irish law to allow someone to be extradited.

Four of the five judges also ruled that he could not be extradited because the offence had been committed outside France. France would not be obliged to surrender a non-Irish citizen to Ireland in similar circumstances. Under Irish law, Section 21A of the European Arrest Warrant Act 2003, as amended, ensures that a person cannot be surrendered for the purposes of investigation. In addition, a court shall refuse to surrender a person if it is satisfied that a decision to charge the person has not been made.

Chief Justice Denham said the legal situation was quite clear:

> [It] is clear that a decision has been made equivalent to charge the appellant. However, no further decision has been made. The appellant is sought for a criminal investigation – for the investigation procedure in France – and no decision has yet been made in France to try him for the murder. Consequently, he may not be surrendered in accordance with Section 21A of the European Arrest Warrant Act 2003, as amended.

Justice Adrian Hardiman was even more scathing in his assessment of the matter, pointing out that, despite several reviews by gardaí and the DPP, no evidence to warrant a prosecution against Mr Bailey was ever identified. 'Mr Bailey has been very thoroughly investigated in Ireland in connection with the death of Madame du Plantier. There was certainly, as will be seen, no lack of enthusiasm to prosecute him if the facts suggested that there was evidence against him. He has been subjected to arrest and detention for the purpose of questioning,' he said.

'He has voluntarily provided, at the request of the Gardaí, forensic samples which have failed to yield incriminating evidence. The fruit of the investigation has been considered not once, but several times by the DPP, who has concluded and reiterated that there is no evidence to warrant a prosecution against him.' This, Mr Justice Hardiman argued, was very significant.

Mr Bailey was awarded his costs not just for the Supreme Court hearing but also for the earlier High Court ruling on the EAW. It was a landmark victory that had enormous implications – the most important of which was that the French authorities, without a conviction, would conceivably have no way of overcoming such a clear-cut Supreme Court ruling. The accuracy of this view would shortly be proved by the fate of a second French EAW.

***

The Supreme Court ruling was a huge setback for Ms du Plantier's family and for ASSOPH. Their greatest concern was now focused on the long-term implications of the decision and whether it could be challenged or overturned at any stage in the future. Sophie's parents were devastated by the ruling.

Their solicitor, Alain Spilliaert, admitted at the time the family was 'shocked and frustrated' by the stance of the Supreme Court in Ireland. The elderly couple had opted not to attend the Four Courts for the ruling and were 'very upset' when they were informed of the outcome at their Paris home. 'Time is our enemy now because of the age of Sophie's parents and their long wait for justice,' he said. 'It is a very big shock for us – it is a step backwards because we were very hopeful, given that the High Court had supported the extradition last year. We were confident – but this is very disappointing. We will have to wait and see what happens next.'

Sophie's parents had visited Ireland the month before, February, to attend a special memorial Mass in Goleen for their daughter. They had planned to visit the previous December to mark the fifteenth anniversary of her death, but Marguerite Bouniol's health had ruled out the trip until two months later. That February, in keeping with their tradition, they laid a wreath of white lilies at the Celtic cross memorial that marks the precise spot where their daughter's body was found. The December visits had become increasingly painful for the elderly couple. 'It is very difficult for them … you can understand perfectly why they do not come [to Ireland] before Christmas,' Mr Spilliaert explained. 'They will travel to west Cork in the new year and will remember Sophie. They are still hopeful of a positive outcome to their battle for justice.'

A friend of the elderly couple, former French consul in Cork Françoise Letellier admitted that the couple's major fear now was that they would not live to see justice done for Sophie. 'They are really old now and worried that they will die without their daughter's killer being brought to justice,' she said.

***

From Mr Bailey's point of view, it was clear what would happen next – he would move ahead with his High Court civil action against the State for alleged wrongful arrest. His partner, Jules Thomas, was also taking a similar action. Mr Bailey's formal complaint to GSOC would also proceed. The GSOC complaint – like the High Court case – had been overshadowed by the Supreme Court challenge.

There was also a suggestion that a third action could arise via an inquiry into some of the revelations as part of the Supreme Court hearing on the extradition matter, in particular the criticisms of the garda investigation and the case file.

It seemed that the pending High Court action for wrongful arrest would prove even more dramatic than the Supreme Court hearing. The journalist had complained of 'breath-taking wrongdoing' by State officials, and it was apparent that Marie Farrell, once the 'star witness' for the newspapers in the 2003 Cork Circuit Court libel action, would now be a key witness for Mr Bailey.

***

Almost nine months after the Supreme Court rejection of the French extradition bid, Sophie's parents highlighted the scale of their disappointment in the Irish judicial system. In a hard-hitting interview for the *Sunday Independent*, Marguerite Bouniol said they viewed the ruling as an insult to their daughter's memory.

[It was] as if the murder had never happened. We are very sad. We have been waiting for so long and we have been used to seeing things progress. But nothing happened, once more. We do not see any end to it. We were hoping a lot after the High Court decision. All of a sudden last year we were faced with that stunning [Supreme Court] decision.

Our daughter was murdered, and it is as if nothing had happened. Sophie loved Ireland. We will never give up. She was so happy here that we have to pay tribute to her by coming every year. We can never do enough for our daughter. We are not going to give up our hopes.

Those hopes were now entirely focused on the investigation being directed by Magistrate Patrick Gachon and his Paris police team.

ASSOPH officials acknowledged that, after the Supreme Court ruling in Ireland, a trial in Paris would not now take place before 2014 at the earliest as the French needed time to fully consider the Supreme Court ruling and potential actions flagged by Mr Bailey as a consequence of it.

***

For Mr Bailey, the Supreme Court victory marked a turning of the tide. In February 2013 he celebrated another boost with his receipt of a Master of Law degree from UCC. There were few doubts about his area of interest in his legal studies. His 25,000-word thesis was entitled 'Policing the Police – Garda Accountability in Ireland'. The master's degree came three years after he received a Bachelor of Civil Law degree from the university, where he had begun his studies in 2007.

Two months later, Mr Bailey delivered a keynote legal address at a special event in west Cork. It was made clear several weeks before the event at Skibbereen's West Cork Hotel that journalists and photographers were more than welcome to attend. As it transpired, almost one-quarter of the total attendance of 30 people were members of the media. The month before, Mr Bailey had even offered his legal opinion on the government's controversial new property tax via RTÉ's *Liveline* programme.

Hosted by the West Cork Philosophical Society, the event was focused on Ireland's post-Celtic boom plight. Journalists present were told, politely but firmly, that while questions would be welcomed at the end of the address, all queries in respect of Mr Bailey's ongoing legal issues in both Ireland and France would be declined.

Mr Bailey's speech was an impassioned defence of the Irish judiciary in their stand-off with the government over various controversial policies in respect of the economic collapse and attempted recovery.

Increasingly the ordinary man, woman and child, supposedly guaranteed so many rights by Bunreacht na hÉireann, are increasingly penalised and victimised by their own government at the command, behest and diktat of that absentee landlord – our new European technocratic masters, 'the troika' of the IMF, ECB and EU – many of whose number are unelected and ultimately answer to no other power or authority than that of Mammon. Going, going, gone are an increasing number of services, safeguards and supports which had been assumed as bastions and dependable norms of our civilised social democratic system and society. Rural banks have been closing by the dozen, rural garda barracks are being closed, public services reduced and child and carers' benefits, despite promises to the contrary, and the principles of Article 45, have been cut, along with a range of basic services.

Mr Bailey said the ECB and IMF had 'a tendril-like grasp' on the economies of sovereign states like Ireland. He argued that the real culprit for Europe's economic meltdown and the Euro crisis was the European Central Bank.

Reckless and negligent lending to the feral and largely unregulated Irish banking sector by the ECB resulted in a disastrous over-inflation of property prices and real estate, which in turn led to the crash and the subsequent pledging by Taoiseach Brian Cowen and the late Brian Lenihan and others of the State's pension reserves to underwrite private equity debts to ensure senior bond holders were not to lose out.

Mr Bailey said that developments in countries like Ireland heralded a grim new era.

What we are witnessing in Europe in general, and in Ireland in particular, is the dawning of an age of regression, retrenchment and welfare austerity, which will lead to significant reductions in wealth redistribution, while the earnings and revenues of future generations have effectively been mortgaged to pay the gambling debts of others.

He was also highly critical of the impact of austerity policies on Ireland and backed the Irish judiciary in their stand-off with the government. 'The Irish judiciary have always been fiercely protective of their independence.'

Sitting in the audience, I wondered whether the remark about the independence of the Irish judiciary was focused more on European judicial protocols than domestic austerity concerns. The Irish judiciary – namely the Supreme Court – had flexed its muscles by rejecting the French EAW in 2012. Such continuing independence was now clearly important to Mr Bailey and his ongoing vow to fight French extradition attempts.

***

Despite his Supreme Court victory, Mr Bailey remained in a difficult legal position. Although the EAW was effectively now void in Ireland, that didn't mean it couldn't be activated in other European countries, including the UK. The journalist still faced the prospect of potential arrest if he ever left Ireland, even to return to his UK home.

Twelve months after his Supreme Court victory, Mr Bailey's elderly mother died on 18 May 2013. He was unable to visit her before her death or even to attend the funeral service in England. She was 88 years old and had suffered a number of medical problems, which left her immobile and increasingly frail. His only sister, Kay Reynolds, said that when doctors informed their mother that she was likely to lose her sight, she began to refuse food.

The family consulted with both Mrs Bailey's carers and her doctors. It was determined that she had her full mental faculties and was capable of making such a decision. Legally, she was entitled to refuse food even though to do so would mean her death was likely within a matter of weeks.

Mrs Reynolds said her brother had maintained contact with his family throughout his time in Ireland and was worried about their mother. She said the pair had a 'very sweet and tender relationship' and she was heartbroken that her brother was unable to attend the funeral in the UK.

Mrs Reynolds admitted that her brother was deeply upset at their mother's death and 'very sad' that he was unable to visit her before her passing. He maintained contact with his family throughout the period and had sent over a special collection of poems he had written for her funeral service. He was also consulted over the specific hymns to be played at the funeral service. Mr Bailey had even written a eulogy in tribute to their mother.

Mrs Reynolds, who had carefully followed the extradition process before Mr Bailey's final Supreme Court victory in 2012, said she was 'very, very scared' for her brother and what might happen next – a recognition that the French were far from finished with their extradition campaign.

10

WRONGFUL ARREST

By 2014 the French investigation had been under way for seven years and there was still no sign of any conclusion. ASSOPH believed that Magistrate Gachon couldn't finish his report until follow-up interviews were concluded in Ireland – and suspected Ireland was delaying the process.

At the same time, Mr Bailey's High Court action for alleged wrongful arrest was about to reach hearing stage. A full Garda Síochána Ombudsman Commission investigation was also under way into complaints lodged by Mr Bailey over his treatment by the police in Ireland. Mr Bailey's legal team were adamant that while these processes were continuing in Ireland, all cooperation with the French investigation should be suspended. Frank Buttimer formally wrote to the Department of Justice and Minister for Justice Alan Shatter on 24 April 2014, demanding that all mutual assistance agreements with the French be suspended immediately given ongoing domestic court actions. Such mutual assistance in the circumstances was, he argued, a blatant abuse of process.

ASSOPH were worried that, amid the flurry of legal proceedings in Ireland, the French investigation could be stalled for months or even years, with disastrous consequences. Jean-Pierre Gazeau, Sophie's uncle and president of ASSOPH, and Jean-Antoine Bloc visited Cork on 17 May 2014 to highlight their worries and to demand that critical Irish cooperation with Magistrate Gachon be maintained.

Georges and Marguerite Bouniol had planned to accompany the ASSOPH members on their trip to Cork for the special press conference but, due to the poor health of Mrs Bouniol, the elderly couple were unable to attend. Mr Bouniol was now 88 years old, while Mrs Bouniol was 86 and in frail health. However, a special message in the form of a personal appeal from Mrs Bouniol would be read out at a press conference in a hotel at Cork Airport that evening.

Mr Bloc did not shy away from detailing the consequences of an Irish decision to suspend cooperation with Magistrate Gachon. '[It would be] a scandal … a catastrophe. It would be extraordinary,' he warned. 'They have suffered terribly for seventeen years. They are very sad, very upset. They do not understand why it took so long.' ASSOPH warned that the treatment of the French family by various Irish agencies was 'a judicial fiasco … a denial of justice'.

In a hard-hitting message read out on behalf of Mrs Bouniol by Mr Gazeau, Sophie's mother warned that 'enough is enough … we, the family, have been suffering a double penalty for almost eighteen years. Sophie was murdered and we … are mute in Ireland. We never had the opportunity to make our case and now we are the victims of serious malfunctions from police and judicial Irish systems.'

Sophie's uncle publicly pleaded with the Irish authorities to continue their cooperation with Magistrate Gachon and his team so that some form of justice could be delivered to the French family. The age and increasingly frail health of Georges and Marguerite Bouniol meant that timing was now imperative. Mr Gazeau told the assembled Irish media that he hoped the authorities would allow the Paris detectives resume their work in west Cork as early as 19 May.

To maintain pressure in France and to keep the case in the public mind, ASSOPH decided to support the publication of a book to highlight Sophie's story and what her family had endured since 23 December 1996.

The book, *L'affaire Sophie Toscan du Plantier – un Déni de justice*, was written by Julien Cros and Jean-Antoine Bloc. Published by Max Milo in Paris, the book also featured contributions from Pierre-Louis Baudey-Vignaud and Marguerite Bouniol.

Copies of the book were brought to the ASSOPH press conference, but the publication was never stocked by Irish booksellers or available for Irish distribution. That wasn't because it was written entirely in French and there were no plans for an English translation. Rather, it was because Mr Bailey had made it perfectly clear that anyone who stocked or distributed the book in Ireland would face possible legal action because of the disputed allegations it contained.

Mr Bailey had strenuously protested his innocence since December 1996 and was appalled that, despite the stance of the DPP, the French investigation seemed to be focused on him. Over time, he would warn that it was a tragedy for the French family for the focus to be wrongly placed on an innocent man while the real killer remained free and undetected.

The ASSOPH press conference didn't succeed in immediately clearing the path for the French team to visit west Cork for a final time. Ultimately, the second round of interviews was finally conducted in September 2015, when three detectives working with Magistrate Gachon flew back to west Cork. These interviews focused on 20 individuals, including several people who had already been interviewed in 2011.

But the press conference generated major headlines in all Irish newspapers and made both RTÉ and TV3 news bulletins. Once again, there was tremendous public sympathy for Sophie's family. Yet little, at least officially, seemed to change.

Meanwhile, Mr Bailey was about to open his long-awaited High Court action for wrongful arrest against the State and Garda Síochána; the Garda Síochána Ombudsman Commission, which was also conducting an investigation into a complaint from Mr Bailey over the conduct of the du Plantier investigation, had paused its probe pending the conclusion of this High Court action.

***

On 30 March 2015, the longest-running, most expensive and undoubtedly most astonishing civil action in High Court history ended in dramatic fashion.

The High Court action had been 64 days at hearing, since 4 November 2014. Mr Justice John Hedigan initially told the jury of eight men and four women that he had been informed by the legal teams involved that the case was expected to last for around six weeks. In the end, the action ran for an astonishing 16 weeks and featured a total of 93 witnesses – 72 called by the defendant, the State; and 21 called by the plaintiff, Mr Bailey. The case was so long that on numerous occasions the jury foreperson, at the request of other jury members, raised the issue of the duration of the hearing with the trial judge. Mr Justice Hedigan said he understood the issues the jury had raised but the action had to be allowed to follow its course. Ultimately, one jury member had to be excused because they had been offered an apprenticeship. Mr Justice Hedigan decided it would be unfair to deprive the juror of the employment opportunity. The ruling was eventually delivered by 11 jurors.

Various legal experts estimated the costs associated with the marathon High Court hearing at more than €2 million. Mr Bailey, having been landed with Circuit Court libel action bills in 2004, now found himself facing High Court legal bills roughly ten times greater.

Coverage of the case in the media had been exhaustive, with a full page in the *Irish Independent*, the *Irish Times* and the *Irish Examiner* almost every day. The case also featured in nightly bulletins on both RTÉ and TV3, as well as hourly radio news updates. Journalists assigned to cover the case found themselves doing little else for five months.

Few who covered the 2003 Cork Circuit Civil Court libel action thought anything could surpass the revelations it contained about the du Plantier case. In truth, the High Court disclosures were of an order entirely above. Had the revelations not occurred in the context of the Four Courts, in direct sworn evidence, they would have been beyond belief.

The allegations were wide-ranging: drugs had been offered by a garda in return for incriminating statements against Mr Bailey; Marie Farrell had been warned about the evidence she offered under oath; sexually inappropriate behaviour by gardaí; attempts by a garda to unduly influence a decision to level a prosecution charge in the case; and claims that detectives engaged in foul-mouthed rants and threatening behaviour during the investigation.

By early 2014 there were sufficient indications that the High Court action would prove extraordinary by Irish legal standards. It had emerged that a telephone system that handled emergency calls, which had been installed in garda stations across Ireland in the 1980s, had a recording function. Such a recording function posed fundamental problems at a garda station – not least for some conversations between gardaí, which should have been treated as confidential. This system with a recording function was discontinued in November 2013.

The garda commissioner at the time, Martin Callinan, had alerted the Department of Justice in March 2014 to the fact that the recording system had been in place. So seriously was the matter taken that it was immediately brought to the attention of Taoiseach Enda Kenny and discussed at a full Cabinet meeting on 25 March. By that time, the retirement of Commissioner Callinan had been confirmed in the wake of the controversy over the treatment of the so-called garda 'whistle-blower' Maurice McCabe.

Bandon Garda Station, the centre of the du Plantier murder investigation, had such a telephone recording system and it had been in operation between 1997 and 2003 – critical periods for the du Plantier investigation.

One month before the High Court action opened, Mr Justice Hedigan held a preliminary hearing in which various evidential matters were discussed. He directed GSOC to disclose statements it had received as part of its investigation into a complaint by Mr Bailey, lodged in December 2011, about his treatment by the gardaí. GSOC was given 12 days to comply with the order.

GSOC was specifically asked to submit statements its officers had received from Mr Bailey, Jules Thomas, Marie Farrell and former British Army soldier Martin Graham. It was Mr Graham who claimed he had been offered drugs and cash by gardaí in return for agreeing to help secure incriminating statements against Mr Bailey. Unlike several of the other key witnesses about to feature in the High Court action, Mr Graham had played no part in the 2003 Circuit Court libel action. A special questionnaire completed by Mrs Farrell in 1997 was also to be located by GSOC.

James B. Dwyer, a legal counsel for GSOC, explained that a single employee was sorting through a large volume of material in relation to the case to assist the hearing. He said this was causing a delay, but GSOC was doing everything possible to work with the High Court. Mr Justice Hedigan accepted the position but said that GSOC should begin handing over an initial batch of material within 12 days. A further two weeks was allowed for the remainder of the material.

Mr Justice Hedigan was also given an undertaking or legally binding commitment by the DPP that any documentation its office had relevant to the Bailey and du Plantier matters would be handed over.

Counsel for Mr Bailey said initial material had been received from the DPP and this 'tended to show wrongdoing'. The DPP had voluntarily submitted documentation and the court said it had accepted an undertaking that all remaining related documentation would be provided without the need for a High Court order.

The State raised the issue of the controversial tape recordings and stressed that there was no objection to their use during the upcoming hearing. Rather, the State said its sole concern was how these tapes were properly described and introduced to the jury during the proceedings.

Crucially, some material would not be allowed into evidence during the hearing – to the detriment, or benefit, of both sides. Elements of a DPP assessment of the garda case (the Sheehan analysis) would not be permitted as it was deemed to be inadmissible opinion. Similarly, elements of the extradition application from the French for Mr Bailey would not be permitted as they were deemed prejudicial to him.

On 4 November 2014, the case opened amid a huge media and legal presence. Many people not connected in any way with the hearing simply attended because they understood that legal history was likely to be made both in terms of the duration of the case and the implications of any rule, particularly for the gardaí. Mr Bailey, aware that he would be required to attend the hearing for extended periods, had arranged temporary accommodation in Dublin for the duration of the hearing. He was again accompanied by his partner, Ms Thomas.

Mr Bailey was represented by Frank Buttimer, Tom Creed SC and Jim Duggan JC. Mr Creed was one of Ireland's most respected senior counsels. A vastly experienced Cork-based counsel, he handled both civil and criminal matters, acting both as a State prosecutor and a defence counsel before the Circuit, High and Central Criminal Courts. Mr Duggan knew the case intimately, having acted for Mr Bailey in both the Circuit Court libel action and the subsequent High Court appeal.

The plaintiff's action alleged that he had been the victim of a garda conspiracy to link him to the killing of Sophie Toscan du Plantier. Mr Bailey claimed that the conspiracy began in December 1996 and was continuing to that very day.

The core elements of the case revolved around garda conduct towards key individuals in west Cork and alleged behaviour by officers in relation to the investigation. It was alleged that gardaí had induced Marie Farrell to make false statements to undermine Mr Bailey's alibi and had put her under duress to commit perjury in the 2003 libel action; that a garda had offered drugs and cash to Mr Graham in order to obtain incriminating statements against Mr Bailey; that another garda had acted to ensure that an assault complaint against Mrs Farrell's husband, Chris, by a local man was withdrawn; that gardaí had actively spread rumours and stories about Mr Bailey so that west Cork locals would be willing to make statements against him; and that gardaí had planned to 'chop up' statements in order to strengthen their case against him.

The key witnesses on the plaintiff's side would be Mr Bailey, Jules Thomas, Marie Farrell and Martin Graham. Other witnesses, including members of Ms Thomas's family, would also be called to corroborate their testimonies.

State defence of the action was led by Paul O'Higgins SC and Luán Ó Braonáin SC. Mr Ó Braonáin was a Dublin-based senior counsel, appointed to the Bar in 1991 and to senior counsel in 2007. He was viewed as one of the foremost of a talented new generation of defence counsels. Mr O'Higgins ranked as one of Ireland's most experienced counsels, having been appointed a junior counsel in 1977 and a senior counsel in 1992. He had been appointed Chairman of the Bar Council in 2010.

The High Court action opened, as the Cork libel case had 11 years before, with Mr Bailey offering evidence and outlining how being wrongly associated with the Sophie Toscan du Plantier investigation had destroyed his life and rendered his every waking moment a nightmare.

As in the Circuit Court libel action, he explained how he had been treated by gardaí, how shocked he was by his arrest, what he perceived as blatant intimidation by certain garda officers, and how his life in west Cork had been transformed into a nightmare as a direct result. Mr Bailey said he believed there was a conspiracy by gardaí to 'stitch [him] up' for something he was totally innocent of. The core of Mr Bailey's evidence was that gardaí had tried to frame him for the killing and that he should never have been arrested in 1997 and 1998, with his detentions amounting to wrongful arrests.

Mr Bailey was in the witness box for almost two weeks. Not long into his evidence there were tetchy exchanges between the journalist and the opposing legal counsel, Mr Ó Braonáin. They engaged in heated exchanges over Mr Bailey's conspiracy claims and, on one occasion, even about how a specific document should be presented in court.

Mr Justice Hedigan intervened. 'This is not a criminal trial – this is a civil trial,' he reminded the court. However, those not familiar with legal proceedings could have been forgiven for confusing the two in the circumstances. Mr Bailey was not on trial – he was taking a civil action against the State for wrongful arrest. But there were times during the marathon hearing when onlookers could easily have mistaken some of the exchanges as more in keeping with a criminal trial. In this, there were echoes of the 2003 libel hearing. Mr Bailey was specifically asked about one of the key issues first raised during the libel hearing – the nature of comments he had made to various people about the circumstances of Sophie's death.

Mr Bailey denied, once again, that he had told Malachi Reed that he had killed the French woman by smashing her head. He denied that he had effectively admitted the crime to Helen Callanan, a former deputy editor and news editor of the *Sunday Tribune* newspaper. He again insisted that his comment to Ms Callanan was dark humour. Seventeen years later, he acknowledged that his remark to the news editor in early 1997 was a 'very regrettable black joke'. The journalist once again insisted that he had been merely repeating what was being said about him locally and that at no stage had he ever made any admissions about the case – he had always protested his innocence and had had his life effectively destroyed through being wrongly associated with the investigation.

Mr Bailey acknowledged that he had said to her, 'Of course, yes, I killed her to resurrect my career as a journalist.' Ms Callanan was so taken aback by the remark she immediately reported it to gardaí. When Ms Callanan took the stand, she explained that she regarded the comment made to her as a 'confession' and had felt compelled to inform gardaí. However, Mr Duggan challenged her interpretation of the remark. In testy exchanges, Mr Duggan queried her motivation. 'You are trying to blacken him,' he argued to the former news editor. The remark visibly annoyed her.

'I am not trying to blacken him. I am telling you I did not take it as black humour. I did not find it humorous. We were not having any conversation that was jocular,' Ms Callanan responded. That conversation between Mr Bailey and Ms Callanan marked the last time he ever worked for the Sunday paper.

Mr Bailey again denied ever making admissions about any involvement in the death of Sophie to Ritchie and Rose Shelly, who had been socialising with him and Ms Thomas one New Year's Eve. He said he had merely been repeating to them what others in west Cork were saying about him. The journalist was also adamant he had never met Sophie Toscan du Plantier and had never had any dealings with her, though he acknowledged that he may have seen her in the distance once while working on a local property.

In a forensic cross-examination, some of his claims were tackled. Mr Bailey was adamant that he was never properly cautioned when he was first arrested. However, he acknowledged he was mistaken about that claim when confronted with an entry in his own diary that indicated he had in fact been read his rights by arresting officers.

While giving evidence during the first month of the hearing, Jules Thomas told the High Court how deeply shocked she was when she was arrested by gardaí. She now believed it was a cynical garda ploy to use her to exert maximum pressure on her partner. The artist also highlighted how she immediately took issue with some aspects of her statement, going so far as to get a solicitor to write to gardaí challenging parts of it.

Once again, major emphasis was placed on the incidents of domestic violence that Ms Thomas had endured at the hands of Mr Bailey. Two attacks, in 1996 and 2001, were outlined in detail to the jury. As she had been during the libel hearing, Ms Thomas was frank about what she endured. 'There is no excuse for violence,' she said. When pressed further about her view of her partner's behaviour towards her, Ms Thomas replied, 'I was pretty disgusted with his behaviour, really. It was appalling.'

Her daughter Saffron also offered evidence. Saffron, who was 17 years old when her mother first met Mr Bailey, said life at Liscaha was happy and content up until Christmas 1996. She insisted that on 22 December Mr Bailey had been helping to kill and pluck turkeys before going into a nearby woodland to cut a tree-top to use for their Christmas decorations. She said that he must have sustained scratches while doing so. She confirmed she was aware of domestic violence incidents her mother had suffered at the hands of Mr Bailey. Mother and daughter had discussed the incidents, but Saffron said that, those incidents aside, she believed that her mother and Mr Bailey enjoyed a good relationship.

Saffron became distraught when she was asked to outline the events surrounding the first arrest of Mr Bailey on 10 February 1997, when her mother had also been detained. She said their entire family was left devastated. Since the arrest, she said, her mother had not enjoyed a decent night of sleep and had been 'overwhelmed'. She started to weep as she outlined the level of ostracisation the family had suffered within the west Cork community as a result of the arrest. She said that Mr Bailey had also changed since he had been living under never-ending pressure as a result of garda actions since 1997. Saffron confirmed that she, along with her sisters, had been questioned a number of times by gardaí in connection with the case. Two officers, she said, had given her 'the creeps' when they visited the family's Liscaha home, and she claimed they had been fawning all over her teenage sister, Virginia.

Saffron said the two officers had insisted to her they believed Mr Bailey had committed the murder of the French woman and warned her that her mother was now in danger. She said that the evidence offered by her and her sisters was never taken seriously by gardaí – and that the three sisters were treated as stupid by detectives. She claimed that detectives would later adopt a more intimidating approach to the sisters in their further dealings with them.

Saffron said that, by 2003, in the aftermath of the Circuit Court libel action, the treatment of her family had been 'absolutely outrageous', with unceasing attention from the media on them and their family home.

Former British Army soldier Martin Graham made for a remarkable witness. He had not featured in the 2003 libel hearing but was now a key element of Mr Bailey's case. Since his discharge from the British Army

20 years before, Mr Graham had been based in west Cork. He lived a bohemian lifestyle, often fuelled by drug and alcohol use. He claimed he was approached by a garda in 1997 and offered both cannabis and cash if he would assist police in securing incriminating statements against Mr Bailey, with whom he had been on casual terms.

The former soldier first met Mr Bailey in an artist's home in Skibbereen, where the journalist had gone to stay in the wake of his release following his February 1997 arrest. Mr Graham said that Mr Bailey was very distraught and emotional at the time and he felt very sorry for him. Within days, the occupants of the house, including himself, were contacted by gardaí and queried about anything Mr Bailey may have said during his time in the house.

'I was constantly being pressed by the police to suggest there was a link between Ian Bailey and Sophie Toscan du Plantier, but I didn't know of any, just what they told me. I just thought it was crazy,' he said. Mr Graham said a garda suggested to him that he 'befriend' Mr Bailey and do what he could to 'loosen his tongue'.

Mr Graham – who warned that he was worried about being perceived to be a 'rat' or informer – claimed that, to assist in this process, a garda offered to supply him with cash, new clothing and drugs, the latter comprising 'seven ounces of high quality Lebanese flat press'.

One of the meetings between Mr Graham and two detectives working on the du Plantier murder case took place, somewhat bizarrely, at a west Cork Marian shrine. Later, he said, he received the cannabis in a garda evidence bag and was asked to attend a Kilcrohane music festival where, it was believed, Mr Bailey would be among those in attendance.

'It was ridiculous,' Mr Graham said, commenting that he came to believe that gardaí were 'stupid' if they had believed giving him cash for drink and drugs would help solve the case. Mr Graham, who had joined the British Army aged just 16, acknowledged during cross-examination that he had once lived in a campsite within a west Cork stone circle and had obtained casual work from a local ladies' commune, one of the many 'alternative' communities that had been established in west Cork and that had contributed so much to the bohemian reputation of the area. He also agreed that since leaving the army, he had experienced great difficulty in settling into civilian life.

Even though Mr Graham was a fascinating witness, the High Court hearing – just like the Cork Circuit Court libel action before it – suddenly began to revolve around Marie Farrell. The former west Cork shopkeeper, who had since relocated to her native Longford, was a core strategic element of Mr Bailey's case.

Her claims about making statements to the 2003 libel hearing under garda duress had been hugely damaging to An Garda Síochána. The High Court action would now hear precisely what she had seen on 23 December 1996 at Kealfadda Bridge – and why she had given evidence at Cork Circuit Court that she had later recanted.

Mrs Farrell was called to offer evidence in December, just two weeks before the High Court suspended its hearings for the Christmas break. Her evidence was nothing short of extraordinary. She claimed a garda had exposed himself to her, that another garda had stripped naked in front of her and asked for sex, that gardaí had put her under unrelenting pressure to support an incriminating statement that undermined Mr Bailey's key alibi – and had threatened her with arrest if she did not comply.

Her time in the witness box proved sensational. Central to Mrs Farrell's evidence was her statement that she had seen seeing someone walking on the road at Kealfadda Bridge outside Schull in the early hours of 23 December 1996. Mrs Farrell had been driving home that night after having met with an unnamed man earlier in the evening.

State counsel Paul O'Higgins demanded to know the identity of the person Mrs Farrell had been with. He argued that this individual could potentially shed vital light on the matters at hand. But Mrs Farrell bluntly refused to publicly name the person. She said that the man was not her husband and she wanted him to remain anonymous.

Mr Justice Hedigan intervened and directed that the witness should answer the question put to her by counsel. The judge said the case ranked as one of the most serious to come before the High Court and there was an obligation on all witnesses to tell the whole truth and nothing but the truth in the witness box. 'Now answer the question,' he directed her.

Mrs Farrell refused – and promptly walked out of the witness box. 'I am not going to tell you that. I am going. I am having nothing more to do with this,' she said.

There was consternation in court as legal teams, journalists, other witnesses and members of the public alike struggled to take in what had just happened. Journalists rushed to file stories on the development while legal teams consulted over what would happen next.

A short time later, a contrite Mrs Farrell was back in the witness box. Mr Justice Hedigan resumed proceedings with a stern warning to her that no further walk-outs would be tolerated by the court. Mr O'Higgins again pressed her to tell the jury who she was with that night.

Mrs Farrell then offered to write the name of the individual on a piece of paper that could be shown to the judge and jury but would be kept from journalists and those in the public gallery. When asked by Mr O'Higgins what all the secrecy was about, she replied, 'I didn't want to make things difficult at home.' Mrs Farrell insisted that no one knew of the identity of the person beyond that individual himself.

The defence team vehemently objected to the witness being allowed to write the name on a piece of paper – effectively adopting a special position while in the witness box. Mr O'Higgins pointed out it was a public trial and other witnesses would have to give difficult evidence in public. Mr Justice Hedigan agreed and told Mrs Farrell to give the name in public as the court would not sanction such 'secret' evidence. The judge said the jury represented the citizens of Ireland and, as such, needed to be publicly told the truth.

Mrs Farrell then identified the individual as John Reilly. It emerged that Mr Reilly was from Longford but had been deceased for almost

14 years. Mr O'Higgins challenged the evidence and pointed out to Mrs Farrell that she had previously given a garda the name of another individual, a Longford musician called Oliver Croghan. She rejected this and claimed the garda had come up with the other name himself. It was also put to her in cross-examination that she had offered gardaí fragments of information which had led them to suspect another individual until their investigations had found it could not have been him.

'So you stormed out of court because you might have to name the 14-years-or-more deceased man who was not very important to you?' Mr O'Higgins challenged her.

Mrs Farrell was adamant the individual was John Reilly, whom she had known growing up. She said she could not remember his exact address but knew he had passed away a number of years ago. 'I stormed out of court because I am here voluntarily. But it feels to me like this is turning into a personal assault on my private life. I am finding this very, very difficult. I am telling the truth. I am gaining nothing by being here – only more personal aggravation, so I am not telling lies,' Mrs Farrell argued.

Mrs Farrell insisted that Mr Reilly was not an invention, but she refused to divulge any more information about him. 'If I knew any more, I would tell you. I don't want to be here any longer than I have to.' When pressed by Mr O'Higgins about who she told gardaí she was with that December evening, she said she had lied in 2002 when she said the man was named Oliver Croghan.

Mrs Farrell also denied that she had revelled in the publicity surrounding her after the 2003 libel trial. She acknowledged she had posed for a photograph for a newspaper with her children as she believed it would keep the gardaí happy. She also insisted she was paid €150 for one particular media interview, not €1,500 as suggested in court.

However, the shopkeeper then found herself being given a formal warning about perjury from Mr Justice Hedigan. In one of her first statements to gardaí in 1997, Mrs Farrell alleged that Mr Bailey had threatened her after meeting her in her Schull shop and that the journalist had told her he was aware of her previous address in London. Mrs Farrell also intimated that Mr Bailey said he was aware of difficulties she had experienced with the UK's Department of Social Services (DSS). In evidence to the High Court, she insisted that this statement was not true. She insisted that the allegations of the threat from Mr Bailey were fabricated at the behest of a garda. Mrs Farrell insisted she had never been in trouble with the DSS in the UK and that, although she had been investigated after a complaint was made against her, she had been fully exonerated after the allegation was found to be without foundation.

Mr O'Higgins put it to Mrs Farrell that she had just told a 'barefaced lie' to the judge and jury. The defence counsel then requested that a video recording of a statement Mrs Farrell previously made to GSOC be played for Mr Justice Hedigan and the jury. The recording was of an interview in which Mrs Farrell told GSOC officials she had had to leave London and return to Ireland because she owed €32,000 (£27,000) to the DSS after claiming both income support and rent support when resident in the UK, despite not being entitled to do so.

A visibly flustered Mrs Farrell explained that she had been confused. She insisted that her evidence to the High Court was the truth and that she had been confused between fact and fiction in the GSOC interview. The shopkeeper said she could offer no explanation for how she had got so mixed up. However, she was adamant that what she had told the High Court was the truth – and she said that State solicitors could check with the UK authorities, if they wished, to verify her story.

Mr O'Higgins said it was apparent that Mrs Farrell was prepared to say virtually anything if it suited her purpose at that point in time. He argued that the two absolutely contradictory statements about her dealings with the DSS were evidence that the jury had been told a barefaced lie. Mr Justice Hedigan interjected to warn Mrs Farrell about perjury and the penalties for not telling the truth under oath. When Mrs Farrell apologised and attempted to explain herself, the judge advised her to think about matters overnight and give careful consideration to the evidence she would offer the following day.

Mrs Farrell's evidence continued to be nothing short of astonishing. She would also claim that, while she was looking after a holiday home in west Cork, Detective Garda Jim Fitzgerald had stripped naked and suggested having sex. When asked what she had told him, Mrs Farrell replied, 'I told him to get the fuck out.' Mr O'Higgins put it to her that such claims were absolutely 'incredible'. The allegation was vehemently denied by the detective, who would claim it had been fabricated by Mrs Farrell because she wrongly blamed him for an incident between her son and a Garda Traffic Corps unit.

Mrs Farrell's retort was that 'everything that happened down there [in west Cork] was wholly incredible.' Although pressed repeatedly over the incredible story she was relating, the shopkeeper insisted, 'I am not a liar.'

***

The evidence offered by three key legal officials may have been less sensational than Mrs Farrell's headline-grabbing testimony, but it was no less important to the High Court hearing. The three officials were former Director of Public Prosecutions Eamonn Barnes; a senior legal officer in the DPP's office, Robert Sheehan; and State solicitor for west Cork Malachy Boohig.

Mr Boohig was the first of the trio to offer evidence. His testimony focused on how unhappy gardaí were with the decision by the DPP in early 1997 not to formally charge Mr Bailey. The west Cork solicitor told the hearing he had been driving home when he received a phone call from Chief Superintendent Dermot Dwyer, who asked him to attend a meeting in Bandon Garda Station at his convenience.

The solicitor said that he met Dwyer and Detective Superintendent Seán Camon, who had since passed away. 'It was clear that gardaí were unhappy that the director had opted not to charge Mr Bailey at that point,' he explained. Mr Boohig said the garda view was that a charge was appropriate. He also said that they suggested that this message could be brought to the DPP's attention.

Mr Boohig said that after the meeting he was followed outside by Camon: 'Superintendent Camon said to me he understood I had been to college with the then Minister for Justice John O'Donoghue. [He asked] would I contact the minister and ask him to approach the director to get him to proffer a charge? I told him absolutely no way was I going to do that – it was completely inappropriate.'

The west Cork State solicitor was so concerned that he brought the conversation to the attention of both Mr Barnes and Mr Sheehan the following day. When he met Mr Barnes some weeks later in Dublin, he said he did not believe there was any discussion of the Bandon meeting and what Camon had said to him.

Mr Sheehan, the legal officer who had conducted a scathing assessment of the garda file in the du Plantier case, confirmed to the High Court that he had had most of the DPP's office's direct contact with gardaí. His evidence would be strictly limited, given a number of legal rulings prior to the High Court case opening in respect of concerns that elements of the assessment he had completed on the garda case file could potentially prove prejudicial.

He was adamant in evidence that, having carefully studied the large garda case file over a number of years, he believed it did not contain the vital ingredients necessary to warrant a murder charge. 'Or any charge,' he pointed out.

Mr Sheehan said he considered the evidence of Schull shopkeeper Marie Farrell to be 'absolutely unreliable' – an assessment he had made years before the drama of the 2003 libel trial and the sensation over Mrs Farrell's statement in 2005 that she had made false statements under duress from gardaí.

The legal officer said he came to this conclusion following a detailed study of the various statements made by Mrs Farrell to gardaí. Initially, she had described spotting 'a man of average height and thin build' at Kealfadda Bridge in the early hours of 23 December 1996.

'Lo and behold, when gardaí wanted Mr Bailey as a suspect, she changed her statement to a very big man, so big was Mr Bailey. Not only was it unreliable – on reflection, it was perverse,' Mr Sheehan said. Counsel for the State immediately objected to the choice of language used by Mr Sheehan in the context of the matters being dealt with.

He acknowledged in evidence that gardaí were 'very anxious' to have charges brought against Mr Bailey. Mr Sheehan said that gardaí made it clear that they were very concerned that if Mr Bailey was not charged, there could be another killing. He said the garda 'certainty' over this was quite striking.

Mr Barnes's evidence was remarkable in that it revealed, for the first time, precisely how concerned some legal officers were about the 2010–2012 extradition process triggered by the French. The former DPP said that, in 2011, he had been on a holiday in Spain reading an Irish newspaper online when he noticed an article about the extradition of Mr Bailey. He realised it was based on information the French investigation team, led by Magistrate Patrick Gachon, had obtained from the gardaí.

'I felt that perhaps not the whole story of the Bailey case was being made known to the French authorities. It was important that it should be,' he said. Mr Barnes said the decision was made in Ireland not to charge Mr Bailey in connection with the du Plantier investigation because there was, in his opinion, no *prima facie* case against him.

On his return from his holiday, he made contact with his successor, James Hamilton. He told the High Court that he 'explained my anxiety' about the matter and said he had given the issue 'a lot of anxious thought while on holidays'.

At the suggestion of Mr Hamilton, Mr Barnes put his concerns in writing and sent an email to the DPP's office. This outlined the garda meeting that Mr Boohig had with officers in Bandon in 1997 and the request to contact the Minister for Justice.

Mr Barnes noted that there was a 'strong and persistent advocacy' by gardaí for Mr Bailey to be charged. However, he confirmed that he took exception to the suggestion that contact be made with the minister to support this advocacy. Mr Barnes said this 'extra step' was something any DPP would object to.

Gardaí are no strangers to courtrooms or offering evidence. However, this is usually done in the context of a prosecution, rather than a High Court civil action defending themselves against claims of wrongful arrest. The key garda witnesses for the State defence of the action were retired Detective Garda Jim Fitzgerald, Detective Sergeant Maurice Walsh, retired Garda Kevin Kelleher and retired Detective Garda Jim Slattery.

Fitzgerald, Walsh, Kelleher and Slattery were specifically named in some of the counts lodged by the plaintiff for consideration by the jury. All had fervently denied any conspiracy against Mr Bailey. Critical evidence was also offered by retired Chief Superintendent Dermot Dwyer, who had supervised key elements of the du Plantier investigation in its early years.

Chief Superintendent Dwyer's evidence directly contradicted key testimony made to the High Court hearing, particularly from Mr Bailey. He also flatly rejected suggestions that Mr Boohig had been asked by a garda to contact the Minister for Justice about the du Plantier case – and said that although a meeting with Mr Boohig may have taken place at Bandon Garda Station in March 1998, its purpose was to address concerns gardaí had over correspondence from the DPP's office. He was adamant that no garda had asked for the minister to be contacted over a potential DPP charge.

He insisted that gardaí believed they had worked hard since December 1996 to develop a strong case file. In light of this strong belief, gardaí considered some of the subsequent correspondence received from the DPP's office to be 'worrying'. However, he denied that any garda had ever attempted to exert undue pressure to bring about a charge. Chief Superintendent Dwyer also stressed that he did not even know that the west Cork solicitor had been at school with the Minister for Justice. He added that, even if had known that fact, he would never have supported any such contact. He insisted that he had never, over the course of his police career, asked a politician to do anything for gardaí in respect of an ongoing case.

The retired superintendent also rejected suggestions that gardaí had at any stage engaged in 'coaching' Marie Farrell before the 2003 libel action, as well as claims that Mrs Farrell was told that if she did not agree to offer evidence at Cork Circuit Court she would be brought there in handcuffs. He denied that the shopkeeper was told to stick to her garda statements when giving evidence.

Dwyer argued it was 'very wrong and unfair' to suggest that the gardaí were determined to have Mr Bailey charged at all costs. 'Our job is to investigate a murder and everything we do comes up in court, so what you are saying is not right,' he said.

He described the killing of Sophie Toscan du Plantier as an 'outrageous murder' that had deeply upset the west Cork community. 'It was shocking to see the woman left the way that she was. It creates panic in an area because people do not want a murderer in their area. So we were concerned – of course we were.' He insisted that the gardaí, like any good police force, try to follow leads and evidence and deliver a result. 'We all need results, we are a police service,' he said.

In evidence, retired Detective Jim Fitzgerald vehemently denied the claims levelled against him by both Mr Bailey and Mrs Farrell. He denied that there was ever any type of close relationship between Mrs Farrell and himself. He said he was 'familiar' with the Schull shopkeeper only through dealings with her in the du Plantier investigation.

Mr Creed, senior counsel for Mr Bailey, had queried the nature of the contact between the detective and Mrs Farrell in a recorded telephone call from 9 October 1997, which was played to the jury. In one part of the tape recording – after a redacted section – Mrs Farrell commented that the detective was a 'pervert'. At that point, the detective is heard to reply, 'I fucking am not – if I am, I am talking to another one.'

Additionally, Detective Fitzgerald denied ever advising Mrs Farrell to have her statement about Kealfadda Bridge 'tidied up' because of the apparent disparity in the description between the man she said she spotted and Mr Bailey's actual physical characteristics. He proceeded to deny that he had ever suggested Mrs Farrell lodge a written complaint with Mr Bailey's solicitor over his alleged threatening behaviour towards her. He also deemed false the suggestion that he had advised Mrs Farrell to use the name of a dead man if ever pressed about whom she had been with on the evening of 22 December 1996.

He was also vehement in his objection to Mrs Farrell's claim that he had stripped naked in front of her in a west Cork holiday home. He said this was a 'completely false allegation', which, he believed, stemmed from a traffic matter involving her son.

The detective said Mrs Farrell apparently blamed him for an incident between her son and a Garda Traffic Corps unit. She believed he had asked for her son to be targeted. He claimed that she had called him and threatened that she would think of an allegation to make against him. The detective said he had been so concerned by the disturbing nature of the call from Mrs Farrell that he formally reported it to the garda authorities in May 2010.

It was then the turn of Detective Sergeant Maurice Walsh to take the stand. He forcefully denied an allegation by Mrs Farrell that he had exposed himself to her in the toilets of Schull Golf Club. She claimed he had told her something along the lines of the fact that stitching up Mr Bailey was a 'turn on'. The detective said the claim was 'the height of fantasy'. He added that the allegations levelled against him by Mrs Farrell were 'revolting' and 'deeply upsetting' both to him and to his family. 'It is an outrageous lie. It is total and utter lies,' he insisted.

The detective said the casual manner in which the shopkeeper had levelled such a damaging allegation was 'horrible'. When Tom Creed challenged him over why Mrs Farrell would put up such a scenario just to 'shaft' him, the detective said he was baffled. 'I have no understanding of how that woman's mind works,' he responded.

His testimony was supported by later statements from two women – Linda Horgan and Bernie O'Shea – who challenged Mrs Farrell's claims that one of her tasks at Schull Golf Club was to regularly check on the condition of the toilets. Both also made statements that Mrs Farrell had never, as she had claimed, told them about the exposure incident.

Detective Sergeant Walsh acknowledged that he had met Mrs Farrell in Dublin for a drink after she had contacted him and told him she was in the capital and knew no one. He was based in Dublin at the time. The detective said they met for a drink at The Hole in the Wall pub – a meeting he said he now viewed as a 'misjudgement' on his part. The detective said he returned Mrs Farrell to the city centre hotel she was staying at but did not accompany her inside.

He strongly denied any suggestion of a conspiracy between gardaí in west Cork over Mr Bailey. Walsh said he had taken a number of statements from Mrs Farrell in both 1997 and 1998. He said those statements were dictated and there was absolutely no indication whatsoever that they were prepared.

Garda Kevin Kelleher was challenged in cross-examination that he had been put under pressure 'to get' Mr Bailey. He said that he had regarded Mr Bailey as a suspect in the probe and could not recall having anyone else under suspicion.

Garda Kelleher denied Mrs Farrell's allegation that he had only invited her to come to his home on 28 January 1997 so he could get her to identify Mr Bailey as the man she had spotted at Kealfadda Bridge from a video that had been taken of a Christmas Day swim in Schull in 1996. Mr Bailey had attended the swim that day to read some poetry during the event.

Garda Kelleher said he had been told to confirm that Mrs Farrell was indeed the anonymous caller called 'Fíona' who had rung a helpline with the information about the sighting at Kealfadda Bridge. He said it was possible he had invited her to his house to view the Christmas Day swim video as a pretext for introducing her to detectives involved in the case who wanted to meet her. But there was no hidden motive in relation to Mr Bailey.

'I was doing my job to the best of my ability,' he insisted. Garda Kelleher noted that Mrs Farrell was 'very good at adding to incidents'. He also said she had a 'very good knack of landing gardaí in trouble after 2005' – a clear reference to how, two years after the Cork libel case, Mrs Farrell had suddenly made a serious of astonishing claims about local gardaí.

In his evidence, Detective Garda Jim Slattery disagreed with suggestions that inducements were offered to Mrs Farrell for testimony she might offer about Mr Bailey. The detective said he had absolutely no recollection of her ever being told a summons against her husband would be taken care of if she identified Mr Bailey as the person she had seen at Kealfadda Bridge. He also denied that a memo of a meeting with Mrs Farrell on 28 January 1997 was 'an invention' that had been compiled by two detectives over a week later. In response to Mrs Farrell's assertion that she had been asked to sign pages and given the assurance that gardaí would 'work it out later', he responded, 'That never happened. No such discussion took place.'

He confirmed the memo was written up by Detective Garda Fitzgerald on 7 February 1997 – Mrs Farrell had not wanted notes taken during the 28 January meeting. But, he said, the memo was an accurate note based on the fresh recollections of the two detectives about the meeting.

Tom Creed, for Mr Bailey, put it to the detective in cross-examination that it was an extraordinary document. The counsel noted that the memo was written in the first person. The detective said it was unusual for an individual to not want to engage in the normal, voluntary question-and-answer format. He disagreed that elements of the statement amounted to 'garda-speak', such as one phrase that read, 'I now know him to be Ian Bailey.'

Detective Garda Slattery pointed out that the memo was not signed by Mrs Farrell and that no one had ever suggested it was what she had said word for word. But he insisted it was an accurate overall reflection of what she had said to them.

Further garda evidence came from a member of one of the Garda Síochána review teams that had examined the du Plantier investigation. Detective Inspector Kevin Gately reviewed the file in 2002. The review team came to the conclusion that Mrs Farrell was not a reliable or credible witness. Gately confirmed he had met with Mrs Farrell a total of five times, and it had been put to her by the team that she had changed her story more than once. On one occasion, he said, Mrs Farrell had walked out of a meeting with the review team when she was challenged over making a false report about the identity of the man she was with on the evening of 22 December 1996.

He also noted that Mrs Farrell had given gardaí conflicting accounts of her movements over the critical period of the evening of the 22nd and the morning of 23 December. Detective Inspector Gately acknowledged that Mrs Farrell's overall account was weakened by her inability to offer corroboration of what she had seen at Kealfadda Bridge that night and the various different names she had given to the individual she was with that evening.

A number of ancillary witnesses were then heard before the State made its dramatic move: in a legal application to Mr Justice Hedigan, the defence argued that the case at hearing was in part or in whole statute-barred. In essence, the time limit for Mr Bailey to take such a case had expired. The State also argued that no case was made for various aspects of the plaintiff's case, including the wrongful arrest element, and it would be perverse to allow these to proceed, irrespective of the statute argument. The State was making a two-fold argument to the High Court – first, that Mr Bailey had exceeded the legal time limit allowed for him to take his action and, second, that he had failed to offer sufficient evidence as to his core argument, namely that he had been wrongly arrested.

The State now wanted the entire case to be withdrawn from the jury – after almost five months and 60 days of hearing.

Not surprisingly, there was uproar in the court. The plaintiff's legal team forcefully objected. Mr Justice Hedigan queried why such an application on statute grounds had not been made earlier. This could have been done at the preliminary hearing stage or even in the opening phase of the trial. It could even have been lodged at the conclusion of the plaintiff's case on the thirty-seventh day of the trial.

Mr Bailey's legal team, in opposing the application, argued that such an application should have been lodged at an earlier stage. They argued that for such an application to be lodged at that late stage, after enormous cost and effort had been expended by both sides throughout a 60-day hearing process, effectively amounted to abuse of process. The plaintiff's team argued that the issues at hand involved matters of enormous public interest and should be put to the jury to allow them to determine a verdict.

However, the State countered that it was open to lodge such a statute-barred application at any stage in the hearing – there was no time constraint involved. Critically, the State also pointed out that the gardaí who were the target of the allegations involved in the case – some of whom had faced allegations even before the case had been heard – were fully entitled to be afforded an opportunity to publicly deny those allegations and present detailed counter-evidence.

This was a reference to the fact that there had been numerous newspaper reports about the nature of the allegations being made about west Cork gardaí between 2005 and 2014, some of which were very serious and deeply upsetting to the officers involved.

The State also argued that it had been necessary to await all the evidence because certain elements of the claim lodged by Mr Bailey had not been sufficiently detailed for a full assessment before all the evidence was presented.

Mr Justice Hedigan, having heard all the State and plaintiff arguments, adjourned the matter to consider the legal position involved. On day 62 of the High Court hearing, he delivered his ruling – and it was a shattering blow to Mr Bailey.

The judge said it was clear on review that many of the claims lodged by Mr Bailey were, in fact, statute-barred. He noted that the case was triggered in May 2007 – more than a decade since Mr Bailey's first arrest by gardaí. Mr Justice Hedigan said that, on the application of the six-year rule, the plaintiff's claim could not involve any issues that occurred before 1 May 2001 – six years before the date he lodged his claim.

The court noted that both of Mr Bailey's arrests – in February 1997 and January 1998 – fell outside that six-year period. Also outside the six-year period between 2001 and 2007 was the meeting at Bandon Garda Station between west Cork State solicitor Malachy Boohig and a number of senior garda officers.

Having heard the evidence, Mr Justice Hedigan ruled that, in his opinion, no case for wrongful arrest had been made. The judge noted that there were, in fact, several grounds for both arrests, totally separate from any issues in relation to the statements made by Mrs Farrell. Mr Justice Hedigan said that to consider either of these as wrongful arrests would be 'perverse'.

He ruled that general criticism of the conduct of the garda investigation in respect of the du Plantier case was not a matter for the court or the jury. He accepted a submission by State counsel that the courts did not have any supervisory jurisdiction on the activities of gardaí in general. The judge also ruled out any issue in respect of Mr Bailey's complaint about the extradition proceedings. He pointed out that the EAW had originated in France and the State could not conceivably be held responsible for that. No evidence had been offered that Ireland had breached or manipulated the processing of obligations under agreed European mutual judicial agreements.

In addition, Mr Justice Hedigan ruled out any issue facing the State over the libel actions taken in 2003 by Mr Bailey and their outcome. No cause of action had been made. This referred to allegations that the State and gardaí had provided assistance to the newspapers in defending the libel actions.

However, the State did lose on two of its applications – namely, that no case of conspiracy had been made and therefore should not be put to the jury. Mr Justice Hedigan disagreed. He noted that the central claim by Mr Bailey was that certain gardaí had worked to get Mrs Farrell to make statements that would incriminate the journalist. These statements, it was claimed, had been made by inducements and intimidation and were aimed at implicating Mr Bailey in the murder investigation.

The judge said such claims were very serious and, if true, represented an 'action that affronts all norms of law and an attack on the rule of law. It would be, if true, an attempt to pervert the course of justice and remains a live attempt, if true.'

Mr Justice Hedigan ultimately rejected the State application for the conspiracy charges not to be put to the jury. He said that the statements taken by various gardaí from Mrs Farrell were 'lying heavily' upon the reputation of Mr Bailey. He said the conspiracy counts should therefore be put to the jury.

In his closing argument, Mr Creed said Mr Bailey's case was about demonstrating to the world that he had absolutely nothing to do with the appalling death of Mrs du Plantier. He argued that his client was the victim of an ongoing conspiracy and that the High Court action effectively amounted to a 'David and Goliath [battle] ... with the forces of law and order'. Mr Creed said there was a very simple reason Mr Bailey had taken the action. 'That is why we are here, this is him saying to the world, "Will someone please say, 'Stop, what you are doing is wrong.'"'

For the State, Mr O'Higgins pointed out that it was clear from the various recordings that had been played to the hearing that in various garda interviews, Mrs Farrell was the one in control. He said the shopkeeper had threatened to withdraw statements, but not once in any of the recordings was there any indication that she had been induced to make the statements or been put under duress by gardaí.

Mr O'Higgins opted for a comedic reference in his assessment of the recordings, which were, as he put it, 'not of the choirboy tenor'. In a reference to the cult Channel 4 show *Father Ted*, he warned that 'if every detective was Father Dougal, you might not solve many crimes, but one might prefer a little less of the language of Father Jack in the tapes'.

***

The jury was ultimately given two questions to answer by Mr Justice Hedigan and both related to conspiracy involving gardaí, Mr Bailey and Mrs Farrell.

The first question was, 'Did Gardaí Jim Fitzgerald, Kevin Kelleher and Jim Slattery, or any combination of them, conspire together to implicate Mr Bailey in the murder of Sophie Toscan du Plantier by obtaining statements from Marie Farrell, by threats, inducements or intimidation, which purportedly identified him as the man she saw at Kealfadda Bridge in the early hours of 23 December 1996, when they knew they were false?'

The second question was, 'Did Detective Garda Jim Fitzgerald and Detective Sergeant Maurice Walsh conspire by threats, inducements or intimidation to get statements from Marie Farrell that Ian Bailey had intimidated her, when they knew they were false?'

The jury was sent out by Mr Justice Hedigan to consider its verdict on Monday, 30 March 2015, after some 64 days of evidence. The 11 men and women were back with their verdict after just over two hours of deliberation. The case had once again confounded the pundits, who had expected the jury to be out considering a verdict for several days.

In answer to both questions put to them, the jury unanimously rejected that the gardaí had engaged in any form of conspiracy against Mr Bailey. There was a brief stunned silence in the courtroom before every eye turned to the journalist to gauge his reaction.

Looking calm and composed, Mr Bailey had his arm around his partner, who was once again in court supporting him. Immediately after the jury verdicts were confirmed, he leaned over to consult with his legal team before leaving the court.

To the surprise of no one, Mr Justice Hedigan also confirmed that he would be referring to the DPP a transcript of the evidence offered by Mrs Farrell to the High Court hearing to determine what action, if any, might be appropriate. However, few journalists present expected any subsequent action given all that had happened in the convoluted legal cases between 2003 and 2015.

After paying tribute to the jury for their diligence and commitment to the hearing, the judge addressed the du Plantier family. He said he felt it important to ensure that Sophie was not forgotten and that her family should know that: 'Throughout this case there has always been the shadow of the late Sophie Toscan du Plantier and her tragic and senseless death. It is a source of dismay and anguish in Ireland and France that her cruel killer has not been brought to justice. I do not want it thought that her life was forgotten here in this court.'

Judge Hedigan's comments served as a fitting reminder to everyone that the various legal actions over the previous years had taken place against the backdrop of an unsolved murder case and a heartbroken family in France still hoping and praying for justice in Ireland.

11

BUILD-UP TO PARIS TRIAL

The High Court verdict was a shattering defeat for Mr Bailey, although he seemed determined not to show any outward sign of it. For ten years, since 2005, it had appeared that every new development in the du Plantier case had been damaging to the gardaí and had appeared to bolster his case for wrongful arrest. Now he faced the aftermath of losing the longest-running civil action in High Court history in Ireland.

Mr Bailey left the High Court with Ms Thomas. He did not comment to the large gathering of reporters, photographers and TV crews outside. His solicitor, Frank Buttimer, issued a brief statement in which he acknowledged their great disappointment at the outcome.

'[Mr Bailey] is obviously very disappointed with the outcome. He gave this case his very best effort. He thought – and in fact still thinks – that he had sufficient evidence to sway the jury in his favour. However, he has a deep and abiding respect for the Irish legal system,' the Cork solicitor said. 'He appreciates the fact that the jury gave this case the attention that it did give the case. That is to be acknowledged. But the result is disappointing. We will have to consider the result, consider our options, and at this point in time I think it is appropriate, out of respect for the fact that the decision has just been handed down, that we should be allowed space and time to consider what might arise from here on in.'

Just two months after the jury verdict, on 12 May 2015, Mr Justice Hedigan addressed the issue of costs arising from the marathon five-month action. He ordered that Mr Bailey pay the full legal costs of the action. While no final financial total was offered at the High Court hearing, various legal experts estimated the overall cost of the action at anywhere between €2 million and €5 million.

Mr Justice Hedigan agreed to place a stay or a suspension on the costs order in the event of Mr Bailey appealing his High Court defeat to the Supreme Court. Few doubted that, similar to the Circuit Court libel action, an appeal would be forthcoming.

It was submitted to Mr Justice Hedigan that the Garda Commissioner and the State should foot at least 50 per cent of the overall cost of the High Court action. This was argued on the basis that the State had only applied to have matters statute-barred on the sixtieth day of the hearing. Had the application been made at an earlier stage, the costs involved would likely have been dramatically lower, as the action would have been substantially shortened.

Tom Creed, for Mr Bailey, said substantial court time and cost would have been saved had the State made the statute-barred application earlier than day 60. He said that around 23 days of the court hearing involved matters that had been ruled on by the jury. The costs involved should be based on this fact, he argued. Mr Creed said that, given the manner in which the State had timed their statute-barred application, they should be responsible for a significant portion of the hearing costs incurred as a result.

Mr Justice Hedigan said such an argument from Mr Bailey was essentially 'unreal'. He found that, given the serious and extremely grave nature of the conspiracy allegations being levelled by Mr Bailey, the State felt that it was vital and in the overall public interest to allow the detailed claims involved to be aired in an open court. The judge said that while it was unfortunate that the case ultimately took so long, he was satisfied that it had been in the public interest – as well as the garda need – to have each individual allegation dealt with in detail in open court.

He also noted that if the case had been stopped at a very early stage on the basis of a statute-barred application, there would likely 'have been an outcry', given the lengths Mr Bailey had gone to in order to have his allegations dealt with in open court.

The State, represented by Luán Ó Braonáin SC, opposed Mr Bailey's costs submission. He argued that the plaintiff or State was fully entitled to make the statute-barred application at any point in the proceedings.

Mr Ó Braonáin said it was manifestly in the public interest to have such serious allegations against the gardaí dealt with in open court – and that the individual garda members involved had a right to defend their good reputations in open court. He argued that such grave allegations as conspiracy, corruption and inappropriate sexual behaviour were so serious that they fully warranted being dealt with in an open court in the public interest. He also pointed out that Mr Bailey had been aware from a very early stage of the proceedings that the State had raised the issue of a statute-barred limitation in its defence submissions.

Mr Ó Braonáin said that, ultimately, the High Court had been asked to resolve the central planks of Mr Bailey's case, which were that gardaí had conspired against him in the du Plantier investigation and that gardaí had threatened or coerced Mrs Farrell into giving false evidence against the journalist.

Mr Justice Hedigan said it was a complex and detailed case that involved a huge amount of documentation and recordings, all of which were necessary if the central allegations were to be properly dealt with. He found that the nature of the allegations was so serious and had such far-reaching consequences for the rule of law that having them dealt with properly and in open court was very much in the public interest. The public, he ruled, 'deserved nothing less'.

Mr Justice Hedigan said he had been presented with no special reasons why the High Court should depart from the long-standing rule that the costs should follow the verdict. The State had won and therefore the costs should go against the plaintiff – Mr Bailey.

He ordered that Mr Bailey pay the full costs of the hearing. This included all discovery costs, hearing costs, the reserved costs, as well as 50 per cent of a holiday that had to be cancelled by one of the jury members. The State had earlier agreed to foot 50 per cent of the juror's lost holiday cost.

Within weeks of the High Court costs hearing, Mr Bailey confirmed that he would challenge the ruling to the Court of Appeal.

***

Almost two years later, on 27 March 2017, Mr Bailey's challenge opened before the Court of Appeal, where the case was heard by a three-judge panel comprising Ms Justice Mary Finlay Geoghegan, Mr Justice George Birmingham and Mr Justice Gerard Hogan. The challenge took two days to hear.

Mr Bailey's legal team had lodged 17 different grounds for appeal – the most important of which was the decision by the hearing judge, Mr Justice Hedigan, not to allow the majority of the issues to be put to the jury on day 62 of the trial on the basis of an eleventh-hour statute-barred submission from the State.

In a detailed hearing, the appeal judges acknowledged that the case raised important and difficult legal issues. On that basis, it was reserving judgment. Four months later, on 26 July, the Court of Appeal published its ruling.

It ruled against Mr Bailey on 16 of the 17 grounds of appeal he had tabled. However, crucially, the Court of Appeal did rule in his favour in one area. While initially described as a minor area of appeal, it quickly became apparent that this could pave the way for a fresh High Court case.

In respect of whether the alleged wrongful disclosure of information by gardaí prior to Mr Bailey's libel case against eight Irish and UK newspapers in December 2003 amounted to conspiracy, the Court of Appeal ruled that this matter should have gone to the High Court jury to decide. It was sufficient, legal commentators agreed, for Mr Bailey to now seek a new High Court hearing, albeit on much narrower grounds than before.

Mr Bailey's grounds for appeal had included submissions that Mr Justice Hedigan erred in allowing the State make a statute-barred application so late in the hearing process and that the judge had incorrectly restricted the evidence that could be offered by key witnesses, including Eamonn Barnes, James Hamilton and Robert Sheehan.

The State challenged those appeal grounds and, in reference to the perjury warning to Mrs Farrell, said it had to be considered against the entire backdrop of Mr Bailey's civil case against both gardaí and the State, as well as the actual circumstances of the hearing itself.

In dismissing the majority of Mr Bailey's 17 grounds of appeal, the three judges also dismissed a cross-appeal by the State. The judges ruled that such was the scale and overarching nature of the conspiracy alleged by Mr Bailey against gardaí, it was not unfair that the State be allowed to raise a motion for statute-barring aspects of the claim on days 60–62.

Mr Bailey's legal team immediately confirmed that they would be reviewing the implications of the Court of Appeals ruling in their favour on one ground of appeal. However, the State also indicated it was also considering the matter.

The State then asked the Court of Appeal to review its decision on the sole ground of the challenge upheld. This was on the basis that the State claimed an error had been made by the Court of Appeal in referring to an observation made by the High Court judge as a ruling.

Sensationally, on 14 March 2018, the Court of Appeal overturned its own ruling – meaning that Mr Bailey lost his sole ground for a new High Court case. This Court of Appeal reversal – which was highly unusual – meant that the journalist had now lost his entire appeal against his High Court defeat and no longer had any grounds on which to press for a new hearing.

Mr Bailey's legal team had opposed the reopening of the decision on the basis that this was only done in exceptional circumstances – and the challenge from the State did not amount to such. However, the Court of Appeal, in reversing its ruling, said that even if the trial judge had failed to deliver a ruling on the matter, it had not prejudiced the plaintiff in his action. Furthermore, the Court of Appeal said there was not sufficient evidence to support a claim that gardaí had disclosed the information complained of for it to revert to the jury for decision.

***

What wasn't fully appreciated at the time was that the Court of Appeal ruling meant that Mr Bailey's legal battles would now switch from Ireland to France. The French had been preparing for a Paris-based prosecution and, critically – from their point of view – this had avoided being damaged by the High Court action for wrongful arrest.

A French prosecution had slowly but steadily moved from a possibility to a certainty. Mr Bailey had appointed a French legal team and began to consider his avenues of challenge should a prosecution be formally sought.

In 2016, he had called on the Director of Public Prosecutions, Claire Loftus, to review matters. Ms Loftus was the third director to handle the du Plantier case, after Eamonn Barnes and James Hamilton. Appointed to the role in November 2011, she had previously served as Chief Prosecution Solicitor in the DPP's office. Mr Bailey had requested that Ms Loftus review the decisions by her two predecessors, based on all the evidence available, not to have him prosecuted. The move was interpreted as an attempt to underline the growing chasm between the Irish and French positions on the case – and to again underline Mr Bailey's innocence in the matter. Such a review would also effectively pre-empt any French decision on the Gachon investigation file. Having first ruled out a prosecution in 2001 due to lack of evidence, there was little doubt that the position of the DPP had not changed.

However, GSOC was yet to issue its report; a GSOC finding in favour of Mr Bailey over the manner in which the garda murder investigation was conducted could jeopardise a proposed French prosecution.

***

The second French extradition request was issued in August 2016, and the Irish courts had begun processing the application. Finally, in June 2017, the latest French extradition bid arrived before the High Court.

Sitting in Dublin, Mr Justice Tony Hunt ruled on 24 July 2017 that Mr Bailey should not be extradited to France to answer a charge of voluntary homicide over the death of Ms du Plantier. In a stark dismissal of the French application, he described the latest extradition request as an 'abuse of process'. Mr Justice Hunt said that the Supreme Court had already decided on the matter in 2012. He also noted the fact that the latest French application had ignored the detailed issues already dealt with as part of the 2012 extradition application and the Supreme Court ruling.

Mr Justice Hunt said that the High Court was bound by the ruling of the higher court – the Supreme Court. He described the Supreme Court ruling as 'conclusive and binding'. He also noted that the issues at hand had occurred some time ago. Ms du Plantier had died in December 1996, some 21 years earlier. The first French extradition application had been tabled in 2010 and was dealt with by the Supreme Court in 2012. He queried the five-year timeframe between that decision and the latest extradition application.

'Apparently neither the minister nor the requesting authorities considered it appropriate to furnish any information by way of explanation for the elapse of this period of time,' he stated. The judge said he did not consider the court to have been afforded any adequate explanation for the period of delay involved – in essence, querying why the French or Minister for Justice did not offer any specific reasons for the five-year delay in pursuing a second EAW after the Supreme Court in Ireland rejected the first EAW.

Mr Justice Hunt noted that there was a major garda investigation into the crime in Ireland and that a detailed file had been submitted to the director of prosecutions. Having considered the file, the DPP ruled that not only was there no basis for a trial but there was no basis for a charge.

He pointed out that the specific reasons for this had been aired during the 2012 Supreme Court hearing.

He said that the current application before the High Court did not materially change anything – and did not actually engage with the historic situation at all. In fact, he said, the new extradition request effectively ignored the fact that the domestic legal process had ruled out any question of a charge. Mr Justice Hunt said it was a 'highly unusual' state of affairs.

Mr Bailey, the subject of the extradition application, was entitled to the protection of Ireland's Constitution and the laws designed to protect individual rights. He noted that the application involved a very serious matter – a crime for which a sentence of 30 years could be handed down. Few were surprised by Mr Justice Hunt's ruling. His comments about abuse of process were, however, unexpected – and an undeniable blow to French hopes. Mr Bailey was present for the ruling and was visibly relieved at the outcome. He spoke briefly to reporters assembled outside the High Court. 'I am pleased with the judgment and grateful to the court. I do not believe that this is the end of the matter. But life goes on.'

Mr Bailey did comment on the fact that solicitors for the State, which had triggered the action on behalf of the French authorities, were not represented in court for the judgment. This was, he argued, 'quite astonishing.' He explained that his life had been rendered a 'living nightmare' and that he had endured a 'form of torture for twenty years, on and off' by being wrongly associated with the death of Ms du Plantier. Mr Bailey again stressed that he had tremendous sympathy for the family of the French woman but repeated his insistence that he had absolutely nothing to do with her death.

While the 2012 Supreme Court judgment on Mr Bailey's extradition garnered headlines for several days in Ireland, the coverage of the High Court ruling in 2017 effectively petered out after 24 hours. Few doubted but that there would be another extradition move by the French. But their third extradition attempt, legal experts indicated, would be after a Paris trial over the circumstances of Sophie's death. The second EAW was dismissed because it effectively did not vary sufficiently from the first EAW rejected by the Supreme Court in 2012. However, legal experts queried what might happen if a third EAW was issued – but this time on the basis of a conviction.

***

In the meantime, the journalist had other more personal considerations to deal with. An avid writer, his poetry had for years been a source of both comfort and strength for him. In the worst of times, his art had offered him solace and refuge from what he called the 'nightmare' of being wrongly pursued by both the Irish and French authorities. Since his arrival in Ireland, he had been writing 'songs without music', as he once described his poetry. His poems had featured in arts events across west Cork over the years, ranging from Christmas Day swims to festivals on Cape Clear Island.

Now, he had completed a special collection of poems, which was to be published under the title *The West Cork Way*. It was a collection he was immensely proud of, and he had been delighted when he was invited to launch the volume at the prestigious Electric Picnic festival in Stradbally on 3 September 2017. Known for its eclectic mix of music, visual and performance arts, Electric Picnic was famed as the biggest outdoor event of its kind in Ireland. It also served as a final farewell to summer, taking place at the sprawling Laois estate on the final weekend of August or the first weekend of September.

The invitation came to Mr Bailey via the music magazine *Hot Press*, which was involved in the programme of events for the festival. In early 2017, the journalist had agreed to a lengthy interview with the magazine about his legal plight and the threat he faced of possible extradition to France.

The West Cork Way was launched on Saturday afternoon during the second day of Electric Picnic. Mr Bailey read several of the poems and participated in a question-and-answer section with compère Olaf Tyaransen in the *Hot Press* tent.

The writings were largely work he had completed in his first five years in Ireland, just before he had been catapulted into the spotlight over the du Plantier murder. The *Irish Times* carried a preview story from Barry Roche about Mr Bailey's appearance at Electric Picnic and the type of poems that featured in his new collection. Later, there would be multiple social media postings of Mr Bailey reading his poems and being interviewed about his writings.

'It is a collection of thirty poems, ballads and odes. It is partly autobiographical and deals with my time in Ireland, specifically in west Cork,' Mr Bailey explained. 'Each of the poems has a footnote to explain how they came to be born. I chose the title because of the manner in which many people, like myself, have come to west Cork, effectively as "blow-ins" and made their lives here. Many are expat British subjects, like myself, and many eke out a living. They undertake a range of tasks and seasonal jobs to make a living.'

A large gathering attended the launch and Mr Bailey was clearly delighted with the interest shown in his work: 'There are a range of topics dealt with in *The West Cork Way*, ranging from love and life, struggle and strife, the growing of barley and the struggle between *préacháns* – crows – on a farm in Waterford where they hired me as a human scarecrow. There is material about the collapse of the herring-fishing industry.'

But the focus always seemed to revert back to the du Plantier investigation and French attempts to extradite him. Mr Bailey told the audience his first arrest by gardaí in February 1997 was horrific. 'It was shocking. It was surprising. It was aggressive. For twenty-odd years I have been associated with a murder I had nothing to do with. And I have been protesting and doing everything I can to clear my name. I'm still doing it. So long as I have life in me, I will continue to try and clear my name,' he said.

He confirmed that he was already working on a follow-up collection of poetry, provisionally entitled *The Peninsula Poems*, which would offer a journey along three of west Cork's most famous headlands: Mizen Head, Sheep's Head and Beara. Other arts projects he was working on included a one-man show and a short film about a west Cork jazz parade.

It was clear that his writing and arts projects offered relief from the pressures of the never-ending judicial battles he faced. *The West Cork Way* was proudly stocked at Mr Bailey's farmers' market stall and by a number of outlets across west Cork and Cork city. He was delighted when orders arrived from overseas supporters.

Although Electric Picnic was a personal triumph for Mr Bailey, legal defeats were again looming on the horizon. In February 2018, the Chambre de l'instruction – the French equivalent of the High Court – found that there was sufficient evidence to allow the proposed Paris prosecution to proceed. This was a major boost for French prosecutors – it signalled that the investigation by Magistrates Gachon and Dutartre was deemed to have met the required standards to warrant a trial hearing in Paris.

Mr Bailey, via his French solicitor, Dominique Tricaud, immediately indicated that he would challenge the Chambre de l'instruction ruling. Unlike in Ireland and the UK, that appeal would be dealt with in a matter of months – there would be no major delay. Sophie's family had said they were hopeful the long-awaited trial would take place in 2019, and that now appeared highly likely.

***

It was against this backdrop that the Amazon-owned media outlet Audible confirmed it would make available a special thirteen-part podcast called *West Cork*. The programme was modelled on the smash-hit *Serial* and represented the first major podcast of its type focusing on a crime that had occurred in Ireland.

Researched and produced by Brian Reed, Sam Bungey and Jennifer Forde, the series had been in preparation for two years. Critically, it involved the cooperation of Mr Bailey. He allowed the programme-makers unprecedented access to his life, which even included travelling with them in a taxi to one of his High Court hearings in Dublin in relation to the ongoing French extradition bid. From Audible's point of view, the release couldn't have been more perfectly timed – the podcast hit the Internet exactly one week after the Chambre de l'instruction ruling.

The series was remarkable in the access it had both to Mr Bailey and to his UK connections, ranging from former work colleagues to friends and neighbours. It also had major contributions from judicial officials connected with the two-decade-long investigation, including forensic officers who had worked on the original garda investigation. But the Audible series made headlines in Ireland largely because of a contribution from the former DPP James Hamilton about the ongoing French investigation and the view taken of it by some within Irish legal circles.

It had been a predecessor of Mr Hamilton, Eamonn Barnes, who had ruled out a charge being brought against Mr Bailey, having studied the garda case file and a special analysis conducted by Robert Sheehan, one of the DPP's own legal staff. Mr Barnes's assessment of the file – as would repeatedly be cited over the years – was its total lack of evidence in the murder case of Sophie Toscan du Plantier.

Mr Hamilton was nonplussed about the French decision not to accept the DPP case file ruling and to press ahead with their own domestic investigation. The former DPP didn't pull his punches in relation to how he viewed the treatment of Irish agencies and institutions by the French in the conduct of their subsequent investigation.

He argued that the French had essentially shown 'contempt' towards the Irish judicial system. He pointed out that Paris investigators, while operating in Ireland, had never made contact with the DPP's office either as a courtesy or for consultation.

'Not a phone call, not a letter – nothing. To be quite frank, I think it is extraordinary. That is a very mild word and I won't say any more than that. It shows a contempt for the office of the Director of Public

Prosecutions, in my view. It shows an arrogance and a contempt,' he stated in an interview for the podcast.

Mr Hamilton also rejected the idea – possibly a reference to gardaí who had strongly supported a charge – that Ireland should have proceeded with a prosecution over Ms du Plantier's death. He said that, under Irish law, prosecutions must be grounded in a careful assessment of the available evidence:

It is a very heavy thing to charge somebody with an offence. It is something you do not do lightly. Sometimes people say, 'Well, why don't you just run the case to the court and let the court decide?' We have always taken the view that that would be quite an irresponsible thing to do. To put a citizen through the ordeal of a trial merely so that public curiosity can be satisfied? Because that is what it would amount to.

Ireland, like the UK, operates an adversarial system, in which evidence is carefully weighed and tested. In France, a completely different legal system applies. This has its roots in the old Napoleonic Code, which allows greater leeway to judges over how matters relating to evidence and witness statements can be handled.

Sophie's family – including her son – said the French prosecution was 'very welcome' and urged everyone in Ireland to support it. ASSOPH bluntly said that Ireland must comply with its obligations under European judicial cooperation in the forthcoming Paris trial and its outcome. 'It is like the train – when the train is late. Then the train arrives so it is a matter of time,' Mr Baudey-Vignaud said. 'It is very good news – it is news that we have waited a very long time for.'

In May 2018, the French Supreme Court moved as quickly as had been expected in delivering a verdict on Mr Bailey's challenge to the proposed Paris trial. The court rejected the appeal for the trial to be halted and the ruling of the Chambre de l'instruction from three months earlier to be set aside. This appeal had been the final legal avenue in France open to Mr Bailey to prevent the trial taking place.

I was covering a teachers' conference in a Cork hotel when I received a phone call from a grave Ian Bailey. He confirmed he had just lost his final avenue of recourse in France. He admitted that to me that even the promise of a European Court of Human Rights challenge to the French prosecution would not now likely halt the planned Paris murder trial. He briefly dictated an agreed statement for the following day's *Irish Independent*. Other Cork-based journalists received similar calls.

I have been informed by my French lawyer, Dominique Trichaud, that I have failed in the French Supreme Court in my challenge to the decision to charge me with the murder of Sophie Toscan du Plantier 22 years ago. Mr Trichaud said he was very surprised at that decision.

I am less surprised, although clearly disappointed, that a prosecution repeatedly rejected by the Irish authorities could make muster in France. I am also angry that as part of the French investigation somebody in authority in Ireland made the decision to not inform me that I had the right to participate in the French investigation.

My French lawyers will in due course take my challenge to the false allegation that I am somehow unexplainedly connected with the murder of Sophie Toscan du Plantier to the European Court of Human Rights. Even if I am tried for murder in France and found guilty under their Napoleonic Code of law all they will have done is convict an innocent person and merely managed in France what the members of An Garda Síochána tried to and failed.

It was obvious that the French decision, although expected, was a disappointing knock to the journalist. Having fought one Circuit Court case and two High Court hearings over the previous 15 years, he now faced the prospect of a criminal trial in France and all the unknowns it might entail, not least in terms of the impact any Paris conviction might have on Ireland's stance on his extradition.

Mr Bailey's solicitor, Frank Buttimer, was scornful in his assessment of what was now likely to happen in Paris. 'It is appalling. It has destroyed his life. It is nothing more than a show trial,' he said.

In 22 years of speaking with Mr Bailey, I cannot recall a time when I felt he was under more strain. From the tone of his voice to the nature of the brief conversations we had, I felt he was under incredible stress. It seemed obvious to me that developments in France were now dominating his daily existence. Even after the 2001 domestic violence arrest and in the aftermath of the 2003 libel trial defeats, I didn't detect the tension that now seemed to be exerting a vice-like grip on him.

Nevertheless, he attempted to put on a brave face in the handful of interviews he gave before the Paris trial opened. In every interview, Mr Bailey was adamant that the French were going to find him guilty despite the fact that Ireland and Irish law considered him an innocent man. In one interview he said that the events in Paris represented a 'horrible and cataclysmic shift in the tectonic plates of my life'.

In an interview with *The Guardian* he said that the French were 'going to bonfire me … It feels like medieval torture. I didn't do it. I had nothing to do with it. In Paris, all they will do is convict an innocent man. But I have just got to stay calm. If I do go down, I'll go like Nelson at Trafalgar, with both barrels smoking. My number one priority is protecting my sanity. I am actually quite relaxed at the moment. I do the Lord's Prayer. I meditate. I find creative outlets.'

He said that he was content with his life in west Cork and only wanted to leave Ireland under one set of circumstances: 'Hopefully I will be leaving in a coffin, rather than on a plane in handcuffs.'

12

GSOC

In August 2018, just after Mr Bailey had lost his final avenue of challenge to his impending trial in France and and had flagged a challenge to the European Court of Human Rights, the findings of the GSOC investigation were published.

A GSOC finding in his favour would be a potent weapon to delay or even halt the impending French trial: Mr Bailey would be able to make a powerful argument that any French action against him was based on a flawed investigation in Ireland.

The GSOC complaint had been formally lodged in December 2011 but the probe had been stalled for a number of reasons, both legal and procedural. It was also unavoidably delayed by the Commission of Inquiry conducted by Mr Justice Nial Fennelly, which dealt with the recording of phone calls at Bandon Garda Station and other garda stations nationwide. That report wasn't completed and released until 31 March 2017, and GSOC wasn't ready to release its findings until 2 August 2018 – more than three years after the conclusion of Mr Bailey's marathon High Court claim and over six years after the review first commenced. Under Section 103 of the Garda Síochána Act 2005, the entire 36-page report was released to the media and was also published on the GSOC website, where it remains for public viewing.

GSOC's final report did not include the names of any gardaí against whom allegations were levelled or specific witnesses who had assisted the commission with its investigation:

In light of the fact that the decision of the Commission is that no conduct of a criminal or disciplinary nature has been revealed in this investigation it was decided it was not necessary to name the various parties. It should be noted that where members of the Garda Síochána have retired it is not possible to bring proceedings under the Garda Discipline Regulations and a number of the original gardaí involved in the investigation in 1996 onwards had retired by the time the complaint was made to GSOC in 2011 and 2012. Other members had died in the interim period.

GSOC noted that its investigation had been complicated by multiple different legal and ancillary factors, not least the Fennelly Commission:

The various and complicated court proceedings and related investigations, such as the Fennelly Commission have added to the investigative process for GSOC. The Commission was not anxious to complete the investigation in the event that matters relevant to its inquiries came into the public arena which could be further investigated by GSOC.

The Commission has also been informed that the garda investigation into the unlawful death of Ms du Plantier is still open as no one has been charged with her death in this jurisdiction. GSOC therefore is conscious that any information released should not jeopardise any future proceedings, if indeed same arises.

This appeared strange to many who had closely followed developments with the du Plantier case as any prospect of a prosecution in Ireland seemed critically undermined, from the Cork libel action through to the revelations of the High Court wrongful arrest case and the fact that the French police team under Magistrate Gachon had been given access to the full garda murder file. In light of all of this, it appeared to many that no prosecution could ever now be contemplated in Ireland. But it was a very different story in France.

The GSOC investigation examined three main strands of complaints in respect of the du Plantier investigation. The first two strands involved the various detailed complaints from Mr Bailey and Ms Thomas. The third strand involved complaints lodged by Marie Farrell. The complaints from Ms Thomas and Mrs Farrell were both lodged in 2012.

Mr Bailey alleged that some of the garda members involved in the du Plantier murder case had conducted a corrupt investigation that had focused on the Manchester-born journalist. It was also claimed that both Mr Bailey and Ms Thomas were the victims of an unlawful arrest in 1997.

Mrs Farrell claimed that she had signed five or more blank statements, which were then 'subsequently created to support the false narrative' by unnamed gardaí. It was further alleged that 'the case against Mr Bailey has been based on this false narrative and that the so-called "evidence" garnered by a large number of officers … was falsified, forged and fabricated with one overriding intention: to "frame Mr Bailey".'

Arguably the most damaging accusation was that the 'new information which has now come to light is indicative and evidence of a concerted, determined and persisting ongoing conspiracy, by ex- and serving garda members, to pervert the course of justice in this case'.

GSOC agreed an investigation strategy aimed at dealing with the key allegations from Mr Bailey, Ms Thomas and Mrs Farrell in tandem. This began with an extensive documentation request to An Garda Síochána. A lengthy review period was then provided to allow GSOC officials to meticulously study the files and reports received by the investigating gardaí in west Cork.

From there, GSOC investigators adopted a three-phase strategy in handling their review. This involved, first, re-interviewing all key witnesses in the original garda murder investigation whose evidence in any way involved Mr Bailey. Second, there would be a re-interviewing of all key witnesses involved in Assistant Commissioner Ray McAndrew's review, which had begun in late 2005. The McAndrew Report had never been made public and it would not be included in the published GSOC investigation summary. Third, and finally, all surviving gardaí who had held key positions in the original murder investigation between 1997 and 2001 would be re-interviewed.

GSOC officers first sought garda files in March 2012 and received the first of the documentation that November. The remainder of the documentation sought was provided in January 2013. There were setbacks for the GSOC officers, most notably in relation to one individual who was identified as a key witness in respect of some of Mr Bailey's allegations:

> Extensive efforts were undertaken by GSOC to trace the whereabouts of a person considered a key witness in this complaint investigation. This witness was eventually traced to a location in England and in February 2014, GSOC investigators attended a pre-arranged appointment with the witness at an agreed location with the intention of obtaining a witness statement from the witness. The witness failed to provide the statement as requested.

The GSOC investigators found no evidence of high-level corruption within the garda force in west Cork – a finding that dominated coverage of the report's publication. The GSOC findings also made headlines in France – and were hailed by the French as hugely significant for their ongoing probe.

While other elements of the GSOC report did not make for pleasant reading for either the government or the gardaí, its core finding had failed to provide Mr Bailey with the verification he sought. Crucially, the GSOC report would not serve as an impediment to the French bid to mount a Paris murder trial.

> GSOC reviewed large amounts of documentation and re-interviewed witnesses in respect of this allegation which was central to the GSOC investigation. There is no evidence to suggest that Ian Bailey was 'framed'

for the murder or that evidence was falsified, forged or fabricated by members of the Garda Síochána.

All relevant documentation was reviewed by GSOC and relevant witnesses were re-interviewed. Whilst concerns are raised by GSOC later in the body of this report in relation to the management of the garda investigation, there was no evidence of corruption in support of this allegation.

The GSOC report noted that, despite major forensic tests being conducted on the basis of Mrs Farrell's allegations about the blank documents she signed, her account could likewise not be supported by evidence:

The original statements made by Marie Farrell were seized by GSOC Designated Officers during this investigation and submitted for forensic analysis which included ESDA 2 testing and ink analysis [for dating and matching purposes]. Nothing was found of evidential value in this testing to support this assertion.

GSOC examined all relevant documentation and re-interviewed witnesses in respect of this allegation. In addition, original materials were seized by GSOC and submitted for forensic examination.

During the course of the GSOC investigation, the existence of recorded telephone calls into and out of garda stations in the Cork area became known and these were also secured and examined by GSOC. These recordings would not be supportive of any suggestion of intimidation towards Marie Farrell by any member of the Garda Síochána at that time.

Despite its overall finding that there was no evidence to support allegations of a garda conspiracy or officers acting to try to 'frame' Mr Bailey, elements of the GSOC report were hugely embarrassing for the west Cork force, especially in relation to the management of a major ongoing murder investigation with international dimensions.

GSOC raised what it called 'grave concerns' over changes to critical garda reports in the investigation into the killing of Sophie Toscan du Plantier. While never specified, it was clear these concerns were procedural and related to how key elements of the investigation administration were conducted. This followed a detailed analysis of the so-called 'job books'. These are reports on major investigations that gardaí maintain and update. These books are specially bound with pages individually numbered for verification and cataloguing reasons. But some of the west Cork job books' pages were mysteriously missing.

It was confirmed that the jobs book was only ever in the possession of gardaí. In one case it appeared that the pages had been deliberately removed. In another case, pages were missing from a report that dealt with a time period when gardaí first seemed to take an interest in Mr Bailey

It was also noted that while the name of Ian Bailey appeared in jobs book 1 at a relatively early stage of the investigation, the first formal nomination of him as a suspect was contained at job number 166, on page 9 in book 2. The next two pages had been seemingly ripped or cut out of the book, leaving a rough, torn stub. Other than the first few pages of the book, there appeared to be no other pages missing. The book continued at page 12.

GSOC also focused its concerns on what appeared to be deliberate changes to official garda documents, including station records, in relation to the murder investigation. The revelation that entire pages were missing from specific vital documents was a focus of significant media attention on the GSOC report.

'It would not be possible for pages to simply fall out of the book by accident or for them to be removed – this would have to have been a deliberate act,' the report noted.

On 13 June 2013, following a request by GSOC to have sight of the original suspect files in the Garda Síochána murder investigation, it was reported by a chief superintendent to a GSOC (designated) officer that five of the suspect files requested were in fact missing. The missing suspect files included [those for] Ian Bailey and Jules Thomas as well as three other files on suspects.It was further reported that the missing suspect files could not be located for the McNally Review group led by Chief Superintendent McNally in 2002.

In other words, key files in respect of the du Plantier investigation had vanished just over five years after Sophie's killing. But the GSOC findings grew even more embarrassing for west Cork gardaí: the report also highlighted what it termed a lack of administration and management oversight of key aspects of the du Plantier investigation. Many were shocked to realise that a total of 139 original witness statements taken in relation to the du Plantier investigation were either missing or not in the possession of the Garda Síochána.

On 25 September 2013, following a written request by GSOC, documentation was received from the Garda Síochána which outlined an extensive list of significant documents including witness statements and 22 exhibits that had gone missing and could no longer be located by An Garda Síochána along with when they were noticed as missing and what steps the Garda Síochána had taken to locate them. It was reported to GSOC that extensive searches had been carried out by An Garda Síochána for the missing items.

Other concerns were raised about potential evidence vanishing at unknown times since December 1996. Given the high-profile nature of the du Plantier investigation and the international interest in it, the fact that such exhibits went missing was identified as an issue of serious concern.

Incredibly, some of the exhibits now missing from garda storage included 'a blood-spattered gate taken from close to where Madame Toscan du Plantier's body was found'. Quite understandably, many were shocked at how an entire metal gate could vanish from supposedly secure garda storage – particularly when it appeared to have bloodstains from the killing.

Other items that had vanished included the French wine bottle found three months after the murder in a field next to the murder scene; a black overcoat belonging to Mr Bailey; the original interview memo of Jules Thomas following her arrest in 1997; an original witness statement from Mrs Farrell provided on 5 March 2004; and an original witness statement from Jules Thomas dated 19 February 1997.

The GSOC revelations certainly outlined a saga of garda operations that did not make comfortable reading for anyone, from officers to ordinary citizens. Although embarrassing, these incidents were not found to be indicative of a conspiracy within the west Cork police force. What had been found, however, were mistakes, haphazard administration and evidential failings, particularly in relation to the preservation of key exhibits.

The police watchdog said it did not find the garda decision to question Mr Bailey to be unlawful or corruptly motivated. 'A number of factors led to Ian Bailey being identified as a suspect at an early stage of the murder inquiry … His subsequent arrest and the arrest of his partner, Jules Thomas, therefore, could not, as the complainants allege, have been construed as unlawful or illegal,' it ruled.

In essence, GSOC found that officers had been well within their powers and operational guidelines in deciding to arrest and formally question Mr Bailey. The report noted that the officers involved had cited a number of factors for considering Mr Bailey as a suspect – although these specific grounds were not set out in the report.

GSOC also found no indication that Mrs Farrell had been forced by gardaí into making specific statements about Mr Bailey.

> GSOC found no evidence that Marie Farrell was coerced or intimidated (as alleged by Ian Bailey and Marie Farrell) into making false statements against Ian Bailey; in fact, a phone call listened to in the course of the investigation could be seen as evidence of a relationship between Marie Farrell and an investigating garda that was not coercive. While it does certainly appear that journalists were in possession of information in advance of Ian Bailey's arrests, GSOC was unable to establish the source of the media's information.

Journalists questioned as part of the GSOC probe had, in keeping with their commitment to protect their sources, declined to reveal where specific information about the case had come from if it had been given in confidence. A key complaint from Mr Bailey had been that some gardaí were deliberately leaking information to the media about him, effectively using the media to increase pressure on him.

> There is no evidence sufficient to sustain either a criminal or disciplinary charge available in respect of this allegation from the documentation reviewed by GSOC and the witnesses that were interviewed. It does seem that certain elements of the media came to be in possession of information in respect of aspects of the garda investigation but it has not been possible to say that if this was leaked by the Garda Síochána as alleged, when this may have been done and by whom, to any evidential standard.

However, GSOC examined the telephone conversations recorded at Bandon Garda Station in respect of the allegations that some garda officers were briefing the media. 'A level of contact was noted between journalists and Bandon Garda Station. This contact is, in the main, enquiries in relation to progress in the murder investigation. No specific inappropriate disclosure of information by garda members to journalists was found by GSOC investigation in the phone calls. However, conversations between garda members indicated a concern that there were members of the press being briefed.'

The report also noted that a total of ten digital audio tapes were supplied to telecommunications experts for analysis in respect of the Bandon Garda Station calls that were recorded. The Fennelly Commission found that just 0.66 per cent of all the available recordings related to the du Plantier investigation.

> There are ten tapes available from the entire period of the investigation. The recordings begin in March 1997 – some three months after the murder – and span to 2003. There are six tapes for the whole of 1997, three for 1998 and one for 2002/2003. The tapes can only give a snapshot and incomplete picture of the investigation. There are significant gaps in the information available on the tapes due to the randomness of the available tapes. Therefore, the significance of the material on the tapes is reduced. There are over 40,000 calls recorded on the available tapes. Some 282 of the calls were considered of relevance to the murder investigation.

GSOC stressed that, given the extent of their inquiry and its findings, no further action would now be taken. However, the watchdog repeated its concerns about how sensitive case material was handled.

> It is a matter of grave concern to GSOC that a large number of original statements and exhibits relating to the murder investigation are missing.

It is GSOC's view that a lack of administration and management are the likely explanation for this state of affairs. GSOC found no evidence of corruption.

From enquiries conducted by GSOC with members of the McNally Review team, it would appear that the [missing] jobs book pages in question may have been removed from the book some time after December 2002 as their absence was not noted during the McNally Review and would have been the subject of comment had they been noticed. (The McNally Review team had access to the original jobs books as part of their review and reported in December 2002.)

In addition, the significant amount of missing original witness statements and physical exhibits in the garda investigation suggested there was difficulty in the administration and management in the incident room (even when viewed through the lens of the time) as opposed to clear evidence of corrupt practice. The witness statements provided to GSOC from the senior garda members did not indicate clearly who was in charge of the investigation from the very outset and throughout the enquiry and who was responsible for making the strategic decisions (including the arrest plans).

Garda bosses were quick to respond to the GSOC criticisms. An official statement from garda management acknowledged the findings and insisted that a lot of the issues had been addressed.

'There have been significant developments in the investigation of crime since the incident subject of the GSOC report occurred in 1996,' a garda statement stressed. 'These include the establishment of the crime training faculty at the Garda College which is tasked with identifying best international practices.' Gardaí also said areas of concern identified by GSOC no longer applied because a 'significant' new management system for property and exhibits had already been rolled out.

Despite the criticism of aspects of the garda murder investigation, GSOC's rejection of Mr Bailey's central allegation of corruption and collusion was a watershed moment. If Mrs Farrell's dramatic revelations that she had been coerced by gardaí had been a boon to his insistence that he was being deliberately targeted by west Cork gardaí, the comprehensive GSOC report would serve to demolish any public perception of a wide-ranging police conspiracy.

The GSOC report also underlined the fact that the future of the case would now rest in France. While the DPP had for years maintained that there was not sufficient evidence for a charge on the basis of the garda case file, the revelation of missing evidence from garda storage effectively guaranteed that there would be no future prosecutorial action in Ireland – any case would be fatally flawed. Nevertheless, there was nothing to delay the next phase in the story, which would be a Paris trial.

Mr Bailey declined to comment on the GSOC report, politely referring all media enquiries to his solicitor. He stressed that he agreed with his solicitor's view of GSOC – and said he was concerned that retired gardaí had no obligation or legal compulsion to work with GSOC officers. The journalist argued that, in effect, this offered retired police officers a form of 'immunity'.

Frank Buttimer said they were not surprised by the outcome of the investigation and launched a condemnatory assessment of GSOC and its powers. He said the report supported their contention that the police watchdog was little more than a 'toothless body'. He said it was extraordinary that there appeared to be absolutely no accountability for the glaring failures of the du Plantier investigation and, in particular, the manner in which key evidence exhibits had mysteriously vanished from garda storage.

Mr Buttimer noted that Mr Bailey's time and cooperation with GSOC over several years appeared to have been a 'totally wasted exercise'. '[Mr Bailey] is very disappointed,' he acknowledged.

The contrast to the reception of the GSOC report in France could not have been more stark. Sophie's family were delighted that the lengthy watchdog investigation had found no evidence of garda corruption or a long-standing conspiracy against Mr Bailey.

French legal officials also insisted that the GSOC report had implications for the impending Paris prosecution. The Bouniols' Paris-based solicitor, Alain Spilliaert, said the GSOC findings were particularly important in relation to allegations about garda corruption and claims that Marie Farrell had been put under duress by gardaí. 'Mr Bailey has claimed from the beginning that the Irish police investigation was flawed. [But] this report is important because it confirms a previous judgment from the High Court of Dublin ruling that the garda criminal investigation was not corrupted.'

He also insisted that the GSOC revelations about evidence having gone missing from garda storage in west Cork would not impact on the planned French prosecution. 'In any case, a French judge thought the evidence was solid enough to send the case to trial. Just because there is no DNA does not mean that the criminal file is over. The case is based on the file built up by the Irish police plus the work of French investigating magistrates who worked with the gardaí over the past decade.

'The French justice system considered that Mrs Farrell's statements and her subsequent retraction were suspicious and helped to justify a trial. This is one more element. The GSOC report goes in our favour,' Mr Spilliaert insisted.

Sophie's son, Pierre-Louis Baudey-Vignaud, told Lara Marlowe of the *Irish Times* that his faith in the Irish and French systems had been well placed.

> The report strengthens my opinion, and I continue to have great confidence in the French and Irish justice systems which are going forward, slowly but surely. I never believed in any kind of plot [against Mr Bailey]. I know there were [garda] failings. Those failings were harmful to my interests. But they do not mean we won't get to the truth. The report goes in the direction of the truth.

For the French, the GSOC report was of paramount importance. While it had highlighted garda failings – not least the embarrassing loss of key exhibits in the case – it had found no evidence of a garda conspiracy against Mr Bailey. Had GSOC found in favour of Mr Bailey's allegations against the gardaí, it would be hard to see how any Paris prosecution could have been untainted, based as it was on the original garda murder file.

The implications of the GSOC findings for Mr Bailey can be judged from his legal team's reaction to its report summary – they dismissed their cooperation with the long-running review as essentially a waste of time and effort.

13

PARIS TRIAL

I f the GSOC report had highlighted failings in the Irish police and judicial systems, it soon became apparent that the French system was not flawless either. Even though Irish witnesses had known since the previous January that the Paris murder trial would start around the end of May, French prosecutors only informed them three weeks before the event that their presence was actually needed. French law allows for witness statements to be read into evidence, even if the individual involved is not present. When they hadn't heard from the Paris authorities by the end of April, many thought the Paris prosecutors didn't require them to attend.

This included gardaí and key witnesses in the original investigation, who only learned in early May that the French authorities did in fact want them to travel to Paris for the opening of the trial, on 27 May. Dozens had holiday or business plans by this stage – and were now unable or unwilling to change them. Furthermore, the French authorities had not appointed a special police or judicial liaison officer to keep the potential Irish witnesses regularly briefed on developments in the prosecution's case in the months leading up to the trial. This was despite the fact that, over the previous years, nearly all the original garda murder case witnesses had fully cooperated with the French investigation under Magistrate Gachon. The overwhelming majority had indicated that they were willing to cooperate with the French trial but would need plenty of time to prepare. Those who were not willing to cooperate largely cried off for reasons of health or age.

The French authorities had offered to cover all travel and subsistence expenses incurred by Irish witnesses who agreed to travel to Paris for the trial. This, however, would be on a reimbursement basis. Many in west Cork – all too familiar with the delays in State payment schemes at home – were concerned that they might face being out of pocket for months before they were finally reimbursed. In some cases, witnesses were simply not in a financial position to pay such travel expenses up front.

On Sunday, 19 May 2019, Pierre-Louis, by now 38 years old, issued an emotional personal appeal in west Cork for everyone in Ireland to support the forthcoming Paris trial. As he made the journey to Goleen parish church that Sunday morning, accompanied by his uncle Bertrand, Mr Baudey-Vignaud was briefly filmed at Sophie's old cottage by RTÉ's southern editor Paschal Sheehy.

When he arrived at the church for a scheduled press briefing, he spoke with RTÉ before indicating he would speak with all other journalists, both Irish and French, after the service, once he had delivered his carefully written appeal. This plea urged everyone in west Cork to repay the faith that Sophie and her family had put in the local community:

Sophie fought like a lioness against the most atrocious violence there is; the violence used by a monster that nothing stops – the one that struck her for no reason, for nothing. I still come back here every year because it is the only way for me to defy this violence and destroy it.

For twenty years I have trusted you. Do not betray me. Do not betray yourselves. This trial isn't just about my mother – it is the trial of the truth. I want to make an appeal to all the people here – anyone who has received requests from the magistrates in France, come and tell [your story]. We must be all together against violence.

If God is love and if this church is his, let us pray for my mother to find peace and that God's righteousness may join that of men. This case is first and foremost about an innocent woman. This is a trial of a crime that you and I did not deserve, whether it takes place here or in France.

It is the trial of a crime that bears the mark of a country in which a woman, my mother, had such confidence that she opened her door to the person who murdered her. She would not have done this in Paris. She opened her door here in Ireland because she was so confident that nothing bad would happen to her. And that confidence was the reason why she chose to come to this country.

It was my last day of being a child. I was eight years old the first time I came here and I was fifteen years old when my mother was brutally killed. It is time today to turn one of the saddest pages of your history – the darkest page of mine. These are just a few words to tell you that in France, in a week's time, our history is at stake.

It is the story of my mother's death and the story of a woman who needed you so much to recharge her batteries. And the reason I stayed with you here is because she was always right to trust you. That is how I have always felt it. We must turn this sad page together because my mother, you and I, must refuse to see these hills sink into one of the worst tragedies and injustices. This land must find peace again. This land must end this crime which is neither a mystery nor a legend. My mother, Sophie, is not a ghost. She is the victim of human cruelty and violence which has no place here. But humans are sometimes capable of the worst. My mother defended herself from the worst up to her last breath to escape the savage and brutal violence.

Mr Baudey-Vignaud pointed out he had kept his mother's beloved holiday cottage at Toormore despite suggestions by some relatives that it should be sold. He now holidays in west Cork three or four times a year with his wife, Aurelia, and their two children. His eldest daughter was named Sophie in honour of her late grandmother. He said he still kept his mother's old duffle coat hanging on a hook by the back door. 'We chose to leave it here. But it is not a museum.'

In the days after Mr Baudey-Vignaud's emotional appeal, Mr Bailey repeatedly warned that the forthcoming Paris prosecution would be a 'tragedy for the truth'. I had spoken to him in the week before the Goleen appeal and he had agreed to take a phone call afterwards to set out his position. He was livid that Goleen church was used as the venue for the French appeal – and was clearly deeply upset at the imminent Paris prosecution. 'It is a most dreadful and frightening position to be in. It is a nightmare – but it has been a nightmare for the past twenty-two years. It is a nightmare I cannot escape from. As far as I can tell, it is a nightmare that will only end with my death,' he said.

He claimed that there were people in authority in Ireland who knew he was entirely innocent but were prepared to stay silent while he was convicted in France based on evidence already rejected in Ireland. 'These people are prepared to see me convicted and sacrificed to public opinion in France. It is like some kind of code of omertà,' he claimed.

***

Sixteen years after it was first mooted, the French prosecution over the death of Sophie Toscan du Plantier opened in Paris on Monday, 27 May 2019. The trial was held in the Palais de Justice, an eighteenth-century court building located on the Île de la Cité, in the ancient heart of the beautiful French capital. The structure traces its history all the way back through five French Republics to the Bourbon monarchy of Louis XVI.

Just a couple of hundred metres down the street stood the imposing Notre-Dame Cathedral. The structure had made headlines across the world just two weeks earlier when it had been substantially damaged in a massive fire that had gutted the roof and part of its interior. For days the world watched and mourned as one of the most famous religious structures on the planet smouldered. The people of Paris were struggling to come to terms with the extent of the damage to the cathedral. The smell of smoke still hung in the air around the courts complex.

Such was the media interest in the trial that the Paris courts service couldn't accommodate all the journalists who wanted to cover the court proceedings. A limited number of journalists would be allowed in the cramped main courtroom – the rest would be required to report on the proceedings via live video-link in an adjacent room.

Irish, French and British TV crews mingled together outside the courts complex while journalists tried to confirm pre-trial indications that the hearing would only last four days, with a verdict expected on Friday. Due to a French public holiday, the court would not sit on one day during the week. Irish journalists, more used to murder trials that took anywhere between two and eight weeks to hear, found the expectation of a four-day hearing hard to believe.

A large Irish media contingent were present, including Lara Marlowe and Barry Roche for the *Irish Times*, Michael Clifford for the *Irish Examiner*, Sarah Collins for the *Irish Independent*, Sharon Gaffney for RTÉ, as well as a number of freelance reporters. Also present was Michael Sheridan, who had penned *Death in December*, the first major book written about the 1996 killing.

The Cour d'assises hearing was allocated to Courtroom K – a small, wood-panelled room – before three magistrates. The presiding judge was Magistrate Frédérique Aline, who would hear the case with her two colleagues, Magistrate Didier Forton and Magistrate Geraldine Detienne. Because Ian Bailey was not cooperating with the prosecution, a jury hearing was not required. Under French law, Mr Bailey's stance was viewed as a 'criminal default'. The three judges alone would decide on the verdict – and a ruling was expected within hours of the trial finishing its evidence.

French prosecutors, led by Jean-Pierre Bonthoux, went to great lengths to stress that the current prosecution was not, as claimed by

Mr Bailey, rooted in judicial codes dating back more than 200 years. The prosecutor insisted that the trial was, in fact, based on a legal code from 2004. That, however, did not stop supporters of Mr Bailey in Ireland from slating the Paris trial as tantamount to a 'prosecution under colonial law' given that the old Napoleonic Code remained the underlying basis for French law.

However, even though the French mother of one died in Ireland and large parts of the evidence at hand involved statements from English-speaking witnesses, there would be no live translation – all evidence would be dealt with in French. A translator was sworn in but ultimately would only be required for a small portion of the trial.

Under France's Napoleonic Code, the prosecution was integrally linked to a complaint made against Mr Bailey over Sophie's death by her family, the Bouniols and du Plantiers. This criminal complaint over her death had been lodged with the French authorities by Sophie's family back in January 1997, but it took the revelations of the 2003 libel trial in Ireland to kick-start events in France. Even then, the investigation proper under Magistrate Gachon did not commence until 2008.

In respect of the prosecution, eight named members of Sophie's family were linked to the case, including her son and her elderly parents. Also present to support the prosecution were the deceased's brother, Bertrand, her aunt, Marie-Madeleine Opalka, as well as her uncle and ASSOPH founder, Jean-Pierre Gazeau. Family members and their supporters took up several rows in the main gallery of the courtroom as the opening statements were delivered.

Core evidence would be offered to the trial by individual family members. Sophie's family were represented by a team of three solicitors: Alain Spilliaert, Laurent Pettiti and Marie Dose.

The trial would hear from a total of 28 witnesses, the majority dealt with via sworn statements made either to the French police team operating under Magistrates Gachon and Dutartre or to gardaí as part of the original murder investigation.

Mr Baudey-Vignaud's concerns voiced a couple of weeks earlier about the number of Irish witnesses set to travel to Paris for the trial proved well founded. Ultimately, just two people made the trip from Ireland to Paris for the hearing – Mr Bailey's neighbour Amanda Reed, whose son, Malachi, was one of the key witnesses in the 2003 libel hearing, as well as Bill Fuller, a former friend of Mr Bailey. Mr Fuller's evidence would challenge Mr Bailey's insistence that he had never met the French mother of one.

The absence of Irish witnesses was undoubtedly a disappointment for the French family, particularly after the lengths they had gone to over the years to make personal appeals for help in west Cork. Each of the witnesses requested to attend the trial had their name read out by the French prosecutor. Again and again, in an embarrassing cycle, the court clerk confirmed there was no answer to the witness call.

There were extenuating circumstances in many cases. A number of the witnesses were only contactable via old and unverified addresses – there were fears many never even received the court summons. Another witness was medically incapacitated and unable to attend. In one clearly embarrassing moment for the prosecution, it was confirmed that two of the witnesses listed – Patrick Lowney and Martin Graham – were now deceased. Mr Lowney had died almost three years earlier.

Other witnesses were annoyed at the lack of notice given by the French. Helen Callanan, a former news editor of the *Sunday Tribune*, took the trouble to write directly to the court to express concern at the lack of suitable notice she was given about the 27 May hearing. Pointedly, Ms Callanan said she had a serious concern that the lack of proper notice offered to potential Irish witnesses and their understandable inability to attend could undermine the entire credibility of the Paris proceedings. Ms Callanan bluntly remarked on the 'fragility of the process'.

The small number of Irish witnesses to answer the French summonses was undoubtedly an underlying source of tension between the prosecutors and Irish authorities. The case opened with criticisms of Ireland's handling of the original murder investigation, how journalists had reported on the crime between 1996 and 1998, and even how information about the current trial process was allegedly being fed back to Mr Bailey at his west Cork home. There was even criticism of the DPP and the decision not to sanction any charge in Ireland over Sophie's death.

Lawyer Marie Dose pointedly challenged the issue of the flow of information to Mr Bailey in west Cork. There were, she complained, journalists present who were texting regular updates to Mr Bailey at his west Cork home, where his reaction to the trial was being recorded by a film crew.

'[Some] Irish journalists are here to send text messages to Ian Bailey who is being filmed live so his reactions to every minute of the trial are recorded. We have no problem with the publicity for the process. Of course, journalists must be able to do their job. But filming Ian Bailey live at home to record his reactions is not acceptable,' she warned.

The complaint caused consternation amongst the Irish journalists present, which prompted a caustic remark from Magistrate Aline. Later, it was clarified that, in fact, the Irish journalists were not offering Mr Bailey live updates from the Paris proceedings. These were being provided by a legal official who was attending the trial with a watching brief.

The judge delivered the opening statement, in which the background to the proceedings was outlined in detail. Having explained the legal circumstances under which the prosecution was taking place, the court then heard an overview of the case against Ian Bailey. In a submission that lasted just under two hours, the judge explained why the British journalist was the focus of the Paris prosecution.

There were essentially five major grounds on which the French had focused attention on Mr Bailey. Interestingly, not a single one of them involved any type of physical or forensic evidence. They were that Mr Bailey had cuts and scratches on his arms and hands in the days after 23 December; that he had varied his story of his precise movements at the Liscaha house on 22 and 23 December; that he had confessed to the crime to several people in west Cork; that he had stopped his car on a hillside near Sophie's home on the evening of 22 December to view the Toormore holiday home; and, finally, that he had lit a bonfire in the back garden of the Liscaha property a few days later over Christmas, essentially a suggestion that he had tried to dispose of material.

Mr Bailey's arrival at the crime scene on 23 December in his role as a journalist was also outlined. The French case was that he had specific details about the killing at such an early stage that gardaí eventually became suspicious. Photos taken at the crime scene and what later happened to them were also raised. This was a reference to photos Mr Bailey claimed were never taken at the scene – but which were referred to by another witness in the garda file who said they were mentioned but never actually viewed.

All three magistrates were then shown photographs of the crime scene and the injuries suffered by the deceased. So graphic was the photographic and post-mortem evidence that most members of the Bouniol family quietly left the courtroom, only to return when the pathology evidence was concluded. Only Sophie's brother, Bertrand, remained behind.

The initial post-mortem was conducted in Cork on 24 December 1996 by State Pathologist Professor John Harbison. A second French post-mortem was conducted 12 years later when, as part of the French investigation, Ms du Plantier's body was exhumed in France. Dr Marc Taccoen conducted the 2008 post-mortem examination following the exhumation.

His report verified the findings of Professor Harbison's initial study, which ruled that Sophie had died from head injuries sustained in a violent assault. She had apparently fought desperately to protect herself and had numerous defensive injuries to her arms. To facilitate his study, Dr Taccoen had painstakingly reconstructed the skull, which allowed for an interpretation of precisely how the blows had been sustained.

He found that the deceased had suffered repeated blows to the right side of her head. The injuries inflicted were consistent with having been sustained by blows from a large, flat rock. A rock of this type was found a short distance from the body. He said the indications were that the blows were aimed in a sideways direction. However, the fatal blow was sustained when a heavy object – likely a concrete breeze block – was dropped directly onto Sophie's skull from a height. Most likely, the block would have been held above the attacker's head and then dropped with force onto the head of the woman lying stunned and bloodied on the ground.

Dr Taccoen added that Sophie's body had lain undiscovered at the scene for several hours. He noted that the body remained at the scene for more than 24 hours after it was discovered, covered by nothing more than a sheet of plastic, until the state pathologist could attend the isolated scene at Toormore.

The garda crime scene photographs were projected onto a large screen in the courtroom. Even for those familiar with trials of violent crimes, they were particularly gruesome. Sophie's entire head and upper torso were soaked in dried blood. Such was the damage inflicted to her head and face it was almost as if her killer had tried to entirely erase her beauty and render her unrecognisable.

Statements from two investigating gardaí – Bart O'Leary and Kevin Kelleher – were read into evidence. These statements underlined that detectives immediately noted the cuts and scratches on Mr Bailey and detailed how Mr Bailey appeared pale, with unkempt hair. Garda O'Leary also noted in his statement that a deep cut to Mr Bailey's head was visible.

Prosecutors were also scathing about Mr Bailey's work as a journalist in the days after the killing – claiming that he had championed a theory that the French mother of one had been murdered by a lover, something that was not supported by any evidence. This theory revolved around the premise that Sophie had been killed by an assassin who targeted her in west Cork knowing she would be alone and helpless. The theory also painted Mr Bailey as the 'fall guy' or local eccentric on whom the crime would be blamed.

For the first time it emerged publicly that gardaí had initially focused on a French culprit. The journalist had, in the days after the murder, passed a tip to gardaí that there was somehow a French connection to the brutal killing. It was suggested that the killer was French and that Ms du Plantier had been deliberately targeted, followed from France and then murdered while in Ireland.

Years later, one of the conspiracy theories about the case was that somehow her husband was involved – despite the fact the couple were in the happiest stage of their marriage and were planning their first child together. Friends of both Sophie Daniel Toscan du Plantier have rubbished the theory as patently false.

The two Irish witnesses who attended the hearing repeated evidence first heard at the 2003 libel hearing before Cork Circuit Court.

Amanda Reid, also known as Irune Reid, confirmed that her son, Malachi, who was then 14 years old, was left very frightened by a conversation he had with Mr Bailey when being given a lift home just a few weeks after Sophie's death. Mr Reid claimed that Mr Bailey turned to him in the car and said, 'I went to her house with a stone one night and smashed her brains out.' The teen was deeply shaken by the conversation and later told his mother what had been said. He confirmed that he believed Mr Bailey had been drinking, but Mr Reid was still convinced he was serious. Ms Reid confirmed to the trial that her son had been left deeply shaken by the exchange. 'Yes, he was very scared. I believed my son and I never questioned his word,' she insisted.

The evidence of Bill Fuller, a former friend and drinking companion of Mr Bailey, was equally stark. Mr Fuller ended their friendship in January 1997, after an exchange with the journalist in Schull. 'He said to me, "It was you who killed her – you saw her at the Spar with her nice little ass. You went to her house around 2 a.m. to see what you could get out of her. This scared her so, to calm her down, you gave her a little punch – but it went too far. It's what happened with Jules. I saw her little ass but she let me in." Bailey used to talk about himself in the second or third person,' Mr Fuller added.

The French prosecutors were critical of the Irish investigation. It was claimed that west Cork gardaí were not used to dealing with such high-profile, violent crimes and the suggestion was raised that the crime scene had not even been properly preserved. The Irish, it was later added, were also very fond of the pub, a reference that offended not just the Irish journalists present but many of those following the proceedings back in Ireland. Additionally, it was claimed that the Irish and UK journalists who had covered the case in the weeks after 23 December 1996 were not objective and had penned articles that were speculative and, in some cases, entirely without foundation.

The claims about Sophie's relationship with her husband, Daniel, were clearly a matter of concern to her family. A special profile of the deceased was prepared for Magistrate Gachon and this dismissed suggestions that she was targeted by a scorned lover. Investigator and psychologist Michel Larousse acknowledged in his report that Sophie had, at times, been unhappy in love. She had been involved in a relationship with another person in France but there was absolutely no evidence that she had had any relationships in Ireland.

He also noted that in 1996 her relationship with her late husband was amicable and that they were essentially reconciled. The court was told that Mr Toscan du Plantier adored his wife and that he had bought the Toormore property for her so she could use it as a retreat from the pressures of their professional lives in France. In the weeks before her death the couple had also been discussing having a child together.

The court was also told that Sophie had called her husband a number of times during her brief stay in Ireland that December. The family were planning on spending the new year together in Dakar, after she had flown back to France from Cork. She also regularly brought family and friends with her to Ireland.

He described Sophie as a highly intelligent woman who prized her independence. Mr Larousse said that friends described her as very sociable, good company and intensely loyal, but also reserved on occasions – she valued her time alone to read and write poetry. He said Sophie was a very warm person who, because of her independence, sometimes took what might be described as risks. For instance, she never worried about travelling alone to Ireland in the depths of winter or staying on her own in the isolated Toormore property.

With reference to what might be perceived as risk-taking behaviour, he noted that Sophie had once decided to help a homeless person. In a kind-hearted gesture, she had allowed the person to sleep overnight in her car for shelter. However, he said that while this might be interpreted as taking 'a risk', the deceased was a trusting person rather than someone who might be described as gullible.

'She was not afraid of much,' he testified. Mr Larousse said that, in his opinion, the evidence pointed to a culprit that Sophie was not afraid of and someone who she likely believed did not pose a threat to her before the sudden and unprovoked attack.

After her murder, her husband chose not to travel to west Cork and did not formally identify the body to gardaí. The trial was told by Gilbert Jacob, a close friend of the late film executive, that the decision was perfectly understandable given how devastated Mr du Plantier was by the circumstances of the death of his beloved wife. The French film executive first learned of his wife's death via a news report on television and initially refused to believe it was true. 'He said, "I cannot go to Ireland to identify her." Psychologically, he was not able to go,' Mr Jacob said. He also described Sophie as a natural beauty who was deeply loved by Mr du Plantier. He said she was elegant, intelligent and very sociable. But she was also reserved and a deep thinker, and, as a result, needed time alone, away from the demands of the French film industry and public life.

Mr du Plantier – who died while attending a film industry function in Germany in March 2003 – made just a single visit to west Cork after the murder, when he travelled to Ireland with his solicitor, Paul Haennig, on 7 July 2000 to be briefed at Bandon Garda Station on the ongoing Irish murder investigation. During that visit he was also accompanied by Pierre-Louis Baudey-Vignaud and his own son, Davide.

Regarding Mr Bailey, the French investigation claimed he had effectively 'confessed' to the crime on a number of occasions to people in west Cork. Magistrate Aline was told that the witness statements of five people – Malachi Reed, Helen Callanan, Ritchie and Rosie Shelly as well as Bill Fuller – had never varied in their account of what Mr Bailey had allegedly said. It was never raised in court that these could have been accounts of him merely repeating hurtful stories of what others were saying about him.

Those five witnesses had been re-interviewed by French detectives as part of Magistrate Gachon's investigation between 2008 and 2011. One senior French policeman, Damian Roehrig, was part of the Irish element of the investigation in 2011. He travelled to west Cork and had interviewed more than 20 people from the original garda murder file. He confirmed that none of the five witnesses mentioned had ever changed their accounts of what they claimed Mr Bailey had said to them. In the case of Mr Reed, he said the teenager had been left terrified of Mr Bailey following the conversation. In all cases, he said, the witnesses had nothing to gain from their statements about Mr Bailey.

The French policeman said that, before December 1996, Mr Bailey had been viewed as the 'local eccentric' who was essentially harmless. But he also said that a number of witnesses in the case told him they were now afraid of the Englishman. Mr Bailey was reportedly viewed as a violent man, who would consume large amounts of alcohol to the point of blacking out. Mr Roehrig mentioned that they had focused their investigation on Mr Bailey after learning of his history of violence towards his partner.

Additionally, he said, the journalist was known in west Cork for his strange and bizarre behaviour. One neighbour recounted to him how the journalist would howl at the full moon like a wolf. Mr Bailey was also known to walk the roads in the dark and would wear distinctive clothing – all adding to the image of the journalist as a strange, bohemian character.

He added that a number of witnesses told French police how Mr Bailey had a penchant for trying to frighten people living on their own. One woman, who saw Mr Bailey howling at the full moon, said she subsequently slept with an iron bar by her bed.

Mr Roehrig laid particular emphasis on the scratches and cuts Mr Bailey had on his hands and arms after 22 and 23 December 1996. He said French police were satisfied the cuts were not on his hands before 22 December and that they were more consistent with having been inflicted by briars and thorns rather than the talons of a turkey, as had been repeatedly claimed by the journalist. The detective pointed out that the murder scene at Toormore was surrounded by briar-filled ditches.

Arguably the core element of Mr Roehrig's testimony dealt with the evidence given by Schull shopkeeper Marie Farrell, which had later been retracted. Mrs Farrell was the one witness, as heard in the 2003 libel trial, whose evidence contradicted Mr Bailey's claim that he had not left the Liscaha property on the evening of 22 December. Mr Roehrig outlined how Mrs Farrell had told gardaí about seeing a tall man at Kealfadda Bridge outside Schull. This man was later identified by her as Mr Bailey. Crucially, there was no mention at the trial of the fact that Mrs Farrell had retracted this statement or that she had steadfastly maintained since 2005 that her original statement to gardaí had been made under duress.

There was also no mention of the concerns highlighted by Ireland's DPP that Mrs Farrell's physical description of the person she saw that night had also dramatically varied. She initially described the person at Kealfadda Bridge as being around five foot eight or five foot ten inches in height. However, just one month later, on 22 January 1997, she revised that description to say that the man was very tall.

The shopkeeper was one of the witnesses requested to attend the Paris trial but prosecutors never received a reply to their letter requesting her presence. Despite this, the magistrates were asked to accept her January 1997 statement and regard her as credible despite her later retraction of sworn evidence. For Sophie's family, Mrs Farrell's evidence about what she saw at Kealfadda Bridge that night was 'credible'.

While significant elements of the Paris trial were little more than detailed elaborations of evidence already heard in Ireland either as part of the 2003 libel hearing or the 2015 High Court claim for wrongful arrest, there were some dramatic new revelations. Many of these came from Sophie's friends, who had never been asked to participate in the Irish legal proceedings.

A close friend of Sophie, Agnes Thomas, told of a telephone conversation she had with her just days before she was due to fly to Ireland in December 1996. Ms Thomas told the trial that during the conversation Sophie revealed she was due to meet a man in west Cork who was a poet. Ms Thomas said her friend described the man as a 'weird guy'.

'She told me that she was going to meet this guy, a poet, to talk to him about his work. She said he was a "weird guy", and I advised her that she should not meet him if he was weird. She thought he was strange. She was wary of him. If she ever met him, it would have been professional,' she said. The conversation was only recalled by Agnes Thomas in 2015 and it had played no part in the original garda murder file. Ms Thomas said her friend had never mentioned the name of the poet to her during their brief conversation.

Agnes Thomas said her friend was kind-hearted and would never refuse to help another person – something that possibly explained why she opened her door on the evening of 22 December or morning of 23 December 1996. 'Sophie took care of other people. If someone needed help and knocked on her door during the night, she would open the door,' she said.

Other revelations involved Irish witnesses who had never played a role in the libel action or High Court cases. One such witness was Patrick Lowney, who had died in 2016. His statements, made to gardaí in October and November 2000, provoked an intense reaction in the court. Mr Lowney operated a garage at Strand Road outside Clonakilty, but he was also a keen amateur photographer. His interest in photography was so great that he even operated his own private photo-developing lab. He explained to west Cork detectives that he had been contacted by a man in May 2000. This man said he needed help from Mr Lowney with 'discreet' photographic work. He asked him to develop film negatives at his Clonakilty lab. Mr Lowney said he thought the man who called to him may even have been wearing a wig.

During the development process, Mr Lowney examined the images and realised that they depicted a woman's body. That body was lying on what appeared to be a country road or pathway. Mr Lowney said he thought the road resembled the area where Sophie's body was found. He also believed that the photographs were taken at night or in low light conditions. He said the images appeared to show a gateway or an entrance to a field in the background.

The man who approached him with the photographs appeared anxious when Mr Lowney started carefully studying the images. The man grabbed both the photographs and negatives and left. Mr Lowney was concerned and made a statement to gardaí the following November. In the original statement signed by Mr Lowney, the individual who called to the lab was identified as Mr Bailey.

However, the trial was not told that, subsequent to his statement, in May 2013 Mr Lowney informed two Irish journalists, Shane Phelan of the *Irish Daily Mail* and Philip Boucher-Hayes of RTÉ, that he believed that the man had not been Ian Bailey.

'I did not actually say it was him,' the amateur photographer told Shane Phelan in May 2013. Mr Lowney also confirmed that he had formally withdrawn his original garda statement. The photographer was adamant that he had never identified the man as Mr Bailey. No trace of the photos described by Mr Lowney were ever found by gardaí.

Mr Bailey, during his 2003 libel action, had vehemently denied ever offering photographs of the crime scene to newspapers, insisting that he had only offered to help with 'pick up' photographs of the deceased, such as from the family, friends or local events. However, during that libel action, both Provision Photographic Agency boss, Mike MacSweeney, and the *Irish Independent* photographic editor, Padraig Beirne, insisted that they were offered crime scene photographs by Mr Bailey.

In an unexpected development, the trial also heard evidence from a psychiatrist and psychologist who had prepared reports on Ian Bailey – but had never met him. Neither was present in court when their studies were presented. The reports had been ordered by the investigating magistrate in 2014 and were compiled without any direct interviews with Mr Bailey. Rather, they were based on a study of his personal diaries and his various garda interviews.

Psychiatrist Jean-Michel Masson and psychologist Katy Lorenzo-Regreny found that Mr Bailey had a 'borderline personality'. This, they said, could lead to both extremes of emotion and impulsive behaviour. Both agreed that Mr Bailey was not psychotic and that he had no impairment that would influence him in respect of the matter at trial. In essence, both found him fit to stand trial in France.

Their report found that Mr Bailey had a 'particularly complex and intelligent personality'. But he was also found to have a personality that was partly based on 'narcissism, psycho-rigidity, violence, impulsiveness, egocentricity, with an intolerance to frustration and a great need for recognition'.

Undoubtedly, the most powerful testimony offered during the entire trial came from Sophie's family. They had waited 22 years for an outlet for their pain and loss. It was apparent that, despite the length of time since the brutal killing on 23 December 1996, their pain and suffering had not lessened in the slightest.

'[Sophie] should be here now, walking free ... she was so beautiful without ever trying to be. The air vibrated around her,' wept her aunt, Marie-Madeleine Opalka. 'It is important for justice to be done.' Until recently, Mrs Opalka had, along with Georges and Marguerite Bouniol, travelled to west Cork every December to appeal for help in bringing

Sophie's killer to justice. Mrs Opalka had for many years been the voice of the family in Ireland in their annual plea for help in identifying their daughter's killer.

The pain still being endured by the family was evident when, during references to the injuries suffered by Sophie that Christmas evening, her father bowed his head in grief while her son cradled his head in his hands.

Mr Baudey-Vignaud said the Paris court now had the opportunity to deliver justice – and to help Sophie's family to 'feel secure'. He still owned his mother's Toormore property and wanted himself and his family to feel safe when he visited it. The father of two maintained the house exactly as it was when his mother left it. Her coat still hangs by the back door and her favourite tea brand still sits on the shelf. 'When I go back to Ireland, I don't go back to a crime scene. The house is how she left it, and her spirit lives on there.'

The young man pointed out to the trial that, at 38 years of age, he was now almost the same age as his mother when her life was cruelly stolen from her. His mother, he insisted, lived on through him and his children.

'[She was] a simple, loving, passionate woman who had given [me] an understanding of the sufferings of the world.' His mother, he added, loved the wildness of the west Cork countryside, the panoramic coastal views and rugged headlands.

He took exception to the manner in which Mr Bailey had dealt with the Paris proceedings. He singled out a man at the back of the court who was monitoring proceedings on behalf of Mr Bailey and his legal team. Mr Baudey-Vignaud said that this approach showed a 'lack of courage' – Mr Bailey had refused to appear before the Paris court or even to be legally represented.

The trial, Sophie's son argued, was 'democracy at work' and an opportunity to offer long-delayed justice for his mother and her family. He also took exception to how his family had been portrayed by some sections of the media. They were, he said, a tight-knit and loving family.

Sophie's brother, Bertrand, said her family had looked for answers over her brutal death ever since the awful events of 23 December 1996, but they were still waiting for justice over 22 years later.

Her uncle, Jean-Pierre Gazeau, said his niece's life was marked by beauty, intelligence and courage. She was never afraid of travelling to Ireland on her own – and never once feared for her safety despite living on her own in such an isolated property.

After three days of evidence – the majority of it spent reading historic sworn statements into the court record – direct testimony concluded. The trial then ended with concluding statements from the prosecutor and the solicitors acting for the family.

Prosecutor Jean-Pierre Bonthoux was scathing in his assessment of Mr Bailey's approach to the Paris trial. He accused him of 'cowardice' in not being present in person and not having legal representation for the proceedings. Instead, he accused Mr Bailey of attempting to manipulate the media to defend himself.

'He is not here but he really is here. He responds via the media, via his previous lawyer, his current lawyer, his future lawyers, his future ex-lawyers. It would be laughable if it were not so tragic. Mr Bailey is making fun of us,' he claimed.

Mr Bonthoux urged the court to consider the statements from west Cork witnesses and the physical evidence from the scene at Toormore. He also expressed exasperation at the loss of potentially crucial evidence from garda storage over the years since the killing, including a bloodstained gate located just metres from where Ms du Plantier's body was found.

The prosecutor was critical of the DPP in Ireland and the 2011 review of the garda case file, which was dismissed as a 'sham'. He slated the 'methodology' applied, which, Mr Bonthoux claimed, took a piecemeal approach to the case rather than an overall perspective of where the facts led. 'If you reduce every element to zero, it does not take a mathematician to work out that the sum will eventually come to zero,' the prosecutor declared. He urged the court to return a guilty verdict. 'I hope one day as soon as possible to see him in court and see his lawyers defend him,' he said.

The three magistrates were also asked to consider Ireland's stance on the Paris proceedings. Solicitor Laurent Pettiti was blunt: 'Ireland does not trust French justice. [This trial] is a humiliation for the Irish system.' The solicitor claimed that the Irish handling of the murder investigation was tantamount to 'a judicial farce'. He warned that mistakes had occurred in the Irish investigation, ranging from the mishandling of evidence right through to critical delays in processing the crime scene. The farce was, he stated, compounded by the ongoing refusal to prosecute Mr Bailey.

To sum up, he pointed out that the tragedy of Sophie's brutal death was that it had occurred in a place she had fallen in love with. 'It was a place she had chosen. It was a place where she recharged and worked. She loved the people around her because they made her relax.'

After these concluding statements, the magistrates retired to consider the case. A verdict was expected within hours.

Less than five hours later, the magistrates returned to the hushed courtroom to confirm the guilty verdict. Their ruling took just over 30 minutes to deliver. Magistrate Aline described the killing as 'extremely violent' and said that due to this extreme level of violence it was apparent that Sophie had been slain with 'homicidal intent'.

She also said it was the opinion of the court that there was 'significant evidence' against Mr Bailey in respect of the charge involved. The court noted the various witness statements offered and, in particular, the original sworn testimony of Marie Farrell.

Magistrate Aline then imposed a 25-year prison sentence on Mr Bailey – just five years below the maximum possible sentence of 30 years. In light of the court verdict, a new EAW was openly proposed. The assembled members of Sophie's family waited in respectful silence as the three magistrates filed from the chamber. Then the pent-up emotion of 22 years swept over them.

Outside the court, members of the family openly wept with relief. They were also adamant that Ireland would now have to act on the French verdict. 'It is a victory for justice, it is a victory for the truth and now Ireland will have to extradite Ian Bailey,' Mr Baudey-Vignaud said.

Alain Spilliaert, the solicitor who had worked with the family on the case for almost 20 years, said the trial was fully justified and conducted in an exceptionally fair and balanced manner. He stressed that the situation in respect of a fresh EAW for Mr Bailey would now have to be carefully studied.

> The judgment was very emphatic and comprehensive. It addressed all the issues that have been raised by Ian Bailey over the years and dealt with in a very thorough way. A trial *in absentia* according to European laws is a valid process and can take place when a person refuses to attend. A trial *in absentia* is entirely in keeping with the presumption of innocence, so it is an entirely credible process. It has been a long process after Mr Bailey made appeals to the Chambre de l'instruction and the Cour de cassation. It is not as if he did not have an opportunity to make his case to French justice.

The only question that remained was whether Mr Bailey would have to face this French justice.

14

AFTERMATH

The news from Paris of the guilty verdict and the 25-year sentence handed down was barely one hour old before Mr Bailey's reaction made headlines. Having denounced the Paris hearing for years as a 'sham' and a 'show trial' at which he was inevitably bound to be found guilty, the journalist now had a few choice soundbites prepared for the media who went looking for him in west Cork.

He wasn't hard to find. Mr Bailey had stuck rigidly to his normal routine and had attended his west Cork market stall that morning, despite knowing a verdict from Paris was imminent. Sporting a fedora-style hat, tan slacks and marine blue jacket complete with blue scarf, if the journalist was feeling the pressure of events in Paris, he was intent not to show it.

Recorded by news cameras as he went about his market stall routine, he agreed to speak with Nicola Anderson and Mark Condren of the *Irish Independent* at his home at The Prairie once he completed his market duties. It was an interview that would dominate the headlines the following day.

Sitting in sunshine amid the wildflowers in his Liscaha garden, he insisted he was 'staying calm in the eye of the hurricane'. Mr Bailey stressed that he was under firm instructions from his 'good lawyer Frank Buttimer' not to offer any reaction or make any utterances about events in France. But, aside from being recorded at the market stall, he had also been filmed by a TV documentary team throughout the day – the self-same documentary team cited by the French prosecution just days earlier at the opening of the trial.

He deftly deflected repeated questions about how he was feeling or what he felt was likely to happen now that the French had sentenced him to 25 years in prison. To the surprise of the journalists, he offered a poem called 'In the Eye', which he said best explained his status at that particular time. 'Actually, this wouldn't offend Frank, because I am a poet and Frank said to me that I couldn't say certain things, but if I put it in a poem?'

He then agreed to recite his poem aloud for the pair: 'There is a full force hurricane, storming, circulating, swirling, angry, aggressive and vengeful, around the outside of my head. Yet because of beauty and love and thoughts of you, I remain calm in the eye of the hurricane. And in the bonfiring of my dreams, at that final moment, between the laughter and the tears, at the tumult of my fears, with thoughts of beauty and love and you, I am able to stay as calm as the stilled mill pond.'

Concluding the poem, he said it perfectly captured where he was at that precise moment in time. 'That is from the heart. I am not acting calmly in a hurricane – I am.' He acknowledged he was a 'bit worried about herself', in reference to his partner, Ms Thomas, who was not participating in the interview but who was painting in her studio just a few metres away. 'She is a bit shook,' he said.

The poetry dominated coverage of the case over the coming days, most likely as intended. The striking photograph taken by Mark Condren, a multiple winner of the prestigious Irish Press Photographer of the Year Award, dominated the front page the following day. Such was the impact of the image it was reproduced several times over the coming weeks for use with various updates on the Paris trial and verdict.

Mr Bailey had explained, when asked how he managed to cope with the stress of recent events, that he had developed a special method of maintaining focus and calm. He now ardently pursued 'Theravada forest Buddhism and detachment meditation'. It offered a form of relaxation that he found hugely beneficial. Many of the journalists to whom he had explained his meditation technique subsequently had to look it up on the Internet for clarification.

As they left his home that day, the photographer and journalist commented to Mr Bailey on an old typewriter rusting in a ditch as a form of garden display. He had, he explained, brought the Underwood typewriter back to west Cork from London and it represented him in 'another life'. Now, he observed, it was 'decomposing – a bit like myself'.

Given his journalistic experience, it was hardly surprising that Mr Bailey's few comments on the matter turned out to be well-chosen sound-bites. To a number of locals, he had joked that his next book of poetry would be entitled *A John Wayne State of Mind*.

He was as good as his word – the successor volume to *The West Cork Way* was indeed entitled *A John Wayne State of Mind* and published by Seanachaí Productions just over six months later.

The quotes on the opening page of the volume were noteworthy. One was from the spiritual self-help guru Pat 'the Barber' Crowley: 'Never react, only respond.' Another was by the author: 'Stay calm in the eye of the hurricane.' Adding a spiritual note was a famous verse attributed to the twelfth-century philosopher Hildegard of Bingen.

The volume included 41 poems and pieces of prose with titles ranging from 'Hardened Steel' to 'Preparing for the Worst, Hoping for the Best' and 'Still in the Ring'. His poem 'In the Eye' was also included.

Mr Bailey also pointedly thanked those who had supported him throughout the difficult weeks, months and years he had endured: 'I have had great support for which I am very grateful. I have been in good company and gotten lots of support. So I am doing my best to stay calm. There has always been a chorus of people going back twenty years – people who believed that I had nothing to do with it and they have been great. More and more people are sending cards, best wishes and miracle medals.'

Referring back to *A John Wayne State of Mind*, he said that he would like to have it ready by the West Cork Literary Festival in July – something that seemed to occupy him much more than a looming third French extradition bid.

His solicitor, Frank Buttimer, was much more forthcoming in terms of what the Paris murder conviction represented not just for his client but for Ireland: 'It is a grotesque miscarriage of justice. It is a shameful episode in Irish criminal justice that we have allowed this to happen. The Department of Justice has questions to answer about how it could have abandoned our criminal justice system. The bigger picture is that it is an abandonment of our independence to a foreign power in this regard.'

The solicitor, in a hard-hitting interview with *The Guardian* newspaper in the UK, repeated his assertion that the outcome of the Paris trial was never in any doubt. 'It is a show trial. A rubber-stamping exercise in determining his guilt. They can read into the record statements that were taken many years ago, including many that are totally discredited or downright bullshit.'

Mr Buttimer said the effective result of the French stance for his client was that Mr Bailey was trapped in west Cork and unable to travel overseas for fear of the outstanding EAW issued by the French. 'He has been a prisoner in a country called Ireland.'

While Mr Bailey had been attempting to put on a brave face in the aftermath of the Paris trial and his conviction, Mr Buttimer was more forthcoming about what it meant on a human level for the journalist.

It has been a nightmare for him, pure and simple. It has been incredibly distressing. I do not know how he has managed to survive over the years. This is just the latest, but one of the worst moments of his life, insofar as he has been caught up in this nightmare.

I truly do not know how he has managed to deal with these extremely difficult matters, but I will continue to support the man and I hope people out there have an understanding of just what has been done to him. And what has been done to the criminal justice system of this independent country.

The French will now return to this country to seek his unlawful removal for the third time, and that will be fully resisted by us. Ian Bailey never expected to receive what we would understand to be justice in the French jurisdiction. This is a French colonial law, in existence for 200 years when France was a colonial power – where France claims to have jurisdiction over the entire world, as if the criminal justice systems of democracies such as Ireland are not fit for purpose.

It is a gross insult to our independence as a country, to the independence of our criminal justice system and to the independence of our public prosecutor. He doesn't have any rights in France, we have to just react to what is next to happen. It is a grotesque miscarriage of justice.

Having dominated headlines in both the Saturday and Sunday papers, the trial continued to generate coverage in both Ireland and France for the next fortnight. Newspapers and magazines carried detailed analysis pieces while radio and TV broadcast programmes offered overviews of all the dramatic events since December 1996.

On 12 June, the Paris court dealt with the subsidiary matter of costs and fines in relation to the week-long murder trial. Under French law, to accelerate the judicial process and ease the burden on victims' families, compensation can be paid out in advance as part of what is known as a 'civil action within criminal proceedings'. Having been convicted by the Cour d'assises, Mr Bailey would now face a civil fallout from the verdict.

Magistrate Aline, in a summary ruling, ordered Mr Bailey to pay a total of €225,000 in damages to the French state and to Sophie's family. More than half of the money – some €115,000 – would go to compensate a state guarantee fund for victims of terrorism and other offences, which advanced the payment to Sophie's family on the foot of a court order in March 2013.

It was the same state-operated fund that was used to aid the multiple victims of the French terror attacks, including the November 2015 Paris nightclub attacks and the July 2016 truck attack in Nice. Almost 220 people died in the combined attacks while a further 600-plus people were injured.

Damages totalling a further €110,000 were awarded against Mr Bailey to seven of Sophie's family members, with the bulk of the money going to her son and her parents. Her brothers, aunt and uncle were also named in an 11 June 'civil judgment'. The court ruled that Mr Bailey now had 10 years to make the payment. After this date, the award would become unenforceable.

Few doubted, as explained by the Bouniols's lawyer, Alain Spilliaert, that the award was nothing more than a symbolic order by the court. He stressed that the French state did not expect either to recoup its €115,000 advance payment or for the family to receive the extra €110,000 awarded. But, he insisted, the award was 'important from a psychological point of view'.

Under the terms of the ruling, €25,000 each was awarded to Georges and Marguerite Bouniol as well as Pierre-Louis Baudey-Vignaud. Sophie's brothers, Bertrand and Stéphane Bouniol, and her aunt, Marie-Madeleine Opalka, were awarded €10,000 each. Her uncle, Jean-Pierre Gazeau, was awarded €5,000.

Explaining the ruling, a court spokesperson said the decision was 'sovereign' and based on applications made by the family and various supporting documents. The appeal for the €110,000 in extra compensation was made after the guilty verdict had been handed down on 31 May.

Magistrate Aline ruled that the court held Mr Bailey 'entirely responsible' for the injury sustained by Sophie's family. The ruling did not spare the journalist, by describing him as being 'on the run' and currently 'wanted' by the court. It found there had been 'actual and certain' harm inflicted on the Bouniol family. This harm, it found, arose 'directly from the acts for which Mr Bailey was convicted'.

The case and the subsequent rulings dominated headlines in France to such an extent that the July issue of *Marie Claire* magazine gave front-page coverage to an interview with Pierre-Louis Baudey-Vignaud. Other magazines gave similar coverage to the trial and its aftermath.

Back in west Cork, Mr Bailey was quick to respond to the French ruling and the financial award against him. A close source to the journalist indicated he had 'absolutely no intention of paying anything'. It quickly became clear that the French civil award had absolutely no status under Irish law and could not be enforced.

But it was criminal rather than civil matters on which everyone in France and Ireland was now focused. The core issue was whether the French court conviction would have any impact on Ireland's extradition stance in respect of Mr Bailey. Would the French now demand an extradition on the basis of the Paris conviction? More important, what would Ireland do with such an application?

The journalist's concern was clearly focused on what the French would attempt with their third EAW. Although extradition attempts had been defeated twice in the Irish courts, none had been levelled on foot of a criminal conviction in a French court. In one conversation, Mr Bailey had warned me that 'The knock on the door could now come at any time.'

Others weren't so sure that action was imminent. It would be unprecedented in European law for an EU member state to seek the extradition of a person from another EU member state for a criminal conviction in the first member state over a crime that had occurred in the second member state. In European judicial terms, it had all the potential to prove a legal minefield. The European Court of Human Rights challenge was also a complicating factor for both Dublin and Paris.

Some legal experts warned that France and Ireland were now heading into totally uncharted European judicial waters. Cork barrister William Bulman said it was impossible to predict what could happen next:

The system of justice is also very different in that Ireland is a Common Law Country and France is a Civil Law System. The function of the judiciary in the two jurisdictions is different.

Mr Bailey had been asked to travel to Paris and voluntarily stand trial in which he refused as his legal team in Ireland held the view that Mr Bailey would not receive a fair trial in Paris. When the French authorities failed to extradite Mr Bailey and Mr Bailey refused to voluntarily travel to Paris a trial commenced in Paris in Mr Bailey's absence. In June 2019 Mr Bailey was convicted of murder by a Paris court in his absence.

It also raises the question how would the Irish courts deal with the matter as there is now a fundamental change in circumstances as the French authorities are no longer looking to put Mr Bailey on trial but have proceeded to try him in his absence and have convicted him. The Irish State has found itself very much in uncharted waters.

The question now has to be posed by the Irish State, and in turn the judicial system, as to what should happen Mr Bailey next? In law, Ian Bailey was convicted of murder in another state and it has been argued by his legal team that it was a show trial, which they did not engage in. But should the decision of the French court be ignored? Is there merit in the argument to actually arrest Mr Bailey and bring him before the High Court and let the Irish court determine whether or not it was a show trial?

Should the Irish courts extradite Mr Bailey to France, who then would have a retrial as set out in French law? These are fundamental questions that need to be addressed as the current situation is unsatisfactory, as the extradition cloud now hangs over Mr Bailey once again. He is a prisoner in this jurisdiction without ever being convicted of a crime in Ireland but convicted of murder in a [second] country. This case could have far-reaching judicial and diplomatic implications for many years to come.

***

The French judiciary issued a warrant on 21 June 2019 for the extradition of Mr Bailey.

It was clear what the Bouniol family wanted. Sophie's son, Pierre-Louis, was adamant that Ireland now had to respect the ruling of the French court. He also expressed confidence that Mr Bailey would end up behind bars in France. In an interview with Michael Clifford of the *Irish Examiner*, he predicted that Mr Bailey would eventually go to jail.

> That man killed my mother 22 years ago and this was the first trial that concentrated on the facts in either France or Ireland. So now we turn to the next step and it is clear that, one day, Ian Bailey, who killed my mother, will go to jail. Of course France will succeed in extradition. And I think Irish justice will see to that, for sure, we are brothers – Ireland and France.

For Mr Bailey, his only option appeared to be to continue to try to live life as normally as possible – and to maintain his hope that somehow, somewhere, fresh evidence would come to light indicating who the real killer was and finally proving his long-stated innocence. He continued to attend his farmers' market stall and sell both organic homemade pizza and books of his poetry. He socialised in Schull, Goleen and Skibbereen and attended arts events across west Cork. He also busied himself with plans for his new book of poetry. It was almost as if he was determined to show the French he was not intimidated or afraid of any forthcoming action.

He attended the 2019 Fastnet Film Festival and spoke enthusiastically of his short film, although it was not part of the official festival programme. Entitled *I Fell in Love with a Dancing Skeleton*, it was inspired by New Orleans-style jazz festival costumes seen in a local parade.

On the evening of 25 August 2019, a Sunday, reports started circulating on social media that Mr Bailey had been arrested in west Cork. I was alerted to the story within 15 minutes of the first cryptic social media posting. A social media storm soon erupted amid claims that the detention was linked to the outstanding French EAW. But it quickly became apparent that the incident had nothing whatsoever to do with France or the Paris trial.

Mr Bailey had been detained on suspicion of drink-driving in Schull and taken to Bantry Garda Station. I rang my news editor – and a privacy issue immediately emerged. While this kind of story would be reported in the normal course of events if it involved a public figure such as a politician or a celebrity, Mr Bailey was not such a figure. He was an ordinary citizen and had the right to privacy. We decided to await developments.

It was a course followed by numerous other newspapers that were aware of the incident, though the *Irish Examiner* did carry a report on the arrest the next morning, following social media speculation.

In response to the ongoing social media claims, Mr Bailey then issued a brief statement about the incident on 26 August. In echoes of 1997, it was his public statement that effectively guaranteed that most Irish newspapers and radio stations would now report on the Schull incident.

I can confirm that on Sunday evening last, I was stopped at a garda checkpoint outside Schull. I failed a roadside breathalyser test. At that point, I was taken to Bantry Garda Station, where I subsequently passed the electronic test. The treatment by gardaí towards me was courteous at all times.

He declined all further comment.

In similar echoes of 1997 and 1998 during the original garda murder investigation, any predictions of rapid developments, this time in the extradition matter, proved wide of the mark. Seven months after the Paris conviction, Mr Bailey voluntarily travelled to Dublin to attend a High Court hearing where the fresh French EAW had its first legal airing.

Mr Justice Donald Binchy was asked on Monday, 16 December 2019 to endorse a French warrant seeking Mr Bailey's extradition on foot of the conviction delivered by the Paris Cour de l'assises. It was a preliminary step required if the extradition was to go to a full High Court hearing.

Mr Bailey, notified of the French application, had voluntarily decided to travel to Dublin rather than stay in west Cork to await developments. As part of the EAW process, Mr Bailey had to be arrested and formally brought before the court on the EAW. Detective Sergeant Jim Kirwan of the Garda Extradition Unit had evidence of the arrest. The detective told the court he gave Mr Bailey a copy of the warrant in both English and French.

He explained to Mr Bailey that the warrant was issued on foot of his conviction *in absentia* in France, for which he had been sentenced to 25 years in prison for the murder of Ms Toscan du Plantier. The detective said Mr Bailey replied to him that he understood what the proceedings were about: 'Yes I do – I just want to say I had nothing to do with this crime.'

Mr Bailey was remanded on bail pending a full hearing on the extradition matter, which was scheduled to take place before the High Court on 20 January 2020. Gardaí did not object to bail being issued. Detective Sergeant Kirwan acknowledged to Ronan Munro SC, who was representing Mr Bailey, that the poet had for years lived 'very visibly in Cork' and was 'easy to keep an eye on'.

Mr Munro had opposed the court endorsing the warrant and said that doing so would simply expose Mr Bailey to another abuse of process. He cited the judgment of Mr Justice Tony Hunt in the High Court in July 2017 when the second French extradition request for Mr Bailey had been dismissed as 'an abuse of process' in light of the 2012 Supreme Court ruling.

However, lawyers for the State argued that the law had changed since 2017 and further pointed out that, in the two years since, Mr Bailey had been convicted of murder at a trial in Paris held in his absence. As many – including Mr Bailey himself – had predicted, the French trial and conviction would now be central to the third French EAW.

Having listened to the arguments, Mr Justice Binchy said it was 'appropriate' to endorse the warrant – a move which would result in a full High Court hearing on the extradition issue. He said that not to endorse the warrant 'would be to eliminate all arguments' in the substantive case and that such a move 'would be premature'. He noted two significant changes since the 2017 hearing – namely a change in the law, and the French conviction.

The High Court hearing catapulted the case back into the headlines – not just in Ireland but across Europe. Adding to the overall impact of the story was the fact that the High Court development came just one week before the twenty-third anniversary of Ms du Plantier's murder.

That evening, I spoke by telephone with Mr Bailey. He insisted he was calm and relaxed about the development – something I found hard to believe. But, as well as being his usual polite self, I found him measured and somewhat philosophical about what he faced in 2020. Once again, he insisted he would 'fight tooth and nail' against the French extradition request and said he felt he was being 'sacrificed' by Ireland to the Paris authorities because of failings in the original murder investigation in west Cork.

'It has been absolute hell. The tragedy here is that the French have convicted an innocent man – and the Irish [authorities] know it. This has been a nightmare that I am afraid will only end with my death. This has been a tragedy for the truth. There are people [in authority] in Ireland who are fully aware of the fact I am innocent. But those devils have remained silent,' Mr Bailey said as he concluded our conversation.

There were also major developments in the case in the area of publicity. Audible were in the process of finalising a number of extra follow-on episodes to their successful *West Cork* series. They would deal with the French trial element of the saga. Two major TV documentaries on the Sophie Toscan du Plantier case were now in the pipeline, one of which will see award-winning Irish director Jim Sheridan unveil his long-awaited documentary series on the case.

Mr Sheridan first confirmed work on the du Plantier story while attending the 2016 Fastnet Film Festival and said he was intrigued by the high-profile case and the controversies it had generated over the previous 20 years.

'We are looking at a documentary about the families of Sophie du Plantier and Ian Bailey – the whole thing. We are trying to examine a cold case, trying to figure out what happened. I think it will be three or four documentaries. I am making it with Donal MacIntyre, the investigative journalist. He is making it for the BBC and TV3,' the director explained.

Mr Sheridan, a long-standing supporter of Ireland's Innocence Project, acknowledged that justice, the presumption of innocence and fairness had been recurring themes in many of his films, such as *In the Name of the Father*, *My Left Foot* and *The Field*. He felt the Sophie Toscan du Plantier case offered similarly rich storytelling potential. 'I have no flag to hold for him. Well, surely there is a situation where it is innocent until proven guilty,' Mr Sheridan said.

Mr MacIntyre, an award-winning investigative journalist, had been intrigued by the case for years because of his close family connections to west Cork, in particular Bere Island. The combination made for an impressive documentary team. The project was strengthened still further by the involvement of Michael Sheridan, the scriptwriter who had written *Death in December* back in 2002.

Mr Bailey agreed to cooperate with the project after being separately approached by Jim Sheridan and Donal MacIntyre in 2015 when his High Court action for wrongful arrest was reaching its climax and dominating national headlines.

'Jim Sheridan approached me during the civil case in Dublin a few years ago and he always knew he wanted to do something but didn't know what. Then Donal MacIntyre – a well-known international investigative journalist – also approached me. I introduced them both. Out of that has come the project which will eventually result in a documentary,' he said.

While no release date has been confirmed for the project, as this book was published the documentary was being considered for a premiere at the 2020 Cannes Film Festival as part of its specialist section. Hardly surprisingly, Mr Bailey has already flagged that, if the film festival participation is confirmed, he will not be in attendance.

Should the documentary feature in the Cannes programme, it will in many ways represent the closing of a circle. Sophie Toscan du Plantier first came to her isolated Toormore holiday home in west Cork to escape the pressures of the French film industry in her life and to seek the private time she craved. For Sophie, Cannes and its world-renowned film festival was an object of both fascination and dread – she adored the professional opportunities it offered but came to be very wary of its celebrity-obsessed social circuit.

Yet, since 1996, Sophie has been the focus of greater publicity than at any time during her all-too-short life. Her death is now the focus of a TV documentary, a Netflix special, an Internet podcast series, multiple books, newspaper crime specials and numerous online conspiracy theories.

For her family, the publicity serves as a constant painful reminder of what they lost. Each December, Georges and Marguerite and their family attend a Mass to remember Sophie and to seek comfort from their deep faith. For years, that Mass was in Goleen parish church and the family would faithfully stay in Sophie's old cottage. Each year, a simple yet beautiful wreath of white lilies, Sophie's favourite flowers, are lovingly placed at the stone Celtic cross that marked the spot where her body was found.

In recent years, Georges and Marguerite are no longer able, for health reasons, to make the long and tiring trek to west Cork in the depths of winter. But each year they attend a Mass for their daughter's memory in Paris. The memorial Mass is now private. But Sophie is remembered by so many.

Having attended the memorial Masses for Sophie in west Cork over the years and got to know Sophie's parents, I found it upsetting that such obviously kind, warm-hearted and decent people should have to endure such a never-ending and painful cycle of hope, disappointment and frustration in Ireland. I felt that they deserved so much better.

It is a truism of the world we live in that bad things can happen to good people. But it doesn't make it any easier to accept when you witness the appalling cost inflicted by violent crime on the families of victims. I remember watching Georges and Marguerite and realising that her death causes them as much pain today as it did on 23 December 1996, when they first learned that their only daughter had been killed.

Sophie's 'Dream of Death' had truly proved a nightmare.

TIMELINE

June 1991
Ian Bailey relocates from his native UK to Ireland to start a new life.

September 1992
Sophie views house at Toormore which boasts dominating views over the Schull–Goleen countryside. Fastnet lighthouse is visible from the upstairs bedroom windows.

January 1993
Sophie purchases the Toormore property.

1993–1996
Sophie enjoys regular weekend breaks and annual summer holidays in Toormore, often bringing her family to share in her Irish vacation.

20 December 1996
Sophie flies into Cork Airport for a brief pre-Christmas break alone at Toormore. She intends to fly back to Paris on 23 December for Christmas and then to Dakar for a New Year's holiday with her husband, film executive Daniel Toscan du Plantier.

23 December 1996
Sophie's battered body is discovered at the foot of the laneway leading from her Toormore home. She had apparently tried to flee from an assailant at her home but was caught near a gateway after her clothing apparently snagged on barbed wire. She died from horrific head injuries.

11 January 1997

Gardaí at Bandon receive the first in a series of calls from a woman identified as 'Fíona' about a suspicious man she claimed she saw at Kealfadda Bridge, not far from the Toormore murder scene.

20 January 1997

A special RTÉ *Crimeline* appeal about the Sophie Toscan du Plantier murder is broadcast on behalf of Bandon gardaí.

10 February 1997

Ian Bailey, a Manchester-born freelance journalist now living in Schull, is arrested by gardaí for questioning in relation to the killing. He is released without charge after almost 12 hours. He is identified by the *Irish Sun* the following day.

12–14 February 1997

Mr Bailey gives an interview to both the *Irish Mirror* and the *Irish Star* before agreeing to a radio interview with Pat Kenny on RTÉ Radio One. Afterwards, he is widely referred to as a self-described suspect in the case.

17 April 1997

West Cork coroner opens and closes the inquest into the death of Ms du Plantier. State Pathologist Professor John Harbison confirms the French woman died from a fractured skull and brain laceration.

27 January 1998

Ian Bailey is arrested a second time by gardaí for questioning. He is again released without charge.

27 June 1998

Daniel Toscan du Plantier (57) marries Melita Nikolic (30), his fourth wife.

7 July 2000

Daniel du Plantier, accompanied by Pierre-Louis Baudey-Vignaud, makes his first and only trip to west Cork after the killing to be briefed by detectives at Bandon Garda Station on the ongoing murder investigation.

January 2002

Garda Commissioner Pat Byrne orders a review of the du Plantier case file by Detective Chief Superintendent Austin McNally.

11 February 2003

Daniel Toscan du Plantier dies at the age of 61 while attending the Berlin Film Festival. He is survived by his fourth wife, Melita Nikolic, and their two young children. He also had three children by his first two marriages.

8–19 December 2003

Ian Bailey sues eight Irish and British newspapers in Cork Circuit Civil Court for libel arising from their coverage of his arrests. He insists he is an innocent man and claims sinister attempts are being made to frame him for the crime.

19 January 2004

Ian Bailey loses his claims against six of the eight newspapers. Total damages of €8,000 are awarded to him against the *Irish Sun* and the *Irish Mirror*. However, Mr Bailey faces estimated legal costs of €200,000.

13 October 2005

Marie Farrell, a west Cork shopkeeper who gave dramatic evidence at the Circuit Court libel action, retracts her evidence after claiming she was put under pressure to make the claims by gardaí.

14 October 2005

Garda Commissioner Noel Conroy orders an inquiry into the matter under Assistant Commissioner Ray McAndrew.

13–16 February 2007

Ian Bailey appeals the libel defeats to the High Court but the action collapses dramatically. He is not awarded damages but does receive a contribution towards his legal costs from the newspapers. He confirms he is now to sue the State for alleged wrongful arrest.

May 2007

Assistant Commissioner McAndrew advises that, having investigated the allegations of Mr Bailey and others in respect of garda operations in west Cork, there is a lack of evidence.

July 2007

Director of Public Prosecutions (DPP) James Hamilton, having studied the McAndrew Report, decides against any prosecutions.

October 2007

Sophie's family press the French authorities to launch their own probe into her killing. Friends set up the Association for the Truth about the Murder of Sophie Toscan du Plantier. Paris-based Magistrate Patrick Gachon is appointed to lead a new inquiry.

1 July 2008

Sophie's body is exhumed from a French cemetery for a fresh post-mortem examination and a battery of forensic tests.

June 2009

Magistrate Gachon and a colleague, Nathalie Dutartre, travel to west Cork as part of their probe. They have already received the garda murder file.

19 October 2009

Two senior west Cork-based gardaí fly to Paris to testify to the French inquiry team.

February–April 2010

Magistrate Gachon issues a European Arrest Warrant (EAW) for Ian Bailey. The legal team for Mr Bailey confirm he will vigorously contest the extradition request.

23 April 2010

High Court endorses the EAW and Ian Bailey is arrested at his home at The Prairie, Liscaha, by Dublin-based detectives. He is taken to Bandon Garda Station before being transferred to Dublin.

24 April 2010

High Court releases Mr Bailey on bail after hearing that he told arresting gardaí he believed the detention to be illegal and based on false information.

7 December 2010

Ian Bailey graduates with a law degree from University College Cork.

18 March 2011

Mr Justice Michael Peart delivers a 54-page judgment in the High Court in which he affirms the French extradition application.

13 April 2011

High Court allows Mr Bailey to appeal the extradition ruling to the Supreme Court.

3 October 2011

Team of French detectives and forensic scientists arrive in Ireland to interview key potential witnesses for a likely Paris trial.

10 November 2011

Planned Supreme Court hearing of Ian Bailey's extradition appeal is postponed after dramatic release of new material to the defence team by the State. Mr Bailey's solicitor, Frank Buttimer, says the material hints at 'breathtaking wrongdoing' by State officials.

January–February 2012

Dramatic new revelations in papers including the *Irish Independent*, the *Irish Times* and the *Irish Daily Mail* about aspects of the original garda murder probe, including that there were other suspects than Mr Bailey, are published.

1 March 2012

Supreme Court unanimously upholds Ian Bailey's appeal against extradition. Mr Bailey – in a dramatic interview – claims he has been through 'hell' over the allegations. The family of Sophie du Toscan du Plantier react with fury to the decision. Mr Bailey indicates he is now to fast-track a civil action against the State for wrongful arrest. He also affirms an earlier formal complaint to the Garda Síochána Ombudsman Commission, which had been stalled due to the High Court and Supreme Court cases. Complaints are also made by his partner, Jules Thomas, and former west Cork shopkeeper Marie Farrell.

12 April 2012

French authorities indicate that their probe continues – amid widespread predictions that Ian Bailey is likely to be tried *in absentia* in France.

December 2013

It emerges that telephone calls at some Irish garda stations, including Bandon, where the Sophie Toscan du Plantier probe was based, were recorded by the telephone system in place.

February–April 2014

It is confirmed that telephone calls between gardaí, between gardaí and witnesses and between gardaí and journalists were recorded in respect of the du Plantier investigation.

June 2014

Sophie's son, Pierre-Louis Baudey-Vignaud, appeals to Ireland via the *Sunday Independent* to continue to cooperate with the Gachon probe despite recent controversies.

July 2014

A planned final trip to Ireland by an elite French detective team is quietly postponed.

4 November 2014

Ian Bailey's High Court action for wrongful arrest against the State opens in Dublin. It is estimated to last six to eight weeks. It ultimately takes five months, including more than 90 witnesses and 63 days at hearing.

30 March 2015

High Court jury finds against Ian Bailey on the two garda conspiracy charges they were asked to consider. The jury was not asked to consider any wrongful arrest issue because it was not taken within a specified legal period.

12 May 2015

High Court orders Ian Bailey to pay full costs of the five-month hearing. The costs are estimated at between €2 million and €5 million. Mr Bailey signals he will challenge the High Court ruling to the Court of Appeal.

27 March 2017

Court of Appeal hears challenge to High Court ruling.

July 2017

Court of Appeal rejects 16 of Mr Bailey's 17 grounds of appeal. But one ruling in his favour could trigger a new High Court trial.

24 July 2017

French authorities have a second extradition bid for Ian Bailey rejected by Irish courts. This application is dismissed by the High Court, which rules that the Supreme Court has already ruled on the issue.

1 February 2018

Three-judge Chambre de l'instruction in France rules that there are 'sufficient grounds' for Ian Bailey to face a prosecution in Paris.

8 February 2018

Amazon-owned media firm Audible releases a 13-part podcast series on the Sophie Toscan du Plantier case entitled *West Cork*.

14 March 2018

Court of Appeal dramatically re-opens its decision and rejects Mr Bailey's sole success in his 2017 wrongful arrest challenge, meaning he has now lost his entire appeal.

3 May 2018

Ian Bailey loses his last legal challenge before France's Supreme Court in a bid to prevent the Paris murder trial over Sophie Toscan du Plantier's death. He immediately flags a European Court of Human Rights challenge to the French prosecution.

2 August 2018

GSOC finds 'no evidence' of high-level corruption within the force over the Sophie Toscan du Plantier investigation on foot of complaints from Ian Bailey. The GSOC report does, however, raise grave concerns over aspects of the garda investigation including apparent changes to key garda reports and the manner in which evidence was lost from storage.

27 May 2019

Paris murder trial of Ian Bailey opens in his absence.

31 May 2019

French magistrates convict the journalist of killing Sophie and impose a sentence of 25 years. He is later fined €225,000.

1 November 2019

Ian Bailey publishes his second book of poetry, entitled *A John Wayne State of Mind*.

16 December 2019

Mr Justice Donald Binchy endorses a third warrant issued by the French for the extradition of Ian Bailey.

Bibliography

Bailey, Ian, *The West Cork Way* (CreateSpace, 2017)

Bailey, Ian, *A John Wayne State of Mind* (Seanachaí Productions, 2019)

Collins, Liam, *Irish Crimes of Passion* (Mentor, 2005)

Cros, Julien & Bloc, Jean-Antoine, *L'Affaire Sophie Toscan du Plantier* (Max Milo, 2014)

Cummins, Barry, *The Cold Case Files* (Gill Books, 2012)

DiMaio, Dominick & DiMaio, Vincent, *Forensic Pathology* (CRC Press, 2001)

Marry, Pat, *The Making of a Detective* (Penguin, 2019)

Riegel, Ralph, *Shattered* (Collins Press, 2011)

Sheridan, Michael, *Death in December* (O'Brien Press, 2002)